Western Canada: An Outline History

WESTERN CANADA
An Outline History

J. ARTHUR LOWER

Douglas & McIntyre

Vancouver / Toronto

Douglas & McIntyre Ltd.
1615 Venables Street
Vancouver, British Columbia

Financially assisted by the Government of British Columbia through B.C. Cultural Fund and B.C. Lottery Revenues

Canadian Cataloguing in Publication Data

Lower, J. Arthur, 1907-
    Western Canada, an outline history

    Bibliography: p.
    Includes index.
    ISBN 0-88894-346-6

    1. Northwest, Canadian – History.   I. Title.
FC3206.L68   971.2   C82-091089-9
F1060.L68

Design by Robert Bringhurst Ltd.
Maps by Claude Roberge
Printed and bound in Canada by D.W. Friesen & Sons Ltd.

CONTENTS

LIST OF MAPS

LIST OF TABLES
(Appendix)

ACKNOWLEDGEMENTS

I wish to thank the many government bodies for their co-operation in providing statistical information used in this book. *Manitoba:* Departments of Cultural Affairs and Historic Resources, Economic Development, Finance; Bureau of Statistics. *Saskatchewan:* Departments of Finance, Industry and Commerce, Tourism and Natural Resources; Bureau of Statistics; Saskatchewan Wheat Pool. *Alberta:* Departments of Agriculture, Business Development and Tourism, Culture, Energy and Natural Resources, Treasury; Petroleum Marketing Commission. *British Columbia:* Departments of Energy, Mines and Petroleum Resources, Environment, Finance, Tourism; Energy Commission. *Northwest Territories:* Department of Information. *Canada:* Department of Indian Affairs and Northern Development; Statistics Canada; Information Canada.

I must also acknowledge the kind assistance of Allan R. Andrews of Vancouver Community College, who made valuable suggestions during the preparation of the manuscript.

Chapter One

CULTURAL CONTACTS

(1700 – 1800)

The Physical Background

W ESTERN Canada is an immense area of land divided into the four provinces of Manitoba, Saskatchewan, Alberta and British Columbia and the two territories, Yukon Territory and Northwest Territories, which lie mostly west of Hudson Bay (see Map 1). The combined area of the four provinces is 1,124,000 square miles (2 912 000 km²), comprising 29 per cent of the total area of Canada, while the territories with 1,512,000 square miles (3 862 000 km²) make up another 39 per cent. Their combined area is more than two-thirds of Canada. They may be compared with all of Europe west of the U.S.S.R. and are slightly smaller than Australia. The air distance from Winnipeg to Vancouver is 1,403 miles (2260 km); from Calgary to Inuvik it is 1,765 miles (2440 km).

Western Canada consists of three predominant geological regions (excluding a small area of the Hudson Bay Lowlands). At the west, trending northwesterly, is the Cordillera, a complex system of high mountain ranges interspersed with valleys and plateaus. The Interior Plains or Lowlands extend from the Arctic Ocean to the Gulf of Mexico. In Canada they broaden towards the south, descending in three levels from the Cordillera. Farther east, the Canadian Shield has a surface of worn-down mountains of Pre-Cambrian rock interspersed with innumerable lakes and streams. The Canadian Shield and Interior Plains meet along a line running approximately through

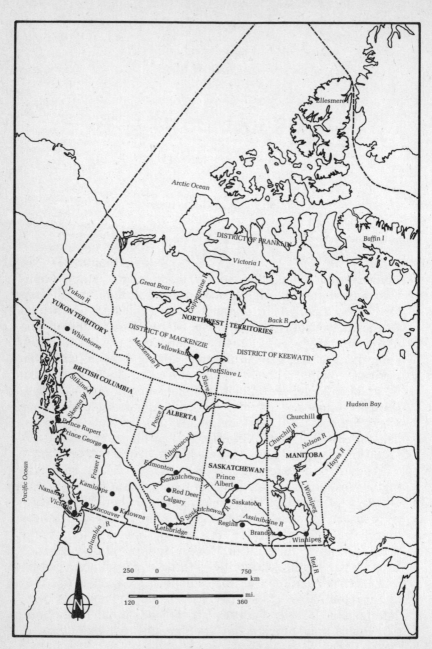

MAP 1: WESTERN CANADA

Great Bear Lake, Great Slave Lake, Lake Winnipeg and Lake of the Woods.

Two-thirds of continental Canada is covered by the Great Northern Forests, or boreal forests, which cover much of the prairie provinces and northern British Columbia, extending northwest from southeastern Manitoba (see Map 2). Both north and south of these great evergreen forests are transition belts. In the north the forests gradually give way to the Barren Lands or tundra. To the south the trees become deciduous across a band commonly known as the Parkland. This in turn dissolves into the prairie grasslands as precipitation decreases, eventually giving way to the dry belt of the southwest which extends sporadically into southern British Columbia. British Columbia is heavily forested, the variety of trees depending on altitude and proximity to the ocean.

Much of this western land is barren and infertile. The first source of wealth exploited by the white men was furs. In the nineteenth century settlers began to occupy the fertile belts, and on the west coast lumbering grew. The common vision of western Canada until comparatively recent times was a land of furs, wheat and vast wilderness. Since these limited resources depend on export trade, western Canada might have remained a poor annex of the prosperous central provinces. In the last century, however, its position has been reversed. The region has proven to contain a wealth of natural resources required by a modern industrial and technical society. Fuels, minerals and electric power are the most vital, and they have given birth to burgeoning secondary industries. With these have grown a spirit of prosperity and demands by westerners for a more influential voice in national affairs.

Nothing has had more influence on the patterns of exploration and settlement in western Canada than its river systems. Within a short distance of Jasper, Alberta, the headwaters of four major river systems can be seen: the Saskatchewan, Mackenzie, Fraser and Columbia. The Saskatchewan-Nelson system crosses the three prairie provinces and is the major water source for this vast region. In two branches it flows from the Rocky Mountains, is joined by waters from the Red River, and empties via the Nelson River into Hudson Bay. The Mackenzie River system, with numerous tributaries, flows northward to

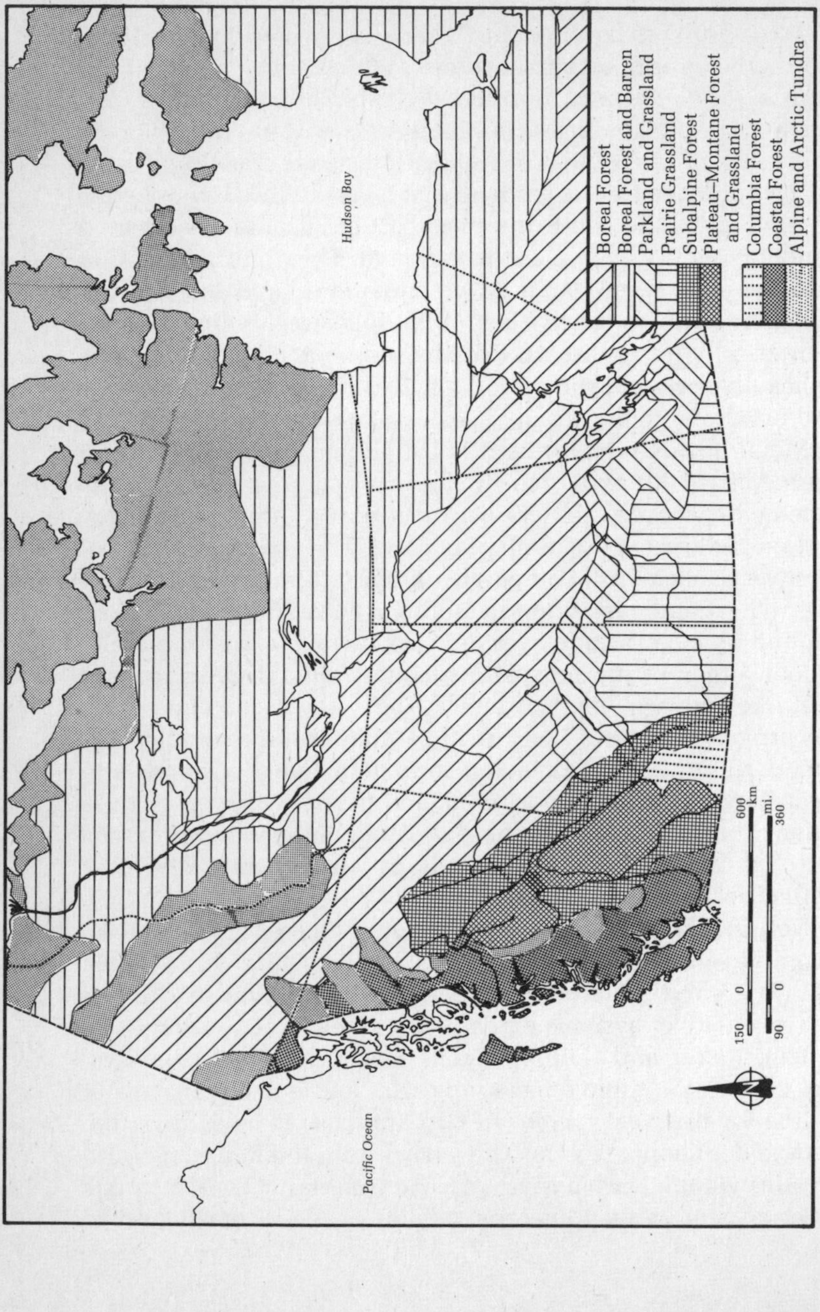

MAP 2: NATURAL REGIONS

Legend:
Boreal Forest
Boreal Forest and Barren
Parkland and Grassland
Prairie Grassland
Subalpine Forest
Plateau–Montane Forest and Grassland
Columbia Forest
Coastal Forest
Alpine and Arctic Tundra

Hudson Bay

Pacific Ocean

150   0   600 km.
90   0   360 mi.

N

the Arctic Ocean. This vast drainage area, which has been opened to settlement only in recent years, is the largest in Canada and covers almost one-fifth of the nation. The Mackenzie is the only major Canadian river without dams and is still free from pollution of cities and industry, but recent industrial developments are beginning to affect the ecosystem of the river basin. Both the Saskatchewan and Mackenzie river systems cross several provincial or territorial borders and therefore the federal government has legislative authority over navigation, fisheries and agricultural uses of the water as well as pollution that results from or affects these uses. Provincial projects on these rivers require interprovincial or provincial-federal agreement. Such agreements are often not achieved until disputes are resolved and a compromise established.

The Fraser and Columbia river systems both flow northwards initially, then turn south and, after tortuous windings through the mountains, empty into the Pacific Ocean. The Columbia is a special problem because its outlet is in the United States. Other river systems that have significance in the history of western Canada include the Churchill and Hayes draining into Hudson Bay, the Coppermine and Back emptying into the Arctic Ocean, and the Stikine, Skeena and Yukon flowing into the Pacific Ocean and Bering Sea. Since the Columbia, Stikine and Yukon rivers flow from Canada through United States territory before reaching the ocean, they require international co-operation in areas such as dam construction, fisheries and pollution control.

A map that shows only the Saskatchewan-Nelson, Mackenzie, Fraser, Yukon and Back river systems would include almost all of western Canada. From the earliest explorations until the construction of modern transportation routes in the twentieth century, the rivers were the arteries of the west and pulsed with the movement of traders and settlers. Although today water transport is of minor importance, rivers remain vital to the region. They open routes for railways and highways through difficult terrain, provide hydroelectric power, permit irrigation of vast areas of arid land, supply necessary water for urban populations and continue to support fish, birds and other animal life. Waterways are one of western Canada's greatest assets and must be preserved and kept free of pollution.

The First Inhabitants

When the first white men arrived in the west they entered a region that was already inhabited. Over 30,000 years ago, towards the end of the Ice Age, the first stragglers crossed land that is now under Bering Strait and spread throughout the Americas. As time passed, these ancestors of the modern Indians and Inuit adjusted to their different environments and became divided into numerous linguistic groups.

Partly because the regions occupied by particular native linguistic groups have changed since the arrival of the first white people, and partly because there is often a melding of borders, authorities differ on the limits of each group. In a broad sense, in the mid-1700s, the western Indians may be divided from north to south, with some of their subgroups, as follows: various groups of Inuit, also called Eskimo; Athapaskan (such as Hare, Yellowknife, Slave, Chipewyan, Beaver, Sarcee); Algonkian (Cree); Algonkian Plains (Plains Cree, Blackfoot, Peigan, Blood, Gros Ventre); Siouan (Assiniboine); the Plateau Indians of British Columbia, who are related to the Athapaskan (Carrier, Chilcotin, Interior Salish, Kootenay); Pacific Coast (Tlingit, Tsimshian, Haida, Kwakiutl, Bella Coola, Salish, Nootka). See Map 3.

Many of these names were not used by the people but were given to them by outsiders, but other names, like "Dene" and "Kutchin" which are both Athapaskan, are their own words meaning "the people." "Inuit" means "the people," while "Eskimo" is an Algonkian name that they never used themselves. Neighbouring groups referred to each other by such names as "people of the mountains," "people of the swamps," "the timid people," and so on. Within the largest linguistic groupings, such as the Athapaskan, for example, which extends even beyond Canada, eastern groups would have difficulty speaking to those farthest west. On the other hand, the use of the Athapaskan and Algonkian languages among widely separated tribes probably indicates ancient associations and incidentally allowed the explorers and fur traders to advance from tribe to tribe with little language barrier.

In the immense area of North America the native peoples, over thousands of years, developed a wide divergence in their patterns of living. Formal boundaries were not mapped, but each band and tribe associated itself with a recognized territory. Although modern ethnographers and linguists have established related language groups, with a common basic dialect, they were loosely organized with no central controlling body. Each band or community was a unit having its own characteristic economic, political, religious and social life adapted to its environment; they could not be considered "nations" in the modern usage of the word. However, common language facilitated trade and the spread of ideas from group to group.

Except on the west coast, where social organization was class-structured, band leadership was established by consensus and usually fell to the those who demonstrated the greatest hunting skill, physical strength or wisdom. The people had no formal system of land title, though on the Pacific coast they observed hereditary claims to hunting and fishing rights in a defined area. There were many rules for social behaviour since people lived in small bands under relatively unchanging conditions. Kinship rules, for instance, were strictly observed. Aggressive behaviour was mainly restricted to intertribal war, and it was the resource-rich and more populous tribes that could afford more than sporadic fighting.

The Indians had no written language and their history was based on legends and stories passed down through the generations. Today historians sift the archeological evidence, the peoples' oral traditions and the written accounts of travellers and missionaries. These all show a wide variety of lifestyles, customs and beliefs, as expected in an environment so vast and varied as western Canada's. Differences of climate, vegetation, geological formations and wildlife meant cultural differences within a single linguistic group. Some Inuit, in a treeless land where winters were long, depended on the sea and its wildlife for most food, clothing and building materials, hunting from boats and sledges made of skins and frames of bone or precious driftwood. Other Inuit were more nomadic and lived much of the year inland as well, hunting the migratory caribou, often travelling along the river systems to intercept the herds at fording places. Conditions made the Inuit enormously inventive, expert in devising specialized hunting weapons and tools for working with ice, rock and animal carcasses. Athapaskan-

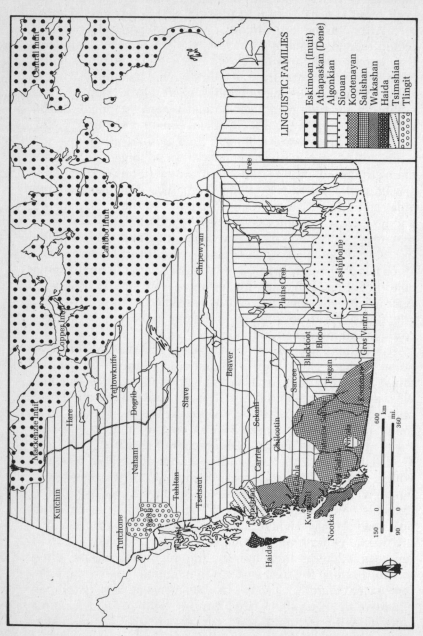

MAP 3: MAJOR LINGUISTIC AND TRIBAL GROUPS

LINGUISTIC FAMILIES

Eskimoan (Inuit)
Athapaskan (Dene)
Algonkian
Siouan
Kootenayan
Salishan
Wakashan
Haida
Tsimshian
Tlingit

speaking peoples are the most widely distributed in North America. They were the hunting inhabitants of the parklands and forest regions north to the barren lands. The Dene, who comprise the most northerly groups, were a peaceful people and had little contact with whites until recent years. The most nomadic Athapaskans, they ranged along the tree line hunting the caribou, though they, too, were essentially a woodland people. The Algonkian Crees were more warlike and were found around Hudson Bay and northern Lake Winnipeg where large animals were abundant. Most of these northern peoples lived in small bands of a few families, travelling by snowshoe and canoe. At certain times of year when supplies were plentiful, many bands would come together to hunt caribou or fish a large run, and perhaps feast and celebrate as well.

The Blackfoot and Plains Cree were also Algonkians. At the time of European contact, the Blackfoot confederacy, which was an alliance of Blackfoot, Peigan and Blood, occupied the plains east of the Rocky Mountains while the Plains Cree spread out from Hudson Bay to the Rocky Mountains. They were bitter rivals since both depended on the buffalo; the latter became powerful middlemen in the fur trade. The Assiniboine came originally from the south and spoke a Sioux dialect. Movements of these plains hunters were determined by the buffalo's, and when the herds left the flatlands the people did the same, breaking up their summer camps of several hundred people into extended families of thirty to sixty to winter in the valleys and hunt together upon the buffalo's return. The Kootenays, in the Kootenay Valley, were once also buffalo hunters but had been driven across the mountains by the Peigans.

The Salish people lived mostly in the southern parts of present-day British Columbia and northern Washington. They were divided into two groups: the Interior Salish and the Coast Salish. The Interior Salish included the Shuswap, Lillooet, Thompson and Okanagan—seminomadic fishermen and hunters who supplemented their diet with the annual salmon run. The Coast Salish occupied the south coast while other groups such as the Tsimshian and Haida comprised the Northwest Coast cultures. These sea peoples were skilled canoeists, sea hunters and fishermen. The densely populated coastal cultures were among the most complex in North America. The people lived in comparatively large groups in permanent homes. They had a high regard for material possessions, both personal and territorial, and ruling families displayed them ostentatiously. With an abundance of marine food, fruits, furs and cedar, they had the time and opportunities to pursue wealth and establish a varied ceremonial and cultural life. Their practical and decorative arts included carving and weaving. The plentiful labour force included a slave class, usually persons taken in war or trade. The several tribes, speaking different dialects, were not held together by any single political structure, and warring was frequent. Some groups became skilled traders, especially with the interior tribes seeking coastal goods. When the white men arrived, they were met by a people who were knowledgeable in trade and had a rich, distinctive culture.

The often illustrated accounts of early white traders preserved their impressions of first encounters with Indian communities; below are three excerpts from the European record of initial contact on the plains, in the north and on the coast.

Anthony Henday, in 1754–55, was the first white man seen by the Blackfoot. He visited the camp of the "Great Leader" where two thousand people were assembled in two hundred tents pitched in two rows:

the Leader's tent [was] large enough to contain fifty persons ... [I] desired of him to allow some of his young men to go down to the Fort with me where they could get Guns, etc. But he answered, it was too far off, & they could not live without Buffalo flesh; ... though all might be got over if they were acquainted with a Canoe, and could eat Fish, which they never do. ... The Chief further said that they never wanted food, as they followed the Buffalo and killed them with Bows and Arrows.

Henday also noted that "the Natives are good Horsemen, & kill the Buffalo on them." He probably did not realize that the horse was a relatively recent acquisition of the plains Indians and had dramatically changed their culture over the previous half century. Before the horse they had followed the roaming buffalo herds on foot, eking out a subsistence living; mounted, they could bring down all the meat they needed and the skins essential for clothing, shelter and even tools like cooking vessels. This new leisure allowed their decorative arts, dance and other cultural activities to flourish. With more available supplies, and able to move their material goods farther distances, the people could gather into larger groups. At the same time, by enlarging the territorial hunting area, the horse led to increased intertribal rivalry.

The Blackfoot were the last Canadian plains Indians to be affected by the white man and until the 1880s were a free roaming people. Their later history is one of almost continuous wars against the enemies surrounding them on every side.

Fifteen years after Henday's plains expedition, Samuel Hearne travelled among the northern Athapaskans and thus describes them:

They are in general above the middle size, well-proportioned, strong and robust but not corpulent. . . . Few of the men have any beard. . . . The tents . . . are generally composed of deer-skins in the raw and for convenience of carriage are always made in small pieces, seldom exceeding five buck-skins in one piece. These tents, as are also their kettles and some lumber are always carried by dogs. . . . [In winter] sledges are used of various sizes, according to the strength of the persons who are to haul them: some I have seen were not less than twelve or fourteen feet long and fifteen or sixteen inches wide, but in general they do not exceed eight or nine feet in length. . . . The many lakes and rivers . . . afford great numbers of fish both in summer and winter. . . . There is a black, hard crumply moss, which is of infinite service to the natives, as [when boiled] it sometimes furnishes them with a temporary subsistence when no animal food can be procured."

On the west coast in 1778 Capt. James Cook found entirely different living conditions. He described the people as being below average stature, with broad noses, black eyes and thick black straight hair hanging over their shoulders. They lived in villages which he estimated contained two thousand people. The houses

consist of a long range of buildings, some of which are one hundred and fifty feet in length, twenty four or thirty broad . . . of very long and broad planks resting upon the edges of each other, fastened by withes of pine-bark. The height of the sides and ends is seven or eight feet; but the back part is a little higher which means that the planks which compose the roof slant forward, and are laid loose so as to be moved about, either to be put close to exclude the rain or in fair weather to be separated to let in the light and carry out the smoke. . . .

The chief employment of the men seems to be that of fishing, and killing land or sea animals for we saw few of them doing anything in the houses; whereas the women were occupied in manufacturing their flaxen or woolen garments, and in preparing the sardines for drying. ... Their weapons are bows and arrows, slings, spears and a small pick-axe not unlike the common American tomahawk. The spear has generally a long point made of bone. The tomahawk is a stone, six or eight inches long, pointed at one end and fixed into a handle of wood.

When the first white people settled along the east coast of North America the Indians brought them furs in exchange for European goods. In turn, the Indians became middlemen as they exchanged these goods for furs with tribes farther inland. In place of wood, bone or stone implements, the people began to use iron products—axes, tools, needles, traps, spearheads, harpoons, knives, scissors and steel to strike fire. Copper or brass kettles were much in demand because they were stronger than clay and lighter than iron. European clothing and blankets supplemented skins. Most desired of all goods were guns and ammunition. As the European presence increased, imports displaced the old materials and became necessities of Indian life, drastically changing their economic patterns of living. As an example, when the Indians' wooden traps and hide snares were replaced by the efficient steel trap, many forest peoples became dependent on trapping for the fur market to obtain European goods, and their traditional movements were abandoned in favour of working their traplines and rendezvousing at the trading posts, which also became the focus of social life for the gathered bands. In many bands leadership now became much more inflexible because the white traders would deal only with a trade chief, whom they appointed and who negotiated the terms of sale for all his people.

But the new economic patterns were never permanent. The heavy demand for furs by the British and French resulted in the decimation of nearby animals and a scarcity of pelts. French fur traders began to travel inland. These expeditions would not have been possible without the assistance of the Indians and their knowledge of life in the "wild unknown" lands. Among the Indian contributions were the canoe, the pack strap, snowshoes, an understanding of animal habits, a recognition of plants suitable for food and medicine, and a knowledge of travel routes including portage sites. Gradually the westward-moving fur frontier would leave the indigenous bands behind as their traditional hunting territories became depleted: life changed more dramatically during the years of European contact than it had for hundreds of years previously.

There had always been trading between tribes; for example, the west coast tribes for years had carried salmon and other coastal products inland. With the new market for furs and the demand for European goods, exchange increased and some tribes became more middlemen than trappers, leaving the gathering of furs to more distant and poorer peoples. The native traders and middlemen often opposed the intrusion of European traders. This was especially true in northern British Columbia and the Yukon where Robert Campbell and later Hudson's Bay Company traders were in bitter competition with the coast Tlingits. Native control from the coast was not broken until the great influx of miners to the Yukon gold rush at the end of the nineteenth century.

The Indians closest to the white men were the first to receive guns. These they would not trade with the inland people, for guns gave them superiority in war; as their own territories were trapped out, they could drive other groups back and take over new lands. Thus for over a century there was a movement of Indian tribes westward from the St. Lawrence. By the 1700s, for example, the Crees pressed upon the Blackfoot, and early in the 1800s the Peigans tried to stop David Thompson from reaching the Kootenay people. Eventually the more western groups obtained guns directly from white traders.

European products made some aspects of native life easier. Less time was spent in making basic necessities such as axes and pots, leaving more time for the development of arts and crafts, in which European tools played an important part. Hunting became more efficient with firearms and steel traps. At the same time, guns made wars between the tribes more lethal and more common. The most devastating result of white contact was the introduction of diseases such as measles, diphtheria and the deadly smallpox. The actual number of Indians in Canada during the sixteenth century is unknown though some estimates put it at 222,000. In 1881 the census of Canada estimated the number at 108,547, a decline of more than 50 per cent. There was little change for sixty years; the 1941 census stated 118,316. From that time the population has

shown a more rapid increase. Status Indians, or those registered on a band roll, totalled 309,590 in 1981. But figures even
now cannot be exact since they do not identify the vast number
of nonstatus Indians and Metis, who are estimated at between
400,000 and one million.

The Inuit, especially the Arctic whalers, also suffered from
their contacts with the white man. Today they are steadily
increasing. The population doubled in thirty years to 17,550 in
1971, and numbered 23,000 in 1982. This three per cent annual
increase is projected to continue.

Hudson Bay

During the sixteenth century Portugal and Spain dominated
the colonial world. Portugal opened and developed the sea
route around Africa to the East Indies while Spain built its
empire in America and restrained passage around Cape Horn.
The Manila galleons extended Spain's dominance across the
Pacific to the Philippines. The surge of English commercial
activity during Elizabeth's reign was frustrated by this Por-
tuguese-Spanish stranglehold on sea routes to the Far East. To
circumvent these barriers other European nations sought a
northern passage to the Pacific. By the early 1500s voyages
such as those of Cabot, Verrazano and Cartier had revealed that
there was no passage through North America south of Labrador. The English initiated a series of expeditions farther north,
but attempts to penetrate the Northeast Passage around Russia
were complete failures; attempts to find a Northwest Passage
(the Straits of Anian) were more persistent.

Eventually Henry Hudson reached Hudson Bay, where he
was left to perish by his mutinous crew. The following year,
1611, Thomas Button was dispatched with two ships and a
letter from King James I to the Emperor of Japan. Button
reached the western shore of Hudson Bay and sailed as far
south as the Nelson River, thus becoming the first white person
to see present-day Manitoba. There he wintered before returning home.

Button's results were inconclusive and other expeditions
were undertaken. A Danish explorer, Jens Munck, wintered in
1619–20 at the mouth of the Churchill River. Only three of his

crew of sixty-four survived, for scurvy was rampant. In 1631 Luke Foxe followed much of Button's route and sailed almost the entire western shore of the bay. In the same year Thomas James reached the southern end of James Bay. These men proved that Hudson had found a great inland bay but not the Straits of Anian.

The Early Traders

Intertribal wars along with British rivalry in the east threatened to cut off the supply of furs to the French and they were forced to travel westward to the fur lands themselves. Two such traders were Pierre-Esprit Radisson and his brother-in-law, Médard Chouart, Sieur des Groseilliers. They made a successful trading expedition into the west in the 1650s. At that time the land west of the St. Lawrence was a vast unclaimed wilderness. Nevertheless, the royal government in Quebec required licences to trade, and when Radisson and Groseillers applied to undertake an expedition, their licence was postponed since they would not accept the rapacious governor's demands that two of his men go along and that he receive half the profits. They decided to set out without the licence. They reached the western shores of Lake Superior and, according to Radisson's account which is regarded as unreliable, went as far south as the headwaters of the Mississippi and as far north as James Bay. In this northern land they did obtain a wealth of thick, heavy beaver pelts.

On their return to Quebec in 1660 they were arrested and fined by the governor for trading without a licence. Their furs were seized and only about 15 per cent were later returned. Disillusioned, the men began to look for someone to finance their next expedition, travelling through Europe and the New England colonies. Eventually they turned to England where they received a sympathetic hearing from Prince Rupert, a cousin of Charles II. The English did not recognize French sovereignty over the North American interior. The *Nonsuch* with Groseilliers aboard was sent to Hudson Bay and returned in 1669 with a load of prime furs. Prince Rupert was able to persuade Charles to issue a trading licence in 1670 to "The Governor and Company of Adventurers of England trading into

Hudson's Bay." By this charter the British government granted to the company all land drained by Hudson Bay. This was the first indirect challenge to the French, who treated all land north and west of the St. Lawrence system as a French fur preserve. The land between the bay and the St. Lawrence was virtually unknown and there was no English-French agreement setting the limit of French claims.

The Hudson's Bay Company charter consisted of five large sheets of closely written parchment which have withstood the many challenges to its legal validity and controlled the destiny of western Canada for two centuries. Parts of it deserve quotation:

grant unto them, and their Successors, the sole Trade and Commerce of all those Seas, Streights, Bays, Rivers, Lakes, Creeks and Sounds, in whatsoever Latitude they shall be, that lie within the entrance of the Streights commonly called Hudson's Streights, ... upon the Coasts and Confines of the Seas, Streights, Bays, Lakes, Rivers, Creeks and Sounds, aforesaid, which are not now actually possessed by any of our Subjects of any other Christian Prince or State. ... We give, grant and confirm ... the sole Trade and Commerce of all those Seas ... with the Fishing of all Sorts of Fish, Whales, Sturgeons, and all other Royal Fishes ... within the Premises and the Fish therein taken, ... and all Mines Royal, as well discovered or not discovered, of Gold, Silver, Gems and precious Stones, to be found or discovered, ... and that the said Land be from henceforth called *Rupert's Land.*

Powers are given to the Company to make laws, impose penalties and punishments, and to judge in all causes civil and criminal according to the laws of England. They may employ armed force, appoint commanders and erect forts.

In return for this grant the company was to make a symbolic payment to the crown: "paying yearely to us our heires and Successors ... two Elkes and two Black beavers whensoever and so often as Wee our heires and Successors shall happen to enter into the said Countreys."

Within a few years the company had established a number of forts on James Bay, as well as York Factory (originally Fort Nelson) at the mouth of the Nelson River. The company followed a policy of "stay on the Bay," expecting the Indians to bring furs to the posts. Without competition, this policy succeeded and the traders did not need to venture inland. Nevertheless, in 1689, nineteen-year-old Henry Kelsey investigated some two hundred miles (320 km) of coast north of the Churchill River and entered the barren lands where he saw musk oxen. The following year he was sent inland: from the mouth of the Hayes River he may have travelled as far as the present site of The Pas. Kelsey spent two years in Indian country and was the first white man to see buffalo. This expedition did nothing to change the company policy of locating posts on the coast.

The northern Athapaskans, such as the Chipewyans and the Yellowknives, as well as the Inuit would not travel as far south as York Factory for fear of their enemies, the Crees. To encourage these northern people James Knight built Fort Churchill in 1717, and to publicize the trading post before it was built, two years previously the company sent William Stewart on a peace mission along the edge of the barren lands. He spent a miserable winter, often near starvation, and may have reached as far west as Slave River and Great Slave Lake, making friendly contacts with the native peoples.

La Vérendrye

Meanwhile the French trader Jacques de Noyon had reached Rainy River and Lake of the Woods in 1688–89. Within twenty-five years a route was known to Lake Winnipeg. In 1717 a trading post was established at Kaministiquia (later Fort William) on the western shore of Lake Superior. Throughout the entire era of the fur trade, indeed even to the present day, the waterways determined the major transportation routes. Exploring fur traders opened the wilderness as they followed the rivers and lakes ever farther westward (see Map 4). The river systems gradually became dotted with trading posts.

It was the La Vérendrye family who opened the land west of the Canadian Shield. Pierre Gaultier de Varennes, Sieur de la Vérendrye, proposed to the officials of New France that an expedition be sent to search for the western sea. In 1731 his appointment as commandant of the western posts gave him the authority to organize and lead such an expedition. He was assisted by his four sons and a nephew, La Jemeraye. From Lake Winnipeg two of his sons travelled south into the Mandan country on the Missouri River where he saw the "Shining Mountains"—probably the Black Hills of Dakota or possibly

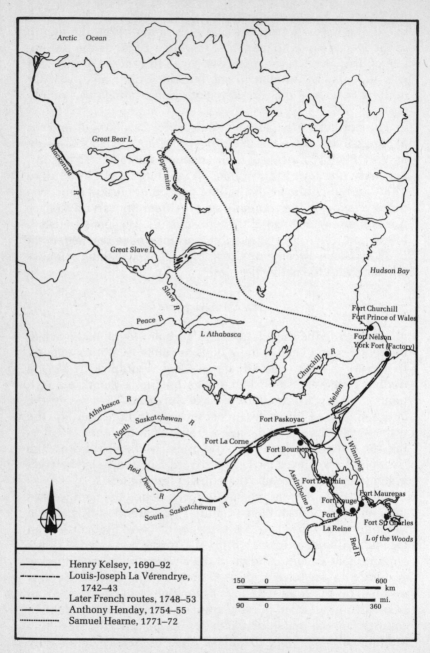

MAP 4: EARLY PRAIRIE EXPLORERS, 1690–1772

the Big Horn Mountains of the eastern Rockies.

Between 1731 and 1743 the La Vérendryes established a
series of trading posts: Fort St. Pierre on Rainy Lake; Fort St.
Charles on Lake of the Woods. Crossing Lake Winnipeg, which
he named, La Vérendrye built Fort Maurepas at the mouth of
the Red River, but it was later moved to the mouth of the
Winnipeg. At the junction of the Red and Assiniboine rivers he
established Fort Rouge. On the Assiniboine he built Fort La
Reine, later moved twenty-one miles (32 km) west to the present Portage la Prairie. Northward near the north end of Lake
Manitoba, his sons built Fort Dauphin, and in 1748 established
Fort Bourbon at the mouth of the Saskatchewan River, on
Cedar Lake, and Fort Paskoyac (The Pas) on the Saskatchewan.
In 1753 the Chevalier de la Corne built Fort La Corne below the
forks of the Saskatchewan. It is believed that in 1751 the temporary Fort La Jonquière was built near Calgary and probably
within sight of the Rocky Mountains, though this surmise is
not verified. The French probably saw the Rocky Mountains
but they were far from La Vérendrye's western sea.

With control in the hands of agents in Quebec and Montreal
the French developed a systematic, efficient fur trade organization. Grand Portage on Lake Superior became the meeting
place for the exchange of supplies from the east for furs from
the west. The French established a firm foundation for the later
English traders.

New France was aware of the British activities on Hudson
Bay, since English traders were taking furs from northern Quebec. With British colonies to the south, the French felt threatened on both sides. In 1686 an expedition led by Chevalier de
Troyes and Le Moyne d'Iberville had crossed overland from
Montreal and seized Moose Factory, Rupert's House and Fort
Albany, but they were soon restored to the English. For the
next twenty-seven years, through King William's War and
Queen Anne's War, the struggle between the French and English for control of Hudson Bay continued. French naval forces
under d'Iberville were a scourge to British ships and forts. At
one point only Fort Albany remained in British hands. In spite
of the French successes, in 1713 the lands drained by Hudson
Bay were finally awarded to Britain by the Treaty of Utrecht.

The French incursions from the south were seriously cutting

into the supply of furs reaching Hudson Bay. In 1732 the Hudson's Bay Company began building Fort Prince of Wales at the mouth of the Churchill River to deal with any future attacks from the sea. This mighty fortress, with stone walls thirty to forty feet (9 to 12 m) thick, was not completed for thirty years. Meanwhile, the company continued to organize a number of inland expeditions to encourage the Indians to bring their furs to the forts on the bay and also to ascertain the extent of French expansion. The expedition made by Anthony Henday was of great significance.

Henday left York Factory with a party of Assiniboines in June 1754. After visiting the French post at Fort Paskoyac, they soon left their canoes and travelled into Blackfoot territory in southern Alberta. Henday did not reach as far south as the Bow River but was the first recorded white man to see the Rocky Mountains, probably near the present site of Innisfail. His appeals to the Indians for trade were unsuccessful. On his return trip he again met the French at Fort La Corne and noted their use of brandy in trading and also the large supplies of choice furs they had obtained. After a year of travelling, Henday returned to York Factory where his report, as that of Kelsey earlier, was discredited and no changes were made in company policy.

The first phase of the western fur trade was an extension of French and British commerce. Furs were the basis of the trade which, in return for products from the home country, would yield a profit. The French trade was controlled by policies set in autocratic France through the king's representatives who licensed agents in Quebec and Montreal. The Hudson's Bay Company, controlled in London, regulated the appointments and actions of its officers and servants in North America through York Factory. In both cases there was monopoly control. From the earliest times western Canada was a market for European goods paid for with its natural resources.

While Henday was travelling through the prairies, British and French forces were already clashing in the east, foreshadowing the Seven Years War (1756–63). With the fall of Quebec and Montreal, the licensed French fur trading system collapsed. The French challenge to the Hudson's Bay Company was ended and, without apparent competition, the company could retain its earlier practices. Dividend bonuses on shares, which had been less than ten per cent since 1745, returned to that figure in 1763 and were maintained for fifteen years.

However, as early as 1760, the year that Montreal surrendered and before the Treaty of Paris was signed, independent traders were already gathering in Montreal to take over the old French trade routes. There were French-Canadian voyageurs, British traders who had experience in the southern colonies, new immigrants, and many men, mostly Scottish, who had been discharged from the British army in Canada. Some had capital behind them. Many were individuals gambling on their ability to survive and to succeed in the wilderness. Within a decade they had reached the Saskatchewan River and had reestablished the old French trading routes. Once again the Hudson's Bay Company found that the supply of furs was being cut off.

The Unknown Pacific

While Europeans were penetrating the interior of North America from the east, the Pacific Northwest remained unknown. Maps were made by guesswork or from the reports of unsubstantiated voyages. One map showed a great inland sea covering modern British Columbia. Francis Drake may have sailed as far north as Vancouver Island before landing on the California coast (New Albion) in 1579. Juan de Fuca may have discovered the strait that bears his name in 1592. The first recognized voyage is that of Vitus Bering, a Dane employed by Russia, who in 1728 sailed through Bering Strait, thus proving that Asia and North America were separated. Thirteen years later, with Aleksei Chirikov, he reached the west coast of Alaska but died on the return voyage. In the following years many adventurous Russian fur traders probed the Aleutian Islands towards America.

By this time the Spanish colonial empire was approaching its greatest extent. On the Atlantic, except for Portuguese Brazil and some Caribbean islands, it stretched from Cape Horn to Florida; on the Pacific it dominated the coast as far north as southern California. It maintained regular transportation routes from Pacific ports to its possessions in the East Indies, and claimed the south Pacific as the "Spanish Ocean." In 1762, during the Seven Years War, Spain obtained Louisiana from France, and eventually inland Spanish settlements were scattered as far north as the Missouri River.

By the end of the sixteenth century, trading ships were reaching the Far East by both the Cape of Good Hope and Cape Horn routes. The military power of Spain had declined in comparison with the growing strength of Holland, Britain and France. These three nations had penetrated the Far East but their expansion was curtailed by the antiforeign policies of China and Japan. The Pacific coast of the Americas was still closed by Spain. Since the time when Balboa had crossed the Isthmus of Panama in 1514, Spain had claimed sovereignty of the west coast of both Americas "from the sea Arctic to the sea Antarctic." The length of the Spanish-controlled coastline discouraged other Europeans from venturing into the northern waters. Probably, had there been any known riches such as those of India and the East Indies, the new emerging trading nations would have challenged Spanish control, but there was no such incentive. Without competition, Spain itself saw no reason to explore or settle north of the Mexican coastline, until the Russian intrusion, so that the northwest coast, aside from the impenetrable Arctic and Antarctic regions, was the last to be explored. See Map 5.

Through its ministers in St. Petersburg, Spain had become aware of Bering's explorations and of the ensuing Russian trading activities in the north. This Russian threat to its claims of sovereignty over the Pacific coast, combined with attempts to revive Spain's prestige under Carlos III, forced Spain to move northwards from Mexico.

Two years before San Francisco was established (1776) Spain began exploratory expeditions to the north. Juan Pérez in the *Santiago*, with eighty-eight men, was ordered to sail as far north as 60° latitude to explore the coastline, to take formal possession of the coast and to report on the people and resources of the country, but he was not to make any settlement; if any foreign settlement or ship was encountered, he was to communicate with them as little as possible. Pérez maintained a course far out to sea before seeing the Queen Charlotte Islands at 55°. Fog, storms and tides prevented his landing or continuing northward, and on the return voyage his men suffered from scurvy. He sailed near Nootka Sound on Vancouver Island but was prevented by weather from landing. Pérez was the first white man to see the British Columbia coast and he saw some of the natives in their canoes, but he had been unable to land or claim sovereignty.

In the following year Bruno de Hezeta in the *Santiago* along with Juan Francisco de la Bodega y Quadra in the *Sonora* led a larger expedition to the north. Hezeta sailed as far as Nootka Sound, having missed Juan de Fuca Strait but noting the mouth of a great river (the Columbia). Quadra continued as far north as 58°. Although they had landed on the Washington coast and claimed sovereignty, neither had landed on the coast of British Columbia.

Capt. James Cook

In an era of French and British commercial and naval expansion the outstanding explorer was Capt. James Cook. In 1770 he was sent on his third major exploratory voyage. He was not only to make scientific studies and claim undiscovered lands for Britain but also to survey the northwest coast of America to ascertain whether there was an outlet to a Northwest Passage. He sailed from Britain with two ships, the 462-ton (419-t) *Resolution* and the 295-ton (268-t) *Discovery*. With him was an outstanding artist, James Webber, and others who would later become famous—William Bligh, Nathaniel Portlock and George Vancouver.

Rounding the Cape of Good Hope and New Zealand, Cook discovered the Sandwich (Hawaiian) Islands. Thence he reached the Oregon coast in 1778 and, sailing northward, landed at Nootka Sound on Vancouver Island where he spent several weeks resting and repairing his ships. He made a study of the friendly natives, and his observations were supplemented by Webber's detailed drawings. In return for paltry amounts of trade goods, his crews received sea otter skins, of which Cook wrote, "The fur of these creatures is certainly finer than any other animal we know of."

Continuing northward, he reached 70° north latitude where he was stopped by the ice of Bering Sea. In this region he met Russian traders who agreed to forward his letters and charts across Siberia to the Lords of the Admiralty in London. His ships returned south to the Hawaiian Islands for the winter, where Cook was killed by the natives. The following year his ships returned north, twice visiting the Russian post at Petropavlosk. Again the ice proved impenetrable so the expedition turned towards home. En route they called at Macao and Canton where the sea otter skins, obtained so cheaply, were sold to the Chinese at enormous profits.

Captain Cook's voyage seemed to have ended hopes for a navigable Northwest Passage to the Pacific. The expedition made the first scientific study of the geography, vegetation, wildlife and natives of the northern coast, and the landing at Nootka gave Britain a strong claim to the region. The profits realized by the sale of the sea otter pelts brought the maritime fur trade.

The activities of Cook and the traders who followed reactivated Spanish determination to claim the coast. Numerous Spanish expeditions were sent northwards in the fifteen years after Cook. They visited the Russians in Alaska and charted Juan de Fuca Strait and the Strait of Georgia. In 1792 Dionisio Alcalá Galiano and Cayetano Valdés met George Vancouver off Spanish Banks, near the present city of Vancouver. Galiano noted the changed colour of the waters but failed to deduce a river mouth—the Fraser. In the following year Estéban José Martínez ascended the Columbia River for fourteen miles (22 km). Meanwhile, critical events were to nullify Spanish ambitions in the northwest.

The Maritime Fur Trade

For many years the Russians had been harvesting the sea otter, a maritime animal with thick, rich fur, found on the coasts of the north Pacific. The Russians were very secretive about their activities in the region. It was not until reports reached Britain of the profits made by Captain Cook's sailors that many individuals recognized the possibilities for successful fur trading enterprises on the northwest coast.

The maritime fur trader faced many problems besides the long, dangerous voyage around the Cape of Good Hope or Cape Horn and the threat of scurvy or other illness due to poor food.

There was the cost of outfitting a ship for three years, the average time needed for the long voyage with stops for rest and refurbishing at Macao or Hawaii plus two seasons on the coast. Trade goods had to be stored, and chosen to appeal to the natives yet not duplicate items that earlier traders had introduced. West coast Indians were experienced and discriminating traders. Trinkets and baubles were little valued but iron and copper were in demand. As European traders became more common, the Indians not only became more selective but also raised the prices of their furs, especially when they became scarce through overhunting. Traders scoured the coast searching for new inlets.

The cargo of furs was taken across the Pacific to China, probably with a stop at Hawaii. Unfortunately, the East India Company controlled all British trade into China and closed the market to independent British traders. They could satisfy the regulations by obtaining a licence from the East India Company on its terms, or circumvent them by flying the flag of some other nation such as Portugal or Austria.

The first maritime trader on the west coast was the Englishman James Hanna (1785–87), sailing under a Portuguese flag. Among the many others who followed were Capt. Charles W. Barkley and his wife, sixteen-year-old Frances Hornby Barkley. She was the first white woman on the west coast and, according to her diary, her husband recognized and named Juan de Fuca Strait. Although the first traders were British they were soon joined by Americans; the first were Capt. John Kendrick and Capt. John Gray. Gray is credited with the discovery of the Columbia River which he ascended for fifteen miles (24 km) and named after his ship the *Columbia*. Martínez, in fact, made the discovery first. There were also an insignificant number of traders from France, Sweden and Portugal. The Americans were not handicapped by the restrictions of the East India Company, and when the British shortly became embroiled in wars with France, the Americans gradually displaced them in the maritime trade.

The Withdrawal of Spain

Spain had accepted Russia's position in the north. Now both countries were alarmed by the influx of British and American traders. Russia established a more eastern permanent post on Kodiak Island in 1784 and sent men to numerous well-supplied outposts along the Alaska coast. Spain was more aggressive.

In 1789 Martínez returned to Nootka Sound with the Spanish ship-of-war *Princesa* and another vessel. The previous year Capt. John Meares, an Englishman, had established his headquarters there for his trading vessels. When Martínez arrived, he found Meares's *Iphigenia* at Nootka. After a week of apparently peaceful relations, Martínez suddenly seized the *Iphigenia* and her crew; he hoisted the Spanish flag and claimed the land for Spain. (His successor later built a small fort, San Miguel, on the site.)

The *Iphigenia* was later released and left for Hawaii. However, when the British *North West America* (the first vessel built on the northwest coast), the *Argonaut* and the *Princess Royal* arrived at Nootka under Meares's instructions, each was seized. The crew of the *North West America* was permitted to accompany the American Captain Gray, who was also at Nootka but not molested, on his departure for China. The two other vessels with their crews were taken to San Blas in Mexico, as were a number of Chinese whom Meares had brought to Nootka as labourers.

Meares had been trading on the coast for several years and the impression one obtains from other traders is that of a scheming and dishonest man. His report to the British government with appeals for redress may therefore be suspect. At this time relations between Britain and the French-Spanish alliance were tense and the British press used Meares's report to stir up public indignation. Both sides prepared for war; but in France, on the threshold of revolution, the states-general refused to support Louis XVI's proposal to enlarge the navy. Unable to depend on its ally and faced by a great assembled British naval force, Spain modified its position. By the Nootka Conventions, opened in 1790, Spain agreed to pay Meares for damages and further accepted the policy that the subjects of both countries should have free access to trade on the northwest coast. Both sides were to send representatives to Nootka to complete the agreement formally. Spain sent Quadra and Britain sent Capt. George Vancouver, but they could not agree on their terms of

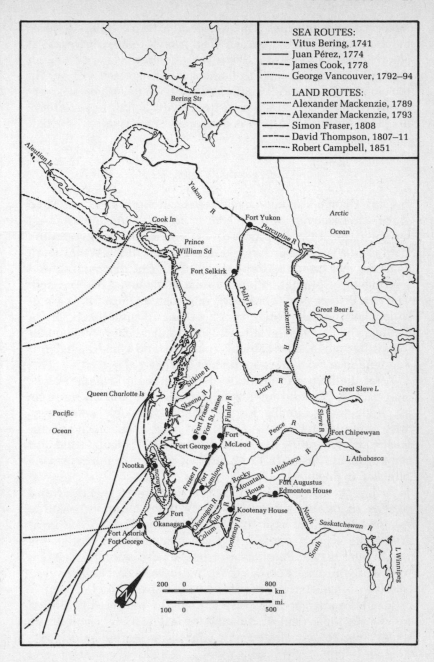

MAP 5: FAR WESTERN EXPLORERS, 1741–1851

reference and returned the problem to their home governments. In 1795 the Spanish flag was formally lowered at
Nootka and the post was destroyed after six years of Spanish
control. Nootka returned to being a quiet, isolated village. By
the Nootka Convention, Spain had given up its claims of sovereignty to the entire coast and withdrew its activities to California. The northwest coast was now open to the rivalry of British
and American traders.

Capt. George Vancouver

Capt. George Vancouver left Britain in April 1791 with two
ships, the Discovery and the Chatham, for the northwest coast
via the Cape of Good Hope. Almost a year later he sighted the
California coast and proceeded northward. Off the Washington
coast he met Captain Gray who told him of discovering and
naming the Columbia River, which Vancouver had missed.
The two British ships continued into Juan de Fuca Strait. Carefully charting the waters of Puget Sound and the Strait of
Georgia, Vancouver eventually circumnavigated Vancouver
Island (for some time called Vancouver and Quadra's Island)
and landed at Nootka where he met Quadra.

After the failure of negotiations, Lieutenant Broughton was
sent back to England for further instructions and en route he
ascended the Columbia for 100 miles (160 km). Vancouver,
after wintering in Hawaii, spent two more years on the north-
west coast, extending his surveys to Prince William Sound and
Cook Inlet in Alaska. In 1795, after an absence of four years, he
returned to England.

Although Vancouver had missed the Columbia, Fraser and
Skeena rivers, his surveys of the British Columbia coastline
established a firm base for modern knowledge of the area.
Along the coast a myriad of place names commemorate his
work. Later his explorations and acts of possession formed one
of Britain's strongest claims to the northwest coast and ensured
that it would eventually become part of Canada.

When Vancouver visited Bella Coola he preceded by only a
few weeks the arrival of Alexander Mackenzie whose journey
by land was to inaugurate a new phase of western history.

Chapter Two

RIVALRY FOR FURS
(1763 – 1821)

The Pedlars

With the collapse of French control in Canada, British traders moved in to join the many French Canadians who continued in the fur trade. Some of this group traded independently, some worked as voyageurs (canoemen) for individual British traders, many became agents for British capitalists in Montreal such as Benjamin Frobisher, Isaac Todd, James McGill and Alexander Henry. Thus from the beginning there were two classes of traders—the inland "wintering partners" and the Montreal agents.

Resumption of trade was delayed at first by Pontiac's rebellion. During the Seven Years War the great Indian leader had been an ally of the French and was determined to prevent British expansion into the Indian lands of the Mississippi Valley. In 1763 his confederacy captured eight British forts and drove the British from all the land west of Niagara except Detroit. But eventually his forces were defeated by superior British forces and in 1768 he had to accept their terms. The rebellion did force the British to recognize the problems of the Indians and was an important contributing factor in the Proclamation of 1763 which limited the boundaries of Quebec and established the west as an Indian preserve. When peace was restored among French, British and natives, the fur trade organizations were ready to re-establish the old French fur routes westward.

By 1765 the traders had reached Lake Winnipeg and three years later James Finlay was on the Saskatchewan River. Soon they had penetrated northward as well as along the Saskatchewan. At first the Hudson's Bay Company did not regard these individual efforts as serious and contemptuously called the newcomers "pedlars."

Following the defeat of New France, the Hudson's Bay Company attempted to restore the flow of furs to the bay. In a period of ten years over forty journeys were undertaken by servants who wintered among the Indians and escorted them, with their furs, to York Factory. William Pink, who made four inland journeys (1766–70), travelled as far west as the modern site of Edmonton. He was the first to report the presence of British-employed French traders and in 1769 he met the Montrealer James Finlay with whom Indians were trading instead of continuing the long journey to the bay. By this time the supply of furs reaching the bay had begun to decrease in numbers and quality.

In 1772–73 Matthew Cocking was sent inland to report on the activities of the pedlars. He passed the forks of the Saskatchewan into lands where the Indians had horses: they were unwilling to travel to the bay since they were not canoemen. He met Montreal traders and noted that they were using rum as well as other trade goods to obtain furs (Cocking himself had brought nothing to trade). His report confirmed the seriousness of the pedlar threat.

The Indians' main routes to the posts on Hudson Bay were the Churchill and Nelson rivers. By 1773 the number of Montrealers was increasing and they began to intercept the fur supply from the Churchill. The Hudson's Bay Company was forced to revise its trade policies and adopt a more aggressive attitude by carrying supplies to the Indians. The man chosen to introduce this new policy was Samuel Hearne.

Hearne had already made a name for himself as an explorer. In 1769 he was sent from Fort Prince of Wales to check on reported copper mines in the north, to take possession of the Arctic coast for the Hudson's Bay Company and to clear up the persistent rumours of a Northwest Passage out of Hudson Bay. On his first expedition he had been gone only five weeks and travelled about 200 miles (320 km) when his Chipewyan guides deserted him; he barely returned alive. A few months later he started his second journey guided by a Chipewyan who proved to know little of the country. For over eight months through the spring and summer the party wandered over the barrens, travelling as far north as Chesterfield Inlet. They often suffered from lack of food, and were raided by a large band of wandering Indians who looted them of most of their supplies. Hearne was forced to turn back, and was fortunate to meet some friendly Indians led by Matonabbee, who took him to Fort Prince of Wales. Part Chipewyan and part Cree, Matonabbee was highly respected by various tribes, was a valued interpreter for the company and had travelled widely through the barren lands.

Hearne's experiences on his first two trips influenced his planning for the third: he dispensed with white companions, who had proved a handicap, and he brought women this time, who were needed to carry goods, pitch tents and sew and mend clothing while the men hunted for food. Hearne departed the fort again in just twelve days accompanied by a group of Chipewyans including Matonabbee and his seven wives. Seven months later the party had crossed overland to the mouth of the Coppermine River. Disappointingly, Hearne found only traces of copper, and he was helpless to prevent his Indian companions from massacring a village of Inuit, their traditional enemies. Returning by a roundabout route, Hearne was the first white man to see Great Slave Lake. He reached Fort Prince of Wales in June 1772, having been away eighteen months. See Map 4.

Hearne was now selected to challenge the growing threat of the Montrealers and establish a post inland. In 1774 Cumberland House, the oldest permanent settlement in Saskatchewan, was built on the Saskatchewan River. Not only was its stock of trade goods and rum a radical change from company policy but it also marked the beginning of the bitter fur wars and the expansion of Hudson's Bay Company forts to the Rocky Mountains and eventually the Pacific Ocean.

At the time of the American Declaration of Independence Hearne was in charge of the massive fortification at Fort Prince of Wales. He was unaware that France was allied to the Americans until, in 1782, a French naval force under Jean François de Galaup, Comte de la Pérouse, appeared off the fort. More than forty years had passed since there had been an armed enemy in the bay. Totally unprepared, with a garrison of thirty-nine men again more than three hundred Frenchmen, Hearne surrendered. After sacking the fort the French vainly tried to destroy the walls, leaving the ruins as they appear today. Then, in the last French attack on Canada, La Pérouse captured and burned York Factory.

Hearne and his men were allowed to return to England in one of the company ships. In 1783, at the end of the war, he established Fort Churchill near the site of the old Fort Prince of Wales. Four years later he returned to England where he died in 1792. Hearne left a vivid, meticulous account of his travels. He had survived the barren lands, found no Northwest Passage and had made the first overland journey to the Arctic Ocean, filling in another detail of that unknown coast.

The North West Company

The long haul from Montreal to the fur lands of the west was undertaken in two phases. Trade goods were transported from Montreal to Grand Portage on Lake Superior in large canoes. There they were reapportioned to light canoes for the various interior posts. Some of the Montreal voyageurs returned with the furs that had been received at Grand Portage while others continued west with the traders. The western Indians' requirements varied from region to region and trade items had to be suited to the individual market. Some trading Indians were warlike in an attempt to prevent the pedlars from passing through their lands to their hunting neighbours. And if they were not satisfied with a trader's offering, they could go to a competing trader.

As more and more traders entered the west and built adjacent posts, competition became keener, profits decreased and the fur animals were depleted. The traders were forced to travel farther in search of virgin lands. One of the most successful was the American Peter Pond who traded from Montreal. In 1778 he reached the Churchill River and followed it to Ile à la Crosse Lake. From there he made the twelve-mile (19-km) Methye Portage to reach a tributary of the Athabasca River, thereby crossing from the Saskatchewan to the Mackenzie watersheds. By following the Athabasca River he may have reached Lake Athabasca. Pond made numerous, often inaccurate maps and suggested that the Slave River might empty into the Pacific Ocean—a surmise that was given much credence and probably later influenced Alexander Mackenzie. Pond was connected with two murders, which he may not have committed himself, but the suspicions that accompanied him to Montreal forced him to withdraw from the fur trade and return to the United States.

The independent traders were not only suffering from the cutthroat competition among themselves and with the Hudson's Bay Company; Americans were maintaining pressure to eliminate them from the lands south of the Great Lakes. Gradually the Montrealers banded into trading groups which amalgamated in 1787 as the North West Company. Among its early members were Peter Pangman, Joseph Frobisher, Alexander Mackenzie and the dominant partner, Simon McTavish. The North West Company controlled the trade from Montreal except for a brief period after 1800 when a breakaway group formed the New North West Company, commonly known as the XY Company from the markings on its bales. This powerful group led by Mackenzie, who believed he had enough influence to form his own syndicate, were dissatisfied with the North West Company management and felt they could do better on their own. The struggle was bitter and only ended after the death of McTavish; Mackenzie withdrew from the fur trade and retired to Scotland. The XY Company rejoined the older company in 1804. With a network of posts stretching to the Pacific Ocean, the North West Company laid the foundation for Confederation.

.Although earlier French agents had sent traders west, the former had neither the drive nor commercial ability of the British traders. Men such as Alexander Henry, Joseph and Benjamin Frobisher, James McGill and Simon McTavish made fortunes from their organization of the fur trade and became leaders of the community in Montreal. They established a policy that was to endure for almost two centuries: the accumulation of wealth by exchanging the raw materials of the west for imported and processed goods from the St. Lawrence centres.

The North West Company was controlled by twenty-two shareholders, though the shares were unevenly divided. The Montreal agents were responsible for ordering the goods from England, as requisitioned by the wintering partners; for storing them and packaging them into ninety-pound (40-kg) bales, and for supplying monies to pay the clerks and voyageurs. Representatives of the two groups met annually at Grand Portage. After the international boundary was established in 1783, Grand Portage was found to be in the United States and the meeting place was moved in 1803 to Fort William where an impressive fort covering several acres was built. Here goods from the east, carried in large thirty-five-foot (10.5-m) *canots de maître*, were exchanged for pelts brought by the men of the *pays d'en haut*, who used the lighter *canots de nord* which were about twenty-four feet (7 m) long, five feet (1.5 m) wide and two feet (60 cm) deep. The clerks and voyageurs were paid set wages and the remaining profits were divided each year among the shareholders.

The far distant brigades were hard pressed to make the return trip before winter set in, so that the timing of the junction of the east and west brigades was vital. At Fort William the goods from the east were sorted for the different inland posts and by July the return trips had begun. Brigades to the most distant posts left first, with two days between brigades to prevent delays at portages. Each brigade consisted of four to eight canoes, each manned by four, five or six men and carrying thirty-five packages.

The trade was developed on the backs of the voyageurs. These men—usually French Canadians, French or English Metis, and Indians—worked long hours, often fifteen hours a day with two short stops for meals. For low wages they carried the goods over a thousand miles (1600 km) and wintered in desolate, unfamiliar territory surrounded by sometimes unfriendly natives. They were responsible for paddling or poling canoes and for carrying the boats and goods across portages. A voyageur was supposed to carry two ninety-pound bales, and some would carry three. The diet of the eastern voyageurs consisted mainly of corn, peas and dried pork (hence "pork-eaters") but the men of the *pays d'en haut* depended on pemmican. This was a concentrated nutritious food made of pounded and dried meat (usually buffalo) sometimes mixed with berries and packaged in animal intestines. The life was full of danger: Indian attacks, sudden lake squalls, unseen rocks in rapids and sometimes, when game was scarce, starvation. At times, wading in icy waters, stumbling through swamps or over logs, pulling canoes with ropes from the river bank, and pestered by swarms of blackflies and mosquitoes, the workers expressed their frustration in a cacophany of oaths.

But the men were proud of their strength as they paddled or poled their canoes or trotted with their packs. They sang to the rhythm of the paddles; when they rested at a post or completed the journey, they were boisterous and noisy. From early spring until autumn the canoemen worked, but in winter they trapped or waited for the new season. This carefree, dangerous life was far removed from that of the cautious, money-conscious agents in Montreal.

Many of the traders had relationships with Indian or Metis women, sometimes marrying them according to the native customs and, in some cases, solidifying the unions with church ceremonies. In later years mixed relationships were encouraged by the Hudson's Bay Company. Not only did the women help with the work but the connections also brought amity between traders and Indians, which in turn increased the number of furs and profits. For the women, the relationships meant prestige and security. If a trader was reposted to a new district, he might not take the woman with whom he had been living for some time, but he probably made arrangements for her and the children's care, either by payment or by arranging for someone else to care for them.

With time and a strong organization, the trade became more systematic. The North West Company developed a spirit of cooperation and loyalty among its servants. The Indians were pacified and controlled. The best water routes were recognized, and as the traders became more efficient in river navigation they were able to penetrate new lands. Pemmican, concentrated and light, became the staple food.

Meanwhile, the Hudson's Bay Company continued building inland posts along the Red-Assiniboine and Saskatchewan river systems. Sometimes within a few miles would be posts of

the North West Company, the Hudson's Bay Company, the XY
Company and an independent trader. It was common practice
for the two major companies to build key posts close together,
a duplication that reduced the profits of both. See Map 6 for
major western posts of the fur trade era.

Alexander Mackenzie

Now that Captain Cook had traced the Pacific coastline, the
Nor'Wester Alexander Mackenzie believed that a shorter overland transportation route to the Pacific would be more practical than the long overland haul to Montreal. Leaving his new
post, Fort Chipewyan, on Lake Athabasca on 3 June 1789, he
began his descent of the Slave River and crossed Great Slave
Lake into the unknown, searching for a river to the Pacific. On
14 July he named Whale Island in the Arctic Ocean at the
mouth of the Mackenzie River. Disappointed, he returned to
Fort Chipewyan, arriving 12 September. He had not found an
outlet to the Pacific but he had added another point to the
Arctic coastline, far west of Hearne's destination (see Map 5),
and his discovery of the Mackenzie River system opened a vast
new trading territory.

Mackenzie spent some time in England studying, among
other subjects, surveying. There he probably heard of the
Pacific maritime fur trade and the misadventures of John
Meares. By 1792 he was back at Fort Chipewyan determined to
find a route to the Pacific. He wintered on the Peace River near
the mouth of the Smoky. On 9 May 1793 his expedition—seven
French Canadians, two Indians and Alexander Mackay, his
clerk—departed in a single canoe. The journey was arduous,
with unexpected rapids, long portages and contacts with
unfriendly natives. Ascending the Peace and Parsnip rivers,
the men portaged to a tributary of the Fraser and descended as
far as the present site of Alexandria. But there, warned by local
Shuswap of the dangers of the river and hostile natives, he
turned back to the Blackwater River, which he called the West
Road. From this river the party cached their canoe and packed
their supplies across the Coast Mountains. After a tortuous
journey, following the advice of Carrier Indians whom he met
on the way, Mackenzie reached the Bella Coola River flowing

west. He made a short stop at "Friendly Village" and feasted on salmon. Upon reaching the ocean in dugouts, the explorers followed North Bentinck Arm to Dean Channel. See Map 5. Here on a rock Mackenzie painted with a mixture of vermilion and melted grease, "Alex. Mackenzie, from Canada, by land, the twenty-first of July, one thousand seven hundred and ninety-three." He learned from the Indians in "Rascal's Village" that some of Captain Vancouver's crew had been in the vicinity forty-eight days before.

Mackenzie was the first white man to cross the Cordillera, closing the gap between land and ocean exploration. Unfortunately, he had not found a navigable route to the Pacific.

Simon Fraser

By Jay's Treaty, 1794, the British finally surrendered their interior fur forts south and southwest of the Great Lakes in what had become American territory in 1783. The North West Company moved north from the American Grand Portage to establish Fort William in 1802–3 which became the meeting place of the brigades from east and west. Trade to the west and north assumed more importance and the Saskatchewan River became a vital trade route. In 1795 the North West Company built Fort Augustus on the North Saskatchewan and soon the Hudson's Bay Company had Edmonton House close by, the first of four posts in the vicinity to bear that name. Edmonton House eventually became the central depot for goods to the Athabasca region and across the Rockies.

This was the greatest era of the North West Company. Employing over 1,500 officers, clerks and labourers, an efficient organization was developed. The company increased its profits and dividends through the business acumen of its men in Montreal, the efforts of the officers in the field, the expertise of the canoemen, and the ruthless harvesting of animals. By holding its annual meetings at Fort William, the company was able to make quick decisions and to move efficiently into new fur lands.

By contrast, the Hudson's Bay Company suffered from an inflexible organization and policies set in faraway London. The wars against France made its European markets uncertain.

In 1778 the company paid a ten per cent dividend, in 1779 eight per cent, but from 1783 to 1785 inclusive there was none. For almost twenty-four years the dividend was usually four per cent (though in a few more years it did rise back to eight). Nevertheless, the company had a stable organization and many years of experience. Pressed by the men in the field, it gradually adopted a more aggressive business attitude.

The North West Company also faced problems: the loss of the American posts, the loss of markets because of the European wars, and the internal dissensions caused by the XY Company. At the same time, however, the Pacific goal of Alexander Mackenzie was not forgotten. In 1805 the company began a policy of steady expansion into the Cordillera. In that year Simon Fraser followed the Peace River and established Fort McLeod just west of the Parsnip River—the first post west of the Rocky Mountains and the oldest in British Columbia. In the following years he established Fort St. James on Stuart Lake, Fort Fraser on Fraser Lake and, in 1807, Fort George at the junction of the Fraser and Nechako rivers.

Fraser, like Mackenzie, believed that he was actually on the Columbia River, and when he received instructions from headquarters to explore the river, he immediately began preparations. His journey (see Map 5) is a story of great dangers and narrow escapes—through treacherous rapids, along precipitous cliffs, in and out of encounters with suspicious Indians. En route he named the Thompson River after his friend David Thompson. Leaving Fort George on 22 May 1808, he reached the Indian village of Musqueam on tidal waters on 2 July. To his surprise Fraser ascertained that he was north of 49°; the Columbia mouth was known to be at 46°. The local Coast Salish Indians were familiar with maritime traders and, presumably, had experienced some mistreatment, for they were hostile towards Fraser. He did not stay but immediately began the return journey.

Fraser called the new district New Caledonia. He was disappointed that his new river was apparently too turbulent to be used as a trading passage to the Pacific, but within a few years a route was found. David Stuart, a cousin of Fraser's companion John Stuart, was employed by John Jacob Astor's Pacific Fur Company. In 1811, after accompanying David Thompson for a short distance up the Columbia, Stuart separated and turned north to follow the Okanagan River to Okanagan Lake whence he crossed overland to the Thompson River. Later, at the junction of the North and South Thompson rivers, he established Fort Kamloops. In 1813 John Stuart left Fort George, followed the Fraser to about Soda Creek and then crossed overland to Okanagan Lake. The two cousins had opened a passable route from the inland posts to the Columbia mouth.

American Rivalry and David Thompson

David Thompson is renowned more for his surveying and map making than for his trading. In 1784 he joined the Hudson's Bay Company and spent some years at inland posts. In 1787 he visited a Peigan camp on the Bow River and thus was probably the first white man to see the present site of Calgary. A leg injury restricted his exploratory work for a while. In 1797, discontented and frustrated, he joined the North West Company which promised to allow him more time for surveying. Thompson spent some time in the south, showed that Grand Portage and Pembina were south of the American frontier, and mapped the Red and Assiniboine rivers. He showed that the international boundary did not cross the Mississippi River as projected in the British-American Treaty of Paris of 1783.

The North West Company hoped to find a southern route to the Pacific in addition to the one expected through the Peace River. In 1800 Thompson, who had a copy of Vancouver's *Voyages* with him, was at Rocky Mountain House; although several passes had been located, no Nor'Wester had yet crossed the mountains south of the Peace River. Rocky Mountain House, built in 1799, was the westernmost post on the Saskatchewan River. Finally in 1807 Thompson penetrated the mountains and reached the Columbia River. See Map 5. Paddling upstream towards the south, he built Kootenay House near the headwaters of the Columbia. For two years he remained in the Kootenay region, establishing posts, mapping, and gathering furs as far south as Spokane in present Washington state. He spent a year in the north at Fort Augustus.

In 1803 the United States had purchased Louisiana from

France and within a year Meriwether Lewis and William Clark were sent overland to the Pacific. On 3 December 1805 they reached the mouth of the Columbia, becoming the second expedition to cross North America north of Mexico. American fur traders were soon moving westward towards the mountains.

Mackenzie and Fraser had attempted to discover a trade route to the Pacific. This scheme was revived by an American capitalist, John Jacob Astor, who was eventually to dominate the American fur trade. Astor planned to establish an overland trade route co-ordinated with coastal vessels which would supply a proposed Columbia River post, trade along the coast and transport furs to China. The project was beset by difficulties. One vessel was wrecked in the Hawaiian Islands, one was blockaded in Canton, and only the *Tonquin* reached the mouth of the Columbia in 1811. Here Fort Astoria was established on the south bank. Shortly afterwards the *Tonquin* was blown up by natives and only two crew members survived. Meanwhile, the overland expedition had a disastrous trip in which they were forced to eat their horses and dogs. After a year's travel the nearly exhausted survivors reached Fort Astoria.

In spite of the difficulties, Astor's Pacific Fur Company, under the guidance of former Nor'Westers such as David Stuart, established inland posts including Fort Okanagan (at the Okanagan and Columbia river junction) and Fort Kamloops.

The North West Company determined to challenge Astor's plans. When David Thompson, who was heading east for a much-deserved furlough, reached Rainy Lake in 1810, he was told to return to the west. Whether he was instructed to forestall the Americans is uncertain but the slowness of his expedition suggests perhaps that he was not so ordered or that he did not expect the Americans to act so quickly. When he reached Rocky Mountain House, he found the Peigans in a warlike mood, annoyed that he had supplied their enemies, the Kootenays, with weapons, and determined to prevent his returning to them. To avoid the Peigans, Thompson went north, crossed Athabasca Pass and reached the Big Bend of the Columbia River at Boat Encampment. These manoeuvres delayed the expedition and it was now December; Thompson decided to construct a rough cabin and winter there. In April

1811 he took his discontented crewmen south against the current to Kootenay House. He crossed Canal Flats to the Kootenay River, followed it south and visited the forts he had established earlier. Then he crossed overland to the Columbia River and reached the mouth on 15 July, where he found the American Fort Astoria already established. The overland commercial system of Montreal was being challenged by eastern American interests using the sea route. After a short friendly visit, Thompson followed the Columbia to the Big Bend accompanied by some Astorians who were planning to trade inland. This completed Thompson's survey of the entire river.

In 1812 Thompson returned to Montreal. Later he was to produce a large map of the northwest and to survey the boundary between Lake Superior and Lake of the Woods. Poor investments dissipated his money and he died in 1857 poor, unrecognized and almost blind. Many more years would pass before he became acknowledged as Canada's greatest map maker.

The establishment of Fort Astoria threatened British expansion on the unoccupied coast. When the War of 1812 broke out, Britain heard the rumour that the American frigate *Essex* was threatening its shipping in the Pacific and dispatched four naval ships to that region. Before any ships arrived on the northwest coast, the North West Company, whose lines of communication were well established, sent men to the Columbia mouth. Outnumbered, the Americans agreed to sell their company and the Nor'Westers occupied Astoria. Thus when the British warship *Racoon* arrived, she found the fort already in British hands. Nevertheless, a formal act of possession was made, the British flag was raised, and the fort was renamed Fort George. This proved to be only temporary, for by the Treaty of Ghent (1814) the fort was restored to the Americans.

By agreement with Astor, the North West Company continued to use Fort George for a number of years and took some Astorians into its employ. In 1814 the North West Company vessel *Isaac Todd* reached Fort George, inaugurating annual voyages. Although some goods for inland posts were sent by ship, the expected maritime export trade did not develop. Trade with China was unprofitable because of the East India Company monopoly of the British trade there. To circumvent

the restrictions, the North West Company made an agreement
with a Boston firm which brought British-manufactured goods
to the Columbia mouth, carried furs across the Pacific to China,
and with the proceeds purchased tea and other Chinese products for the American markets. This arrangement was highly
profitable to both companies.

The main transportation routes continued overland. From
Fort George (Astoria) and later from Fort Vancouver on the
Columbia, the brigades went eastwards either through Athabasca Pass or by the Okanagan Lake–Kamloops–Fort George
route, to connect with the brigades for Fort William.

Following the Treaty of Ghent, in 1818 Great Britain and the
United States completed a number of border agreements. The
forty-ninth parallel was accepted as the boundary from Lake of
the Woods to the Rocky Mountains. The territory west of the
mountains, between the Spanish possessions in the south and
the Russian in the north, was to be held in "joint occupancy."
This agreement was renewed in 1827 for an indefinite period.

The Selkirk Settlement

Thomas Douglas, fifth Earl of Selkirk, was a young Scottish
landowner with humanitarian interests. When he married Jean
Wedderburn in 1807 she had some shares in the Hudson's Bay
Company; her brother Andrew Wedderburn Colvile was a
powerful official in the company. Selkirk gradually purchased
enough shares to gain control. In Scotland, crofters were being
evicted as the land was converted to sheep raising, and Selkirk
believed these displaced persons could be settled in America.
A colony on Prince Edward Island was moderately successful
but the one in Upper Canada at Baldoon was a failure. Selkirk
envisioned a more ambitious colony. In 1811 the Hudson's Bay
Company granted Selkirk the land of Assiniboia, consisting of
116,000 square miles (300 000 km²) of territory which today
would include parts of Manitoba, Minnesota and North Dakota
(see Map 6).

The Selkirk grant threatened to sever the North West Company's communication network and to disrupt the whole organization. Therefore the company began a period of propagan-
dizing in order to discourage British settlers. Although 125

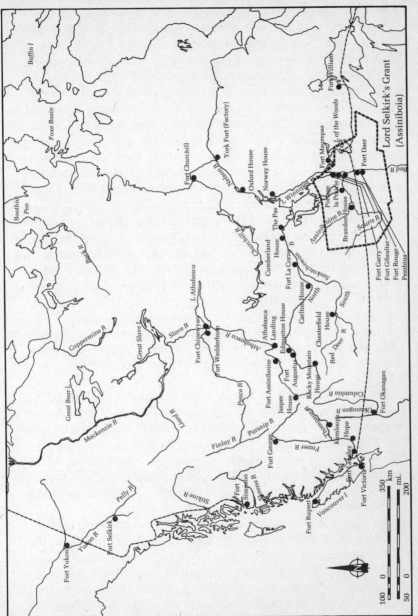

MAP 6: MAJOR FUR TRADING POSTS

people had collected at Stornoway in Scotland, the first shipload only amounted to 70 because of adverse publicity. The
sailing date was delayed several weeks. After a crossing of
sixty-one days, the immigrants arrived in late September at
York Factory where they were not welcomed. Selkirk's party
had been recruited indiscriminately from Scotland, the Ork-
neys and Ireland, and now they were quarrelsome and rebellious. The Hudson's Bay officials at York Factory, by contrast,
were fur traders and did not welcome undisciplined strangers
bent on settlement. They provoked dissension among the newcomers by inviting certain ones to join them instead. It is
doubtful whether York Factory could have accommodated this
sudden influx, but in any event the new arrivals were coldly
received and forced to spend the winter at the mouth of the
Nelson River in makeshift quarters. The following spring
twenty-three men under the leadership of Capt. Miles Macdonell, followed later by the others, took fifty-five days to
reach Red River. Here they established Fort Douglas, three-
quarters of a mile (1.2 km) north of the junction with the Assiniboine. Later they built Fort Daer near Pembina. The newcomers obtained some assistance from the Nor'Westers at Fort
Gibraltar, but because of the uncertainty caused by the War of
1812, the traders needed to conserve most of their supplies.
Unfortunately for the settlers, their first year's crops were a
failure.

Settlers continued to arrive from Scotland and Ireland. In
1813 typhoid struck those on shipboard and they were forced
to spend a difficult winter at Fort Churchill before trekking to
Red River. By this time, under instructions from headquarters,
the North West people were no longer co-operating with the
settlers. That year most crops except potatoes and turnips were
injured by early frosts, but with plenty of buffalo meat the
people survived.

Along the Assiniboine, especially in the La Souris district,
the Indians and Metis received most of their income from the
sale of pemmican to the traders. Miles Macdonell, whom Selkirk had appointed governor of the Red River settlement, was
determined to obtain a food supply for the settlers and in 1814
he posted notices from Fort Douglas along the Assiniboine to
Brandon House forbidding the export of pemmican. When the

Metis resisted, he sent men to seize the pemmican bales and carry them to Red River. Although his proclamation affected all traders, the North West Company suffered most since it depended on the pemmican supply for the long journeys to the west. The company officials had opposed the settlement from the beginning and Macdonell's action precipitated a crisis. North West agents stirred the Indians and Metis with propaganda against the settlers in their midst and resistance increased. Macdonell was forced to agree to provide pemmican to the company that year, but this did not stop the Nor'Westers from warning the Metis that the Selkirk settlers would eventually force them out of their homes.

The North West leader at Fort Gibraltar, Duncan Cameron, also began to spread doubts among the suffering and disillusioned settlers, who were often subject to vandalism. He offered them free passage in company canoes to the more propitious life in Upper Canada. Many accepted his offer. Next, with a warrant issued by a Canadian justice of the peace, and supported by a large force of Indians and Metis, he appeared at Fort Douglas. Threatened with violence, Macdonell surrendered the fort and was sent as a prisoner to Montreal. The remnant of the settlers were forced to flee to the north end of Lake Winnipeg where they survived another winter. Their homes and crops at Fort Douglas were destroyed.

While the inexperienced Macdonell was en route to Montreal, a large Hudson's Bay Company trading party was heading from that city to the Athabasca country under Colin Robertson. When he reached Red River he sent the fur traders on but remained himself to lead the dispossessed settlers back from the north. The colony was rebuilt and the Metis temporarily pacified.

In November 1815 a new band of colonists reached Red River from Hudson Bay under the new governor of the colony, Robert Semple. While Semple was visiting outside posts, Robertson captured a North West winter express and found confirmation of his belief that the company was plotting against the colony. He seized Forts Gibraltar and Pembina. Meanwhile, the Metis on the Assiniboine, under North West employee Cuthbert Grant, had destroyed Brandon House; they now marched towards Fort Douglas. A short distance from the fort they were met by thirty or so men under Governor Semple. Who fired the first shot is uncertain, but in the resulting "Massacre of Seven Oaks" twenty-one settlers and the governor were killed; only one Metis fell. Once again the colonists were herded northward.

Lord Selkirk spent the winter of 1815–16 in Canada attempting to clarify to the British authorities the Hudson's Bay Company's proposals for the Selkirk settlement. Because Montreal was dominated by North West Company officers, Selkirk was frustrated by their continuous opposition. However, Governor Sherbrooke appointed Selkirk a justice of the peace and assisted him in gathering together a group of prospective colonists, some of whom were French Canadians. Selkirk also enlisted a number of demobilized men from the De Meuron regiment who had fought in the war against the United States. Trained men could be of great value in protecting the colony against further depredations.

In the spring of 1816 Lord Selkirk set out with about one hundred prospective settlers. After learning at the Sault of Semple's death, he then seized and occupied Fort William. His subsequent actions would later create numerous legal battles. Papers were seized and the fort officials, including William McGillivray, were arrested and sent to Montreal as prisoners. Weapons and furs were confiscated as recompense for the actions of the Nor'Westers; other supplies were purchased through a minor North West Company clerk. Miles Macdonell was sent ahead to reorganize Red River while Selkirk stayed back until the following May. Fort William was soon reoccupied by Nor'Westers from Montreal.

Selkirk spent a year in Red River organizing the colony. Land was subdivided, crops were planted, transportation was improved and plans were made for roads, bridges, mills, churches and schools.

In the Canadian courts at Montreal began a long series of claims and counterclaims. The North West officials were not only the leaders of business and social life but they were also members of the Legislative Council. The ensuing costly struggle imposed a great strain on Selkirk's health and he died in 1820, only forty-nine years old. It has been estimated that the various lawsuits cost the Selkirk family $100,000. But Selkirk's work was to endure, for in the following years, in spite of drought, floods and insect plagues, the settlement at Red River expanded and prospered.

A Decade of Violence

The Napoleonic Wars and the entrance of the United States into the war strained Britain's trade routes. Both the North West Company and the Hudson's Bay Company suffered. From 1809 to 1814 the latter company again paid no dividends.

The violence at Red River was a phase in the increasingly aggressive and vindictive trade rivalry which marked the Hudson's Bay Company's attempt to expand into Athabasca. By its charter, the Saskatchewan Valley was technically Hudson's Bay Company territory (though this had been ignored by the North West Company). The Mackenzie River watershed was not, however, and the North West Company was determined to stop any invasion of this region which it considered to be its special reserve. Thus when John Clarke established some Hudson's Bay Company posts, including Fort Wedderburn near Fort Chipewyan on Lake Athabasca, he faced determined opposition. By various means, including threats, the Nor'Westers persuaded the Indians not to trade with the newcomers and, more effectively, not to supply them with food. As a result, a number of Bay men sent to outposts died of starvation. The following year, 1816, Clarke was opposed by Archibald Norman McLeod, a trader who held the office of justice of the peace. After a winter of harassment McLeod seized Fort Wedderburn and arrested Clarke.

In the following years both companies perpetrated individual acts of violence: kidnappings, seizures of supplies and forts, and ambushing of rival brigades. Each side attempted to lure the Indian traders with higher prices and greater supplies of rum. The results were ruinous to both companies, but especially to the Nor'Westers dependent on the long overland haul. Moreover, this firm's policy of dividing all the profits each season left few reserves, while the Hudson's Bay Company, by limiting its dividends, continued to maintain a strong financial base. Some of the disgruntled wintering partners, distrusting the Montreal agents, considered joining the Hudson's Bay

Company. The internal dissension further weakened the North West Company.

The British government, beset by the claims and counter-claims of both companies, supported some form of compromise and insisted that an effective method of law enforcement be introduced. In 1821 the two firms were amalgamated as the Hudson's Bay Company. The charter was supplemented to give it control not only of the lands drained by Hudson Bay but also of the former North West Company territories as far west as the Pacific Ocean.

By this time British North America had become the two provinces of Lower and Upper Canada by the Constitutional Act of 1791. Their boundaries extended as far as Hudson Bay Company lands, or the height of land separating the drainage basins of the St. Lawrence and Hudson Bay. Lower Canada contained about one-third of the present area of Quebec. The boundary of Upper Canada followed the Ottawa River and included a comparatively narrow strip of land around Lake Superior and Rainy Lake. All the land north and west of the Canadas was now controlled by the Hudson's Bay Company.

Chapter Three

COMPANY EMPIRE
(1821 – 1850)

Reorganization

AMALGAMATION of the Hudson's Bay Company and the North West Company involved a number of adjustments before the union was complete in practice. The agreement, which was to last for twenty-one years, divided the net profits of the company into 100 equal shares apportioned among the North West Company proprietors, the estate of the late Earl of Selkirk and others. The 40 shares that went to the "commissioned gentlemen" in the field were divided into 85 smaller shares of which each chief factor received two and each chief trader one. The North West Company had fifteen chief factors and seventeen chief traders for a total of 47 shares, while the Hudson's Bay Company had ten chief factors and eleven chief traders for a total of 31 shares. The remaining seven shares were reserved for old servants of both companies. The result was that the more experienced and independent Nor'Westers retained their right to share in the profits while the status of the Hudson's Bay men in the field had been improved by profit-sharing.

The company's territories in North America were divided into four departments: the Montreal Department in Upper and Lower Canada; the Southern Department, south and east of James Bay; the Northern Department of Rupert's Land, from Hudson Bay to the Rocky Mountains; and the Columbia

Department (at first part of the Northern Department) west of
the Rocky Mountains. These in turn were divided into districts
controlled by the chief factors and chief traders. A governor
was appointed over each department, and an annual council
meeting of the governor and his chief factors was held, similar
to the earlier Fort William meetings of the North West partners.
Each department had wide powers and submitted recommendations to the governor, deputy governor and committee in
London, though its decisions were subject to the control of
London.

During the early years, two major decisions were made:
which officers from both companies would be retained and
which of the numerous competitive trading posts would be
maintained. The rival fur traders, who were embittered after
years of ruthless competition, had to be appeased and encouraged to co-operate. In the first four years the number of
employees, both officers and labourers, was reduced from
about 2,000 to less than 900; many of the unemployed were
granted land and supplies at Red River. At the same time, the
company wanted to impress its strength and fairness on the
Indians, who were being asked to change their allegiance from
one set of traders to another.

Nicholas Garry, the deputy governor, was sent from England
to the Nor'Wester wintering partners to explain the new regime
and placate the discontented. He reached Montreal via New
York and, accompanied by Simon McGillivray who had been
the North West Company's representative in London, followed
the old North West route through Fort William to Red River.
Returning, Garry took the Hudson's Bay Company route via
York Factory, having successfully allayed the men's uncertain-
ties and brought about a spirit of co-operation among the factions.

The Southern and Northern departments were the most
important. William Williams had been governor-in-chief of the
Hudson's Bay Company territories and a bitter opponent of the
North West Company in the Athabasca district. Since McGil-
livray was opposed to the appointment of Williams to the
Northern Department, he was appointed governor of the less
prestigious Southern Department. A comparative newcomer,
George Simpson, was appointed governor of the Northern

Department. He would become one of the greatest names in the history of the fur trade.

Sir George Simpson

George Simpson was an illegitimate child whose mother is unknown. Born in Scotland, he was raised by his father's family. Through their influence he entered a London firm of sugar importers controlled by Andrew Wedderburn (who later changed his name to Colvile), a powerful member of the board of the Hudson's Bay Company. (His sister Jean married Lord Selkirk, leading, as we have seen, to his interest in the company.) The years of training under Colvile had a lifelong influence on the young Simpson. It was through him that Simpson entered the Hudson's Bay Company, and his loyalty to both Colvile and the company never wavered. At the same time, he was at heart a businessman who emphasized organization and profits and opposed waste.

During the last years of rivalry the strife between the two fur companies was almost open war: loads of pelts were ambushed and seized; Colin Robertson of the Hudson's Bay Company was captured by Nor'Westers but escaped; a warrant for the arrest of William Williams for seizing North West furs was sworn out in Montreal. In 1820, with their trade in disarray and their governor threatened with arrest, the Hudson's Bay Company sent Simpson to support Williams and to take charge of Athabasca. He travelled via New York to Montreal where the North West agents, already negotiating a peace, entertained him at the exclusive Beaver Club. En route to the Athabasca region he had his first experience of travel by canoe and listened to the stories and advice of his seasoned companions. At Fort Wedderburn he proved his qualities as a leader: challenged by a threatening group of Nor'Westers, Simpson faced their threats with a combination of tact, courage and bluff and gained their respect, if not their friendship. The Indians came to trade and the Hudson's Bay Company was established in the region.

Simpson stands above his contemporaries in intelligence, leadership ability and business understanding. Like all great men he had his detractors and supporters. Though egotistical, he would accept suggestions from any employee. On the other hand, he could be outspoken and would criticize any man to his face for errors or misjudgement, but would not bring embarrassment by ridiculing him in front of others. Only a man of tact could have dissipated the lingering hatred of strong, often violent, independent men and welded them into a loyal unit. Simpson could be ruthless, too, and had no qualms about destroying any individual who was a troublemaker or uncooperative.

Meticulous by nature, he was a capable writer and kept detailed records; his reports to headquarters in London vividly described the life of the fur traders in the west. He also kept a secret file, known as the "Character Book," in which he noted his impressions of the chief factors, chief traders, clerks and even postmasters; mostly written in 1832, they range from such opinions as "a frothy trifling conceited man who is perfectly useless here" (Colin Robertson) to "has every reason to look forward to early promotion" (James Douglas).

Simpson rose to become the most influential man in the Hudson's Bay Company territories. After amalgamation, he was governor of the Northern Department and five years later of the Southern Department, too. In 1839 he was made governor-in-chief of Rupert's Land as well, which gave him judicial and other authority over all of British North America north and west of the Canadas including parts of present-day Montana, Idaho, Oregon and Washington. The following year he was knighted.

Simpson undertook a complete reorganization of the company. Duplicate or unprofitable posts were closed or moved and district boundaries were changed where necessary. Surplus employees were discharged, though some compensation in land or money was granted. Salaries were reduced, as were the payments for furs. Employees were classified by pay levels from steersmen, guides, interpreters, voyageurs, postmasters and clerks to commissioned gentlemen. Skilled labourers and artisans such as coopers, blacksmiths, plumbers and miners were brought from England and Scotland for five-year terms at fixed rates of pay. Wages varied from district to district, and employees were granted a discount in company stores. Waste of any kind was anathema to Simpson. He opposed employees' use of imported luxury items because they took up transportation space. And he could not see why an employee should carry his Indian mate and children in a company canoe when the space could be used for trade goods.

Company policy opposed the sale of liquor to Indians and traders. Gradually alcohol was eliminated from the trade except where it was thought necessary—for example, in the south where American competition might be damaging. In some cases, carefully controlled amounts of rum would be supplied when the Indians came in for trade goods in the fall and when they returned with furs in the spring.

Because he was not the kind of administrator to direct affairs from behind an office desk, Simpson insisted upon being familiar with all aspects of the trade in all regions. During the first twenty years as governor he was continually travelling and inspecting. In 1822 he visited Brandon House, in 1822–23 Peace River, in 1824–25 the Columbia River, and in 1828 New Caledonia. In 1841–42 he made his famous nineteen-month voyage around the world visiting California, Hawaii, Alaska and crossing Siberia.

Simpson was always a driver and resented time lost. His hand-picked canoemen were the best in the service and worked long hours. Once, in 1824, Simpson left York Factory twenty days after John McLoughlin, chief factor of the Columbia Department. Six weeks later, at seven o'clock in the morning when McLoughlin's men were still loading, Simpson, who had already been travelling for two hours that day, caught up with him. On this journey Simpson completed the distance from York Factory to Fort George (Astoria) in eighty-four days, twenty days faster than any previous trader.

Simpson's crews started before five o'clock in the morning; after loading and travelling, a short stop was made for breakfast about eight. The next stop was at noon for a rapid lunch, about an hour. The men continued until dark. Before reaching a post, they would don red outfits and make a spectacular approach in their brightly coloured canoes with vermilion-red paddles, the governor wearing a large cape and beaver hat. The singing of the voyageurs could be heard long before they came in sight. Preceded by a young Scottish piper in full regalia, Simpson would disembark and march into the fort. His rapid travels to all parts of the country kept the traders alert, for they knew he was quick to perceive slovenliness, waste or lack of efforts to lessen the post's dependence on imported stuffs.

As his authority increased, Simpson became more autocratic and domineering. During his travels to Europe he was entertained by the wealthy and aristocratic; in Canada he mixed with government officials and members of the Family Compact, so that he gradually lost his close contact with the working traders and became more aloof. In later years he widened his interests by investing in numerous commercial enterprises. Not unexpectedly, he opposed radical ideas and was unsympathetic to the protests that led to the uprisings of 1837.

Although Simpson had relationships with a number of native women, in 1830 he married his cousin, the sister-in-law of Chief Factor Duncan Finlayson. He brought Frances Ramsay Simpson to Red River where he built her a fine house, but she never adjusted to frontier life and was often ill. Their first child died. They left their home in Lower Fort Garry and moved to Lachine, Quebec. From these new headquarters the "Little Emperor" ran his empire. He died there on 7 September 1860.

For forty years the history of western Canada was dominated and controlled by Sir George Simpson. The company profited: in 1825 the capital increased from £103,950 to £400,000 and from that time the rate of dividends never fell below ten per cent, in spite of the fact that by 1840 the fashionable beaver hat had been displaced by hats made of silk. As the country developed, Simpson recognized the inevitable changes and adjusted his planning and direction to the times.

The Fur Empire

There were practical reasons for Simpson to move his headquarters to Lachine. Montreal was the commercial centre of the growing colony of Canada, with banks and leaders of commerce, and had become the trade centre for both Americans and Canadians from the Great Lakes. Here were the warehouses of the old North West Company as well as the powerful ex–North West officers. By working with them, Simpson was able to forestall the possible establishment of another rival fur company. There was also the fact that Montreal, having a longer navigation season, was a more suitable terminus than York Factory for Simpson's frequent trips to London. Montreal continued to be the supply depot for the Southern Department and regular express canoes were sent as well to Red River.

The main outlet for the Northern Department, however, became York Factory, and Fort William lost its dominating position in favour of Norway House. This post, on the Nelson River near the outlet of Lake Winnipeg, was the meeting place for the brigades from Fort Garry and the western posts with the canoes from York Factory, and became the site of the annual council meeting which determined company policies. Here goods were transferred from the lighter inland canoes to the slower freight canoes—later York boats.

Posts were strung along the North Saskatchewan as strategic depots. Cumberland House was the crossing place from the Saskatchewan north to the Churchill River. Fort La Corne, below the junction of the North and South Saskatchewan rivers, became a storehouse for pemmican, as was Carlton House on the north branch. From Edmonton House the Mackenzie brigade went overland to Athabasca Landing and Fort Assiniboine on the Athbasca River, leading to Fort Chipewyan, and other northern or western posts via the Peace River. From Fort George canoes and pack horses were used by the brigades through the Okanagan Valley to the Columbia River, thence to Fort Vancouver, or, later, the lower Fraser River. Another western route from Edmonton House crossed to Jasper House and the Athabasca Pass.

Along these routes canoes continued to be used for their speed and lightness. In about 1800 the Hudson's Bay Company had begun to use boats from York Factory which Simpson now promoted. These York boats, though slower than canoes, were capable of carrying larger loads with fewer men. Each boat had a crew of nine, and brigades of nine or ten boats became common. The larger ones had a crew of ten and could carry one hundred pieces of ninety-pound (40-kg) baggage. Sometimes forty feet (12 m) long, with a shallow bow and stern for launching off beaches and rocks, they drew only two or three feet (less than 1 m) of water, comparable to canoes. They were propelled with twenty-foot (6-m) sweeps and also had a square sail that could be used in favourable winds. They were better than

canoes in lake storms, were stronger against ice and rocks, and
were safer in small rapids. At portages they were dragged by
men or horses over log rollers.

Edmonton House and Fort Augustus were combined and
moved near the site of the present city of Edmonton. Fort
Edmonton was the largest and most important post west of Red
River. Hexagonal in shape, with 300 feet by 200 feet (90 m by
60 m) of twenty-foot (6-m) palisades, it was an imposing sight,
located at a bend of the North Saskatchewan. As Paul Kane
described it:

All the Company's servants, with their wives and children, numbering about 130, live within the palings of the fort in comfortable log
houses ... every one was busy; the men, some in hunting, some in
sawing boards in the saw-pit and building the boats, which go as far as
York Factory. . . . The women find ample employment in making moc-
casins and clothes for the men, putting up pemmican in ninety-pound
bags. . . .

In charge of Fort Edmonton and the Saskatchewan district
was Chief Trader John Rowand, a legendary man whom Simpson described as "the most active and best qualified." Rowand
was not only a shrewd businessman but was also able to handle the ever-dangerous Indians. To quote Paul Kane, "Seven of
the most important and warlike tribes on the continent are in
constant communication with the fort, which is situated in the
country of the Crees and Assiniboines, and is visited at least
twice yearly by the Blackfeet, Sar-Cees, Gros-Vents, Pay-gans
and Blood Indians." A spectacular sight in Edmonton was
Rowand's "Great House," sixty feet by seventy feet (18 m by 21
m), three storeys high with real glass windows (most were
parchment). It included a large room for the officers' mess and
another for entertainment where at Christmas as many as 150
guests were gathered. When Rowand died, Simpson had his
body placed in a keg of rum. Probably not trusting the voyageurs with such a valuable cargo, he had the keg transported
to York Factory in his own canoes, then shipped to England
and back to Lower Canada where Rowand wished to be buried.

Extending the Boundaries

The Hudson's Bay Company encouraged exploration into
the land north and west of Peace River. Its objectives were to

map new territory, open new fur lands and check Russian penetration from the coast.

John McLeod in 1823 ascended the Liard River to the Nahanni. The following year Samuel Black ascended the Finlay beyond its source. He found this river difficult to travel and he almost starved in a region of little game and few furs. Ten years later McLeod returned to the area and crossed overland west to the Stikine River.

Robert Campbell was one of the great western explorers and spent seventeen years in the region northwest of the Peace. In 1838 he followed McLeod's route along the Liard to Dease Lake, discovered and named the Pelly River, and continued on to the Stikine. Here at the time of the inland salmon run he met the powerful Tlingit Chief Shakes and entered the largest Indian camp he had ever seen. Indians from the coast had come to trade Russian goods with the assembled inland tribes. The coast Indians opposed Campbell's proceeding farther in case he disrupted their trade, but he became friendly with a powerful chief of the Nahannis: "She was a fine looking woman rather above the middle height & about 35 years old. . . . To the kindness and influence of this Chieftainess . . . in all probability we owed our lives more than once." Faced with strong opposition from the Tlingit middlemen, Campbell withdrew, but two years later he returned and, the following year, followed the Pelly to the Lewes River.

Meanwhile, in 1846, John Bell had crossed from the Mackenzie to the Porcupine River which he followed to its confluence with the Yukon; the following year a strong Fort Yukon was established here by Alexander Hunter Murray, a trader who was also an artist. Fort Yukon was the westernmost Hudson's Bay Company post and was inside Russian trading territory. It was so remote that seven years might be required for the furs to be replaced by trade goods from Britain.

While the north was being opened, Campbell established Fort Selkirk at the junction of the Pelly and Yukon rivers. After three years in this post he was instructed by George Simpson to follow the river downstream (see Map 5). After a long journey, he was amazed to reach Fort Yukon, managed by William Hardisty who had served under Campbell at Fort Selkirk three years before: neither the company nor these two men had realized that Fort Selkirk and Fort Yukon were on the same river.

Campbell returned by the easier Porcupine-Mackenzie route
and the Liard, but in 1852 Fort Selkirk was destroyed by hostile Tlingits who resented the instrusion of eastern traders into
their Russian market. Campbell and his men escaped but the
fort was abandoned. When the company refused his pleas to re-
establish the post, Campbell retired. Later he returned to the
company as chief factor in less arduous regions.

The Arctic Coastline

In spite of earlier failures Britain still hoped to find a North-
west Passage to the Orient. Before 1800 the only known locations on the Arctic coastline were those mapped by Hearne and
Mackenzie. With the end of the Napoleonic Wars, Britain had a
large number of experienced seamen and a powerful navy,
which prompted the government to offer numerous awards for
new discoveries in the north and authorize several exploratory
expeditions.

The first expedition, in 1818, was commanded by Capt. John
Ross, accompanied by his second-in-command, Lt. William
Edward Parry, and his nephew James Clark Ross. All three men
were eventually knighted for their Arctic explorations. With
two ships, the *Isabella* and the *Alexander*, they entered Lancaster Sound, but when Ross decided that there was no pass
the ships returned home. The following year, Parry sailed
through Lancaster Sound as far as Melville Island. His were the
first royal navy vessels to winter in the Canadian Arctic. On
this voyage he reported great difficulty with his compass, since
he was north of the magnetic pole. His voyage is noted for the
absence of scurvy as a result of the antiscorbutics he carried.

The British government's plans became more elaborate. A
sea expedition under Parry was to return to the Arctic while a
land expedition under John Franklin was to proceed eastward
along the coast from the mouth of Hearne's Coppermine River
and meet Parry. The latter followed the west coast of Hudson
Bay northward through Foxe Basin until he reached the straits
which he named Fury and Hecla after his ships. Unable to
penetrate the ice in these straits, he crossed them on foot. Parry
returned home after three futile summers in the Arctic.

John Franklin had led an adventurous life before being appointed to this project. He had fought with Nelson at Copenhagen and Trafalgar, accompanied Capt. Matthew Flinders on explorations in Australia, was present at the Battle of New Orleans during the War of 1812, and accompanied Capt. David Beecham on an abortive attempt to sail to the North Pole. His new assignment was the first of three to the Arctic coast.

Although the struggle between the rival fur companies was acute, both agreed to assist the venture. From York Factory, Franklin made his way to Fort Chipewyan thence to Great Slave Lake and on to the Yellowknife River where he wintered. The weather was so cold that even the rum froze. In June he proceeded by the Coppermine River to the ocean and, using small boats, travelled eastward along the coast. He mapped over 500 miles (800 km) of irregular coastline before he began his return from Point Turnagain. Following the Hood River and then portaging overland to the Coppermine, the explorers experienced extreme hardship, at times eating scraps of leather, old bones and soup made from lichens. Only nine survivors of the original twenty men reached Fort Chipewyan.

The next attempt to map the Arctic coastline was a three-pronged effort. Captain Parry was to approach from the east, but he never got past Boothia Peninsula. Capt. Frederick William Beechey was to penetrate from the Pacific but only reached Point Barrow, the most northerly point on the mainland. The third section was to start from the mouth of the Mackenzie River and make connections with the other two: Captain Franklin and Lieutenant Back travelled west to 141° longitude, in Russian territory, before returning; Dr. John Richardson reached only the Coppermine mouth.

Shortly after these failures John Ross and James Clark Ross spent three years (1829–32) in the Arctic. John Ross's ship was the first in Arctic exploration to use steam engines, but the boilers leaked and almost every part wore out or broke down. Eventually the dismantled engines were abandoned overboard. The *Victory* remained ice-bound near Boothia Peninsula where Ross discovered the magnetic pole. He survived four winters in the Arctic, a record not equalled until the twentieth century. He did so by adopting the ways of the Inuit, following their

diet, using dog sleds and living in igloos. Eventually, after
travelling many miles across the ice, the weary explorers met a
whaler who took them home.

Thomas Simpson, a cousin of George Simpson, with the fur
trader Warren Dease closed the gap from the Mackenzie River
to Point Barrow in 1837, using boats and hiking the last section. The other gap to the east was completed by Dr. John Rae
in 1854 while searching for Franklin.

Franklin, now Sir John, had sailed in 1845 in two ships, the
Erebus and the *Terror,* with 120 men and provisions for three
years, in the most ambitious British attempt to discover the
Northwest Passage. After being seen by a whaler in Baffin Bay,
the vessels disappeared. About forty expeditions sought him,
and gradually—from relics, discovered documents and Inuit
reports—a desolate picture emerged. The ships apparently
reached Franklin Strait where they were frozen in for almost
two years. Here Franklin and several others died. The desperate survivors attempted to escape by travelling overland to the
Back River but all perished.

For about nine years probing expeditions searched for
Franklin and added many details to northern maps. In 1851 Sir
Robert McClure, from the west, wintered at Banks Island where
his ships remained frozen for a year. After travelling over the
ice on foot, he and his crew met five ships from the east at
Melville Island. During the ensuing winter four of the ships
were lost and the remaining vessel carried the crews to England. Because he was the first to cross the Northwest Passage,
McClure received the £10,000 award.

The first completion of the Northwest Passage by a vessel
was in 1903 when the *Gjoa* under the Norwegian Roald
Amundsen completed the journey from east to west in three
years.

Assiniboia

The only white settlement west of the Great Lakes by 1821
was the Red River Colony, or Assiniboia as it was named in
1822. Located inside Hudson's Bay Company territory, it had
its own company-appointed governor who was subject to the
authority of the governor of the Northern Department, George

Simpson, to safeguard company interests. Simpson was not supportive of missionaries because he believed they diverted the Indians from fur gathering, but under pressure from zealous missionary societies in Britain, the company finally agreed to sponsor them. It brought the Anglican Rev. John West to Red River in 1820 and assisted him to minister to the needs of the Protestant settlers. Most of the settlers were Presbyterian Scots but for many years they attended St. Andrew's Anglican Church. Methodist missionaries arrived about twenty years later followed by Presbyterians. The Catholic Church had had missionaries in the west since the times of the early French traders and their churches were attended by the French and Metis in the settlement. The ways of the frugal, sober Presbyterian Scots contrasted greatly with those of the carefree uninhibited Metis.

The population extended for almost seventy miles (110 km) along the Red River and a hundred miles (160 km) along the Assiniboine River to beyond Portage la Prairie. As more settlers arrived from Scotland and the United States, the publicity encouraged a number of continental European immigrants.

Paul Kane has left us his impressions of the settlement. He found a mixture of languages: English, Gaelic, Swiss, French and native. In 1821 the population was estimated at 2,000, whereas in 1846 "the Scottish farmers . . . now number about 3,000 who live as farmers. . . . The half-breeds are more numerous than the whites, and now amount to 6,000." As time passed the diverse groups tended to establish ethnic settlements. Thus the Scots were at Kildonan, the French near the Catholic Mission at St. Boniface, the Metis on the White Horse Plains to the west, and retired Hudson's Bay officers and servants as well as the "British half-breeds" near Fort Garry and Lower Fort Garry. The last two became the sites for officers' pretentious homes and government offices and thus became the centre of social and commercial life.

While the Europeans and English-speaking Metis established prosperous farms, other Metis found this type of life difficult. "Their Indian propensities predominate," wrote Kane. They continued to hunt the buffalo and to manufacture pemmican. An example of George Simpson's tactfulness was the appointment of Cuthbert Grant, who had been a leader in

the opposition to Selkirk, as "Warden of the Plains," a gesture
of conciliation towards this former North West Company
Metis.

Natural disasters like those of the early years continued. In
1820 and 1821 the crops were levelled by grasshoppers, in
1823 they were destroyed by prairie fires, in several years the
buffalo were in short supply and hunters had to travel far distances, and in 1826 a great flood covered the valleys. These
events were not altogether calamitous for they discouraged the
misfits and discontented to leave the colony—many migrating
to the United States. As conditions improved the farms became
more productive and the dependence on buffalo meat
decreased.

Through the eras of the French and the North West Company, the main trade route to the west was through the Great
Lakes. With the amalgamation of the fur companies this strong
connection was ended and communication in and out of Red
River was channelled through Hudson Bay. Goods ordered
from Britain for the isolated colony would often take two years
for delivery and luxuries were almost unknown. The people
had to be self-sufficient, making their own homes and furni-
ture. In 1836 the Hudson's Bay Company bought Assiniboia
outright from the Douglas family, Lord Selkirk's heirs on the
board, and organized it as the District of Assiniboia under a
governor and council, while at the same time withdrawing
much support and special privileges for the settlers. As the
number of employees declined in proportion to the newcomers, resentment against the domination of the company
steadily increased throughout the colony.

A new threat to the company came from the south where
waves of American settlers were moving west. Fort Snelling
(renamed Minneapolis in 1852) and St. Paul had become
important trading posts. In 1823 the first steamboat arrived
from St. Louis. These towns could supply goods to Assiniboia
cheaper than the Hudson's Bay Company could through York
Factory. Using St. Paul as a base, American traders under the
strong leadership of John Jacob Astor were able to challenge
the company's trade in the west. Independent traders were
appearing in Assiniboia via the American route, not only selling goods to the settlers and thereby challenging the company's

monopoly but also buying furs. It was impossible to stop these numerous petty traders, encouraged by the settlers, from infiltrating the colony, but Simpson was determined that they should not enter the fur trade.

In Assiniboia most of the agricultural produce was used locally, leaving few goods that could be sold for cash. Simpson tried to encourage industries, such as the manufacture of buffalo wool, but none were successful. Pemmican remained the major cash commodity, and buffalo hides for winter coverings were increasing in demand.

The buffalo herds were being driven farther and farther from the settlement, necessitating a more organized hunt. Each spring the Metis undertook a large-scale search which established a system of Metis democratic self-government: the expedition was divided into groups each having an elected captain and subordinates to help him keep order; one captain was appointed leader of the drive. The rules were very rigid, and punishment for those who did not abide by them was severe. Every evening the captains and their assistants met, reviewed the day's march and made plans for the morrow. In 1840 an estimated 4,000 people and 1,200 Red River carts collected over a million pounds of meat.

The Red River cart was an early development of the Metis. A flat box was mounted over two large wheels so that it could cross swamps and shallow creeks. The entire vehicle was made of wood, with no nails, so that it could be repaired from nearby trees. Strips of wet buffalo hide wound around the wheels served as tires. Power was supplied by horses or ponies ("shaganappis"). Since grease was not used, the most obnoxious experience for the unaccustomed traveller was the perpetual high shrieking of the wheels on their wooden axle.

Buffalo hides were bulky and therefore unprofitable to ship in canoes or small boats but the Red River carts could accommodate them. Although the Hudson's Bay Company could not profitably export the hides through York Factory, there was a ready market in St. Paul. Increasingly, the people of Assiniboia trekked to that city which was an outlet for their hides as well as providing a wider range of goods at cheaper prices. By 1850 over one hundred Red River carts were making the annual spring journey.

Simpson had never liked Americans and this threat to the company's monopoly only intensified his aversion. He believed that radicals importing republican ideas from the United States were influencing the discontented settlers. He would have liked to suppress dissension by a police force or even a military force, but the British government was unsympathetic.

In the 1840s when the Americans were claiming the entire west coast—the height of the Oregon Dispute, Simpson pointed out that Americans were also as close as Pembina. So with the possibility of another annexation drive, the British sent 300 officers and men of the Sixth Regiment of Foot to Assiniboia. For two years there was less trouble in the colony; but when the troops were withdrawn, the discontent resurfaced.

In 1849 Pierre Guillaume Sayer was accused of illicit traffic with the Indians. During his trial the court was surrounded by several hundred threatening Metis. The governor of Assiniboia, Maj. William Caldwell, found the prisoner guilty, but recommended no punishment. Although Sayer had been found guilty of breaking the law which supported the Hudson's Bay Company's monopoly, the Metis concluded from the suspension of sentence that these monopoly rights had ended and that trade, even in furs, was to be open. Their interpretation was never challenged and independent trading increased.

The Columbia Valley

In 1818 Britain and the United States agreed that the territory west of the Rocky Mountains and between Spanish and Russian territories should be under "joint occupancy." In 1819 the Spanish and Americans agreed on a dividing line of 42° latitude. The Russians were bolder than the Spanish: in 1821 the Czar's ukase proclaimed Russia's southern boundary to be 51° (just north of Vancouver Island) and also forbade foreign ships to come within 100 miles (160 km) of Russian shores. This closing of the northern ocean and of trade to Alaska brought protests from both the United States and Britain. (It was partly the threat of Russian expansion that led the United States to issue the Monroe Doctrine in 1823 opposing any expansion of European powers into the Americas.)

In 1824, the Americans and Russians set 54°40′ (Dixon Entrance) as the boundary, and the Russians granted freedom of navigation and trading rights in Alaskan waters. They had actually gained an advantage by dealing with the Americans: the British had wanted 60°, but faced by a *fait accompli*, in 1825 they also accepted 54°40′. Russia in turn accepted 141° longitude instead of 139° as the eastern boundary of Alaska, which conceded the mouth of the Klondike River, and Britain gained the right to navigate Alaskan rivers to its inland posts. In 1839 the Hudson's Bay Company leased a section of the Alaskan "panhandle." In return, the company agreed to supply food and manufactured goods to the Russian posts and pay a rental of sea otter skins. This contract was between the Russian and British fur companies, not their governments, and included a clause by which both companies agreed to remain neutral in the event of war. As a result of this neutrality clause, the Crimean War (1854–56) had no effect on the British fur trading posts scattered along the coast of the North Pacific from Port Simpson near the Nass River to Victoria. Close co-operation between the companies continued until Alaska was sold to the United States in 1867.

When George Simpson visited the mouth of the Columbia in 1824, he was accompanied by Dr. John McLoughlin who was to be in charge of the Columbia Department. Under Simpson's instructions, McLoughlin began a thorough reorganization, hoping to make the territory self-sufficient by encouraging agriculture, decreasing the number of employees, developing exports and eliminating American competition. Simpson believed that the eventual international boundary would be the Columbia River and therefore decided to move the headquarters from Fort George to a new site, Fort Vancouver, farther up the river on the north bank. Steps were now taken to eliminate American traders. The inland fur animals were almost exterminated in order to deter American traders coming from the east. To check the American maritime trade, posts such as Fort McLoughlin, Fort Simpson, Fort Stikine and Fort Taku were established along the coast.

Simpson was convinced that a fort should be built on the lower Fraser River, as a more accessible coast depot for the inland trade of New Caledonia, and in 1827 McLoughlin arranged for the establishment of Fort Langley on the south bank. Surrounded by fertile land, Fort Langley became a major centre for agricultural products, some of which were sent to the northern Russian posts. The colony also developed a method of salting salmon which were exported to the Sandwich Islands in barrels made by a local cooperage. After the last brigade left the Columbia in 1847, Fort Langley became the terminus for interior brigades.

The company introduced trading vessels to service the maritime posts, and in 1836 the *Beaver*, the first steamship on the Pacific coast, joined the small sailing fleet. The Americans were eliminated from the fur trade in the northwest for several years.

The Oregon Treaty

Imbued with the doctrine of "Manifest Destiny," Americans believed that it was only a matter of time before the joint occupancy of the northwest would result in its eventual absorption by the United States. During the 1830s American missionaries and a number of settlers arrived at Fort Vancouver and settled in the Willamette Valley south of the Columbia. They were in dire straits, and the humane Dr. McLoughlin supplied them with necessities, often on credit. This was contrary to Simpson's policies and was one cause of the rift between the two men that intensified through the years. When McLoughlin later retired to the Willamette Valley, he was by now unpopular with both the company and his American neighbours, but eventually he would be recognized as the "Father of Oregon."

By the early 1840s the number of American immigrants arriving over the "Oregon Trail" was in the thousands, and they were demanding union with the United States. Negotiations over a boundary had dragged on for many years. As early as 1824 the United States had suggested 51° but their objective was probably to register a counterproposal to the obvious British claim to the Columbia River at 46°. See Map 7. In the critical year 1844, James Polk was elected president on the slogan "Fifty-four forty or fight," a demand that would have eliminated the entire British coastline. After the election fever

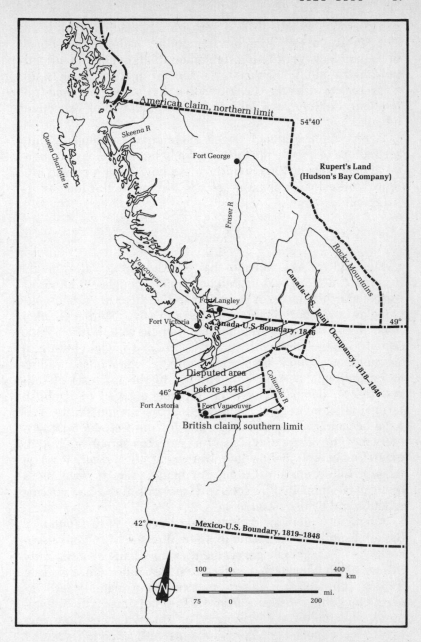

MAP 7: THE OREGON DISPUTE, 1818–1846

had passed, a more realistic approach was made by both sides. The Treaty of Washington (commonly called the Oregon Boundary Treaty) of 1846 established the boundary at 49° latitude to the middle of the straits separating Vancouver Island from the mainland. The Hudson's Bay Company had not retained the Columbia Valley but it did have all of Vancouver Island.

George Simpson had never encouraged settlement, only agriculture to supply the forts, for he believed it was detrimental to the fur trade. First Red River and now Oregon proved him right as the influx of farm settlers drove out the long-established fur traders.

Victoria

McLoughlin had worried that the Columbia Valley might become American and dispatched James Douglas to choose a fort site farther north. In the protected harbour of "Camosack" Douglas began building Fort Victoria in 1843. Similar to other major forts, it was surrounded by a stockade 330 feet by 300 feet (100 m by 90 m) with corner bastions. The eight buildings included accommodation for the men, warehouse, trading store and separate officers' quarters. In the interests of self-sufficiency, company servants were encouraged to establish farms in the environs of the fort. After the Oregon Treaty, Victoria became the new headquarters for the Columbia Department and the centre of trade in furs, surplus agricultural products, timber and fish which were sent to Hawaii, Russian Alaska, California and China. For many years it remained a quiet place inhabited by company servants and a few visiting whalers and British naval vessels.

American ambitions for Manifest Destiny were fanned by the annexation of California in 1848 after the Mexican-American War. The British government, recognizing that its only influence on the north Pacific coast depended on a private trading company, took steps to strengthen claims of sovereignty. In 1849 Vancouver Island was proclaimed a crown colony with Victoria as its capital. The Hudson's Bay Company was to have special privileges—exclusive licence to trade and control of resources—in order to forestall an expected influx of

American settlers. In return, the company would pay a nominal rent, sell land to British colonists at fair prices, and turn over 90 per cent of the proceeds from land and resource sales for public works. Settlers were to purchase at least twenty acres (8 ha) of land at one pound per acre, and anyone buying one hundred acres (40 ha) had to bring out five single men or three married couples.

Richard Blanshard was appointed first governor of the colony. Young and inexperienced, he had no salary, no law officers and at first not even an official residence. At the time of his arrival, Hudson's Bay Company employees had settled most of the land near Victoria. Capt. Walter Colquhoun Grant, who had brought with him eight workmen, was the only independent settler, and when he emigrated briefly to the Sandwich Islands and his workers left, the only white people on the island were connected with the company. Since Douglas was the company's agent on Vancouver Island, Blanshard had little to do. During his tenure a few independent colonists arrived and agriculture expanded. In 1851 he appointed a council of three—James Douglas, John Tod and James Cooper, all connected with the company. Frustrated by the controlling power of company officials, he resigned after two years and was succeeded by James Douglas. Only a few independent colonists arrived each year, but by 1853 the number of settlers on Vancouver Island was estimated at 450. As a result of protests from the colonists and pressure from England, in 1856 Douglas unhappily agreed to the election of a Legislative Assembly, the first west of Canada West. Only property owners had the franchise and the voters numbered about forty.

In 1850 New Caledonia was still a fur trading region. The annual Hudson's Bay ship called at Victoria and serviced the coast. With the loss of the brigade route from the Columbia, Douglas determined to develop an inland route from Fort Langley, from where goods could be barged as far as Hope. Attempts to portage around the Fraser rapids had proved impossible and between 1849 and 1861 various routes were developed overland from the mouth of the Coquihalla River at Hope. Some of these took a southern route (near the present southern highway) towards Princeton and thence to Kamloops, while others farther north followed the Tulameen River and then crossed the divide to Kamloops.

There were signs of change. Coal, which was essential to the increasing number of steamships, had been found at Fort Rupert on northern Vancouver Island. In 1852 the Hudson's Bay Company opened richer mines at Nanaimo and brought out miners from Britain. The company also had extensive agricultural interests spreading from Washington Territory to Fort Langley, supplying the Russian fur company in the north as required by their agreement. In 1849 Rev. Robert John Staines was sent to Victoria as company chaplain and headmaster of the first school.

While life on the British west coast continued at a slow pace, dramatic events were taking place to the south. The California gold rush began a year after the American annexation. San Francisco suddenly became a teeming city. Commercial interests expanded as far north as Vancouver Island: regular steamship services were inaugurated, and soon lumber was being exported from the island to satisfy the needs of the new booming city.

Within a decade the discovery of gold on the Fraser River would agitate Victoria as thousands of miners passed through the settlement on their way to New Caledonia. On the mainland the organization of the fur trading preserve would be overwhelmed by this flood of newcomers, bringing the end of the era of the Hudson's Bay Company.

The Wilderness of 1850

In midcentury the west was still an almost unknown wilderness to Canada and Britain. Although the major river systems had been traced and the fur brigades were making their regular crossings of the country, little was known about the land south of their prairie posts, which were mostly on the North Saskatchewan. To the north the tundra was untouched, though the British had revived their search for a Northwest Passage through the Arctic.

Various accounts written in these times estimated the population between Lake Superior and the Rockies at less than 60,000—almost all of whom were nomadic or seminomadic natives and Metis. In this vast region the only settlement of any size with an agricultural base was in Assiniboia. On the Pacific coast, Fort Langley was the centre of farmlands while Victoria was still little more than a fur post. Scattered along the fur routes were trading centres. Though designated as forts, most were little more than one or two log cabins. There were a few stockaded forts but even the largest of them, Edmonton, seldom had as many as 150 people. West of Assiniboia the only white people were fur traders, explorers who were probably en route to the Arctic, missionaries intent on bringing Christianity and civilization to peoples they considered inferior heathens, and the odd adventure-seeking traveller.

Many of them have left written descriptions of the country. There are full detailed reports of the fur trader's activities— lists of furs and supplies along with financial details. The visitor's account was often widely read in Europe. The most vivid and colourful passages were those dealing with the dangers and hardships—the severity of the climate, the mosquitoes, the scarcity of food, the treacherous rapids, the undeveloped trails, the dangers of mountain passes and, of course, the Indians. Exciting reading, but not the type of material that would encourage settlers to the "Great Lone Land."

At one time the Canadas had derived most of their wealth from the western fur trade. Early leaders in Upper Canada were opposed to the Selkirk settlement not only because it threatened the North West Company fur routes but also because it attracted potential Protestant settlers away from their own nascent colony. But after 1821 Fort William was no longer the centre of trade as the Hudson's Bay Company looked to England through Hudson Bay; the tie between Upper Canada and the west deteriorated to a seldom-used trail. In the ensuing years Upper Canada, renamed Canada West after 1841, lost interest in the west, having empty land of its own to be filled by the flood of immigrants. The British Corn Laws of 1846 which introduced free trade had caused a reorganization of commercial interests, who were now attempting to penetrate the expanding American states. In an effort to attract American trade, Canada West planned to improve the St. Lawrence seaway. The west had little to offer.

By 1850 a change was immiment. The age of steam came to North America: the steamship encouraged immigration while the railways tied communities together and created new industries. The arable lands of Canada West were almost all filled. Books describing adventures in the far west were being widely read. There was growing opposition to the Hudson's Bay Company monopoly as a result of complaints from Assiniboia and the criticisms of British antimonopolists. A few people in Canada West, mostly Protestant, English-speaking, began to consider annexation of the west; in fact, a few visionaries even talked of a railway to the Pacific. But on the whole, in 1850, to Canadians the west was still an unattractive, unprofitable wilderness. The following decade would see a change in this attitude, an increasing awareness of the possibilities of the lands west of Lake Superior.

Chapter Four

OPENING THE WEST
(1850 – 1871)

News of Gold

IN 1858 news reached San Francisco that gold had been discovered on the Fraser River. The California rush had faded out, and this latest find revived aspirations for rapid wealth. Soon thousands of hopefuls, possibly as many as 20,000, were heading for the new gold fields. Most came in overloaded ships from San Francisco, some came overland from Washington and a few travelled west across Rupert's Land. Placid, unprepared Victoria became a scene of turmoil and restlessness as shipload after shipload of people landed and erected tents and shacks. With the miners came builders, merchants, printers, express companies and steamship agents. To most arrivals Victoria was just a transfer point on the way to the gold bars of the Fraser.

Whereas Vancouver Island was a British colony with established laws, the mainland was still Hudson's Bay Company property. The great wave of immigrants entered a land where there were no established government and no local law authorities other than the company officers attached to the scattered posts. Into this vacuum stepped James Douglas.

Sir James Douglas

James Douglas was born in 1803 in Demarara, British Guiana. His father was a Scottish merchant who had interests in a

sugar plantation, and his mother was probably a native. James
attended school in Lanark, Scotland, and at the age of sixteen
became a clerk for the North West Company. Upon the union
of the two companies he was sent from Ile à la Crosse Post to
Fort McLeod and then to Fort St. James, where he married
Amelia Connolly, the Metis daughter of Chief Factor William
Connolly. In 1830 he was posted to Fort Vancouver under Dr.
John McLoughlin; four years later he was promoted to chief
trader. This rank entitled him to one of the eighty-five shares
designated for traders in the field and brought a sizable
increase in salary, augmented again in 1840 when he reached
the rank of chief factor. When McLoughlin retired in 1846,
Douglas succeeded him as controlling officer of the Columbia
Department, which mainly comprised New Caledonia after the
American border had been established that same year. He
moved the western headquarters from Fort Vancouver to Victoria, where the company was granted special privileges in the
newly proclaimed colony of Vancouver Island. In 1851 Douglas acquired another appointment governor of the colony for
Britain.

His two positions often led to conflict of interests, for he
remained loyal to the company and continued to expand its
influence, at the same time recognizing his responsibilities as
governor. He was autocratic and often quarrelled with the Legislative Council and, later, with the Legislative Assembly that
the British government forced him to initiate.

The colony progressed. Surveys were carried out and roads
were built; industries such as sawmilling were encouraged.
Although he had a minimum formal education, Douglas was a
widely read, self-educated man who believed in building
schools and hiring teachers.

During the early years there were several threats to the
security of the colony. At this time bitter Indian wars were
being fought south of the border and Victorians feared similar
disturbances. In 1844 while the post was being established by
Roderick Finlayson, the local Salish had been subdued by
threats and force when, for instance, goods and cattle were
stolen from the fort. Douglas was more sympathetic to the Indians, though usually firm. By buying land from them, establishing reserves for their homes, cajoling and threatening to restrict

trade and at times showing force, he appeased the local groups and discouraged the more warlike northern tribes from disturbing the town.

In 1854 the Crimean War began, with Britain and France opposing Russia. Not for the last time westerners perceived that the Pacific could be the source of a foreign invasion of British soil. A British-French naval force planned an attack on Petropavlosk, a strongly fortified naval base on Kamchatka Peninsula. The British government asked Victoria to supply provisions, coal and a temporary hospital, which was built at Esquimalt. (Only one casualty from the Petropavlosk expedition was ever treated there. From this modest beginning, Esquimalt within a few years would be the major British naval base in the north Pacific.) Victorians feared reprisals, but since the Russian and British fur companies had agreed to remain neutral, their alarm was groundless.

Meanwhile, another border crisis had arisen over the San Juan Islands in the Strait of Georgia where a number of British and Americans had settled. The San Juan group consists of three islands; the problem was whether the main international channel passes outside them or between them. The Hudson's Bay Company had a fishing station and a sheep farm on the main island of San Juan when in 1854 the American government posted a customs officer there to strengthen its own claim. Five years later, the quarrel called the "Pig War" was precipitated by an American settler killing a company pig. Both James Douglas and the American commanding officer in Oregon were aggressive men. Douglas in particular, with memories of the loss of the Columbia Valley, was strongly anti-American. When the Americans landed soldiers on the island, Douglas asked the British navy to intervene; three naval vessels were dispatched but no troops landed. Though the threatened military confrontation did not happen, both sides agreed to a temporary joint occupancy of the island and each installed a force of one hundred men. After long negotiations, in 1873 the German emperor, who arbitrated in the dispute, awarded all the islands to the United States.

During the rush of gold miners to the Fraser River Douglas feared a repetition of the lawlessness prevalent in the California gold rush. And remembering Oregon and Texas, he feared that the large influx of Americans might demand annexation to the United States. Although he did not have political powers on the mainland from the British government, Douglas nevertheless took steps to assert British authority north of the border. He proclaimed new regulations, such as the requirement of permits for American ships entering the Fraser and licences for anyone intending to prospect for gold. He visited the miners along the river, impressing upon them that they were now subject to British laws. He quietened the Indians who were opposed to the spread of miners inland, partly by the appointment of both British and Indian magistrates to maintain the law. Local revenue officers and later gold commissioners were appointed to collect licence fees and regulate mining. He launched road works and planned townsites. He also arranged for the Hudson's Bay Company ships *Beaver* and *Otter* to augment the American ships carrying miners and supplies to Yale, which became the head of navigation.

The Colony of British Columbia

Douglas's dispatches to Britain outlining the threat to British sovereignty posed by the influx of American miners soon had results. On 2 August 1858 the British government established the new colony of British Columbia, having withdrawn it from the company's licence for exclusive trade. Douglas became governor of the colony on condition that he sever all connections with the company.

On 25 November 1858, at Fort Langley, the new colony of British Columbia was officially proclaimed. James Douglas was now the governor of two colonies, and he was assisted in asserting Britain's authority by several capable men. The tall and imposing chief justice, Matthew Baillie Begbie, became a legend as he rode throughout the mining camps on horseback in his official robes, dispensing justice as he interpreted it. By his presence, law and order were maintained in a remote region occupied by men accustomed to the lawlessness of other frontiers.

Col. Richard Moody commanded a detachment of 150 Royal Engineers. Their duties were "to survey those parts of the country which may be suitable for settlement, to mark out allotments of land for public purposes, to suggest a seat of government, to point out where roads should be made, and to render such assistance as may be in their power." Instead of the expected Fort Langley, Colonel Moody selected New Westminster as the capital in 1859. The Royal Engineers also worked with private contractors on the Cariboo Road. This wagon road, 400 miles (640 km) long and 18 feet (4.8 m) wide, was a major construction project, winding around precipitous mountains and crossing numerous rivers and ravines. Begun in 1861, it was completed from Yale to Barkerville four years later.

The gold miners gradually worked their way up the Fraser, panning the various bars and banks. Soon the simple gold pan was replaced by more sophisticated sluice boxes and rockers. By 1860 the miners reached the Quesnel River and in the next few years opened the richest mines in the Cariboo district. In 1862, at Williams Creek, Billy Barker found his mine and nearby grew the town of Barkerville, the largest city north of San Francisco and west of Chicago. The Cariboo Road became a thoroughfare travelled annually by thousands on foot, with packhorses, on stagecoaches, and even with camels. Some people were heading north to the land of opportunity, others were returning south disgruntled and penniless. To serve these many wanderers, Barkerville and other communities produced business establishments, hotels, theatres and housing.

Union of the Colonies

By 1864 the Cariboo gold rush was beginning a rapid decline, but miners were still spreading to the Stikine and the Peace rivers. In 1863 the boundary of British Columbia was extended from the Nass-Finlay rivers to 60° latitude and the northeastern boundary was set at 120° longitude. Meanwhile, Governor Douglas faced growing dissension. Besides the routine problems of government, he had to deal with the opposition of many newcomers who demanded more voice in government. Two of these were Amor de Cosmos, publisher of the Victoria *Daily Colonist*, and John Robson, publisher of the *British Columbian* in New Westminster.

At first British Columbia's only governing body consisted of

Douglas advised by his friends. Protests from the colonists led Britain's secretary of state for the colonies to order Douglas to establish a Legislative Council of fifteen: five government officials, five magistrates, and five representatives from electoral districts yet to be established. The first council of British Columbia met on 21 January 1864. Later in the year Douglas retired and was succeeded by Arthur Edward Kennedy as governor of Vancouver Island and Frederick Seymour as governor of British Columbia.

The collapse of the gold fields brought a period of depression to both colonies, now burdened with heavy roadbuilding debts and the costs of government. In 1866 the colonies were united under Governor Seymour; after a short spell at New Westminster, the capital was established in Victoria.

James Douglas, knighted in 1864, spent his last years in Victoria before his death in 1877. "The Father of British Columbia" had seen Victoria grow from a survey site in the bush to a city of 6,000 people, with paved roads and gas lighting. He had opened the interior of British Columbia, seen the two colonies united, and before his death he saw them become part of Canada. He had maintained the British presence on the Pacific coast making possible a Canada stretching from sea to sea.

Travellers to the West

In 1849 Minnesota, with an estimated population of 6,000, was proclaimed a territory. By this time Mississippi steamboats were serving communities during the ice-free period of the year and railways reached the river from the east. (Not until 1871 did a railway connect Duluth with St. Paul.) When Minnesota became a state in 1858 the population was over 150,000. In contrast, Assiniboia was growing by only a few hundred people a year, with a total of roughly 5,000 in 1850. The majority were Indians and Metis but there were also Scots, Canadians and Americans.

The expansion in Minnesota affected Red River. Many young people left the colony, attracted by the greater opportunities to the south. Communications between Red River and St. Paul increased as the latter's eastern connections developed. In St. Paul could be found luxuries and necessities formerly unavailable. In 1859 the steamship *Anson Northrup* was brought up the Mississippi to Crow Wing, then dismantled and dragged in winter by thirty-four oxen to the Red River. Here she was reassembled and descended the river to Fort Garry. A new phase of communications had begun. At the same time, the overflow of American settlers landed in Assiniboia, where they became the vocal proponents of annexation by the United States.

Using the American route, Canadians began to reach Fort Garry. The French Canadians and Metis had strong ties with Canada East (Quebec) through the Catholic Church, which had been established in the west by missionaries during the fur trade era. Most of the newcomers, however, were Protestants from Canada West.

Although Assiniboia was the most densely populated British holding west of the Great Lakes, trading posts were scattered all the way to the Pacific, and around them were varying numbers of settlers, mostly Metis. Regular caravans of Red River carts and ox carts travelled from Fort Garry northwest to Fort Edmonton. The main route, the Carlton Trail, followed the Assiniboine River to Portage la Prairie, crossed to Fort Ellice on the upper Assiniboine and struck overland to Batoche. It crossed the South Saskatchewan River and continued overland to Battleford, then followed the North Saskatchewan to Fort Edmonton. From there the brigade trails divided, some going north to the Athabasca-Peace-Mackenzie routes, others heading west to Rocky Mountain House. The fur traders from York Factory travelled in boats from the Nelson River to the Red or Saskatchewan rivers.

Besides these regular travellers across the prairies, a number of other expeditions added to the knowledge of the west and brought new attitudes as well. In 1841, as a check to American immigration into Oregon, George Simpson successfully arranged for eighty British subjects from Fort Garry to be sent to the Columbia Valley, the only attempt to bring out a group of British settlers. At the time of the Oregon crisis in 1845, Britain wanted to know whether it would be practical to send troops overland. Two officers, Lt. Mervin Vavasour and Lt. Henry James Warre, were sent with the Hudson's Bay Company brigade, ostensibly as company employees, to make a secret survey. They were definite in their conclusions that an overland movement of troops was impossible and that Fort Victoria was almost defenceless against attack.

Paul Kane travelled with the fur brigades in 1846–47, crossing the continent from Toronto and spending some time visiting the posts of the Pacific coast. He left a lucid journal of his travels, describing the various posts and the natives of the west, but most important were his paintings which capture on canvas the fur traders and the Indians in their natural environment.

Viscount Milton and Dr. W. B. Cheadle travelled for two years in the west and their memoir, *The North-West Passage by Land,* describes the country and people in detail and with considerable humour. Leaving England on 19 June 1862, they sailed to Quebec, took another steamer to Niagara and then Toronto, travelled by railway from Detroit to La Crosse on the banks of the Mississippi, by steamer to St. Paul and by "stage wagon" to Georgetown on the Red River. Here they decided not to wait for the steamer but started downriver in a canoe. This proved to be more difficult than they expected and they were glad to embark on the steamboat *Enterprise* when it caught up to them. By this means they reached Fort Garry on 7 August. They estimated the population of Assiniboia at 8,000, and noted that the Hudson's Bay Company was still powerful: "Nearly the whole population with the exception of a few store-keepers and free-traders live by the Company and the Company is king."

Milton and Cheadle travelled with "over 1500 carts" on the fall buffalo hunt. After wintering near Fort Carlton, they left in April for Fort Edmonton. Eventually they reached the Pacific coast from where they made a trip to the Cariboo gold fields. They returned by steamer via San Francisco, crossing Panama and boarding another steamer for England.

John Palliser

Because the Hudson's Bay Company charter was subject to renewal in 1858, a British parliamentary committee first examined the state of the territories under the company's jurisdiction. The committee meetings, in which both supporters and opponents of the company were heard, aroused interest in the western lands, of which little was known. Thus when the Royal Geographical Society proposed sending an expedition to study Rupert's Land, the British government assisted. The leader was John Palliser, a man who had been to the American prairies and now wanted to explore those of the north. With him were four scientists: Lt. Thomas Blakiston, as magnetical observer (who withdrew before the project was complete); Eugene Bourgeau, botanist; Dr. James Hector, geologist and naturalist; and John W. Sullivan, mathematician, sextant observer and astronomer.

The group would study three distinct regions: from Lake Superior to Red River, where they were to investigate the possibilities for a road or railroad; Red River to the Rocky Mountains; and the Rocky Mountains to the Pacific coast. They would not enter the United States unless it were necessary. Careful magnetic and meteorological records as well as botanical, zoological and geological data were to be kept. Maps would be made of all regions, and areas suitable for settlement would be designated. Finally, the report should include a list of natural resources.

Their route indicates the advances that had been made in eastern transportation. From New York they went by train to Detroit where they embarked on a lake steamer. They sailed to Lake Superior and finished the journey to Fort William in canoes supplied by George Simpson. The old fur route took them to Red River, where they next embarked in two wagons and four Red River carts; but the wagons were unable to withstand the strain of the rough terrain and river crossings and were abandoned in favour of the carts. Blakiston travelled via Hudson Bay, since it was believed that extended land travel would be more harmful to his delicate instruments.

Sometimes together, at other times separately, the five men crisscrossed western Canada from Red River to the Pacific coast and from the American border to the Athabasca country throughout 1857-59, gathering an immense amount of scientific information. They were the first to make a thorough study of the Blackfoot country. Their report stated that the Red River and North Saskatchewan valleys (the parklands) were suitable for settlement, but that the southwestern prairies, except for isolated fertile spots, were not fit for agriculture. This arid region, which Palliser considered to be an extension of the central American desert, became known as Palliser's Triangle: the base was the American border between 100° and 114° longitude and its apex 52° north latitude. For many years this report deterred settlers from the triangle. Palliser also noted the coal and valuable northern forests of present-day Alberta.

He did not believe that a railway was feasible from Lake Superior to Red River nor across the Rocky Mountains, though he thought a wagon road was possible through the mountains. He visualized communication from Lake Superior to Red River through the United States. He forecast the decline of the buffalo and recognized the drastic complications this would have for Indian life. One important achievement of the expedition was its proof of British involvement in the region; it demonstrated that Rupert's Land was not open territory for American expansion.

Hind and Dawson

At the same time that the British Palliser expedition was studying the west, another expedition had been organized by the Canadian government. Although nominally under the command of George Gladman, the leader in reality was the geologist and chemist Henry Youle Hind, ably assisted by Simon James Dawson, a noted geologist and topographical expert. Their instructions were similar to Palliser's and in addition they were to construct a map on a scale of two miles to the inch (1.26 km = 1 cm).

The report of Hind and Dawson gives a picture of life at that time. They gave the population of Assiniboia as 6,526 and noted that the majority of the people were Indians and "halfbreeds." The people, they wrote, tended to settle in ethnic and religious communities. Most were Catholic but there were a large group of Episcopalians and a smaller group of Presbyterians. The settlers had divided their land in the pattern common to Quebec, that is, each farm was long and narrow and had river frontage; homes were built by the river. Hind believed there were large areas of fertile land suitable for settlement along the Assiniboine to the Saskatchewan, while beyond this belt were sections suitable for grazing. Attention was given to the small settlements near posts and missions; for example, the report noted that the farms near Cumberland House produced barley, potatoes, rhubarb, cabbage, peas and carrots.

Transportation was described, including Red River carts and their routes and how the York boats were "tracked" or dragged through rapids. The comparative distances from Fort Garry to both Hudson Bay and St. Paul were estimated. The growing importance of steamboats south of the border and the implications to Red River were pointed out. There is one major difference between the Palliser and Hind reports. The latter believed that a road and possibly a railway could be constructed between Lake Superior and Red River.

The Overlanders

Of the few adventurers who travelled overland to the Cariboo gold fields from the east, the most famous are the Overlanders of 1862. Most of them came from Canada West but a few were from Canada East, Britain and the United States. Approximately 200 people assembled at Fort Garry; during the journey some returned home, others dropped out, while some diverted to prospect the Peace River, so that about 160 completed the trip.

The Overlanders were gold seekers who expected to make their fortunes and leave. Women were not encouraged to make the strenuous journey, but Mrs. Catherine Schubert and her three children persisted. The groups were organized at Fort Garry under the leadership of Capt. T. R. McMicking and a committee of 13. Provisions, horses, oxen and Red River carts were purchased, and on 2 June 1862 the first group of 97 carts, 110 animals and 136 people left Fort Garry, followed by two smaller groups. They took the regular overland route across the prairies to Fort Edmonton, arriving on 21 July.

At Edmonton the carts were exchanged for horses. After an eight-day rest, the Overlanders pushed on to a trackless country where trails had to be chopped through the forest. A month later they were at Tête Jaune Cache, where a difficult decision had to be made. Should they follow the Fraser River to the mouth of the Quesnel or should they take the unknown overland route to the North Thompson River and Fort Kamloops? Most decided to risk the Fraser: they built rafts and embarked on a journey that included many dangerous rapids and canyons. On 4 October they were at the mouth of the Quesnel River.

Twenty people had chosen the more difficult Thompson River route, cutting a trail to the river through unknown territory. The trip down the river was disastrous: rafts were wrecked, supplies lost and starvation was close. Eventually, on 11 October, the group reached Fort Kamloops. The next day Mrs. Schubert's fourth child, Rose, was born—the first white child born in the interior of British Columbia. Altogether in the Fraser and Thompson river journeys only six lives were lost.

When the Overlanders reached their destinations, the Cariboo gold rush had passed its peak and already many miners were leaving. A few of the Overlanders went to the mines while others returned home. Most remained in British Columbia, and after working as labourers in various jobs many of them became important pioneering farmers, businessmen and government agents.

Growing Insecurity

Under the paternalistic supervision of the Hudson's Bay Company life in Rupert's Land was generally peaceful and orderly. In the United States, by contrast, the rapid advance of white settlers was being met by active resistance from the Indians. These bitter wars had repercussions in Assiniboia.

Following the Sioux uprising under Little Crow in the United States, all the Sioux were to be transported westward out of Minnesota. In 1863 a small group of 86 entered Assiniboia, but their reception was cool and they soon returned to the United States. Shortly afterwards another band of 600 Sioux, fleeing from American soldiers, entered Assiniboia. Governor A. G. Dallas refused to accept them as refugees and they scattered, some to western British territory. This threat of large bands of warlike Indians alarmed the local authorities and renewed the demand for stronger British control on the prairies.

In 1863 the Hudson's Bay Company was sold for £1.5 million to a syndicate of capitalists, the International Finance Society. Although the new organization stated its intention to improve road and telegraph communication across the territory as well as to encourage settlement, in reality it was a group of promoters seeking speculative profits, as was shown by their prompt increase of capital shares from £500,000 to £2 million.

The Canadas

The 1850s in Canada West was a decade of boom, coinciding with the greatest era of railway building. Trade with the United States was thriving because of the Reciprocity Treaty of 1854; and the Crimean War increased demands for goods. The prospect of successful crops and waiting markets brought capital and immigrants flowing into the colony. The great influx of settlers filled the vacant arable lands of Canada West, whose population soon surpassed that of Canada East. When land became scarce, many immigrants continued on to the United States, but some Upper Canadians began to look to Assiniboia and farther west as areas of development.

In the 1840s Canada West assumed that the western regions would remain a wilderness, but that was no longer the attitude in the 1850s. A strong nationalistic, pro–British Empire, expansionist movement emerged which stressed that the land belonged to Canada—that it was Canada's duty to take over the land in name. Supporting this view were manufacturers who envisaged a wider domestic market and railway interests who enviously watched new lines expanding across the United States.

With improved access through the United States, emigrants from Canada West began to settle in Assiniboia. They brought a new perspective to the west, seeing it not as a wilderness but as a potential area for agriculture and settlement, with possibilities for mining, trade and railway construction. They formed an aggressive British Protestant group. Their leader was John Christian Schultz who had contacts with the Orangemen in Canada West. William Coldwell began the first newspaper in Fort Garry, the *Nor'Wester*, which was in reality the voice of the British newcomers. Such men as these had no connection with the Hudson's Bay Company, and as independent farmers, traders or businessmen they were opposed to company restrictions. Fearing American annexation of Assiniboia, they advocated either the status of a colony of Great Britain or union with Canada. They had little sympathy with the French-speaking Catholic Metis to whom Red River had always been home and to whom Canadians and Americans were alien transgressors.

Encouraged by reports from the Canadians in Assiniboia, a growing number of Canadians in the east began to support the idea of annexation. As early as 1857 a group of Toronto businessmen sent William Kennedy to Red River to make arrangements for trade and to encourage the inhabitants to support union with Canada. George Brown of the Toronto *Globe* became a leader in this campaign. Petitions were sent to the British government asking for cancellation of the Hudson's Bay Company's trade monopoly which was up for renewal in 1858.

The company's influence in the west at this time consisted of three elements: its chartered territory of Rupert's Land, the land drained by Hudson Bay; its Licence for Exclusive Trade in the North-West Territories; and its grant of Vancouver Island, a crown colony. In a period of increasing political and social liberties and antimonopolistic sentiment in Britain, complaints were received in London from western settlers about the company's influence on Vancouver Island and in Assiniboia. Canadian businessmen wanted trade in the west, including the fur trade, to be openly competitive, while the government of Canada regarded the company as an obstacle to western expansion. As time approached for the renewal of its rights in 1858, the company was in an uneasy situation.

As mentioned, in 1857 the British House of Commons established a committee to investigate the company's activities. This influential committee listened to returned soldiers, settlers, Arctic explorers, clergymen, representatives of the Canadian government and company officials, the most knowledgeable of whom was Sir George Simpson; as might be supposed, he claimed that the west was unsuitable for agricultural settlement.

The final report gave a concise summary, which included among its recommendations: the company's rule of Vancouver

Island and the land west of the Rockies should be terminated (the colony of British Columbia was established in 1858); provisions should be made for Canada to annex the Red and Saskatchewan river valleys; if colonial Canada was not ready to take over the Red River settlement, then some other agreement for its government should be made; in the territories where there was no prospect of permanent settlement (as Simpson claimed), the company should have the privilege of exclusive trade in order to ensure the preservation of peace and the conservation of fur-bearing animals. During the enquiry Hon. William Henry Draper, chief justice of Canada West, stated, "I hope you will not laugh at me as being a visionary, but I hope to see the time, or my children may live to see the time, when there is a railway going all across the country and ending on the Pacific." Apart from proposing some changes in the government of Red River, the committee otherwise was satisfied with the policies and practices of the Hudson's Bay Company. The exclusive trade licence was not renewed, however, pending negotiation of the committee's recommendations for annexation.

The boom years of the 1850s ended and during the 1860s the united province of Canada East and Canada West experienced economic depression and other problems at home and abroad. The inherent distrust remained between the agricultural French-Catholic Canada East and the commercial and industrial interests in Canada West. Their equal representation in the Legislative Assembly and the "double majority" principle—an understanding that all bills must receive a majority of votes from the representatives of both provinces— practically stifled any important legislation. To complicate matters further, the Conservatives under John A. Macdonald and George-Etienne Cartier had almost the same number of seats as the Clear Grits (Liberals) under George Brown, and by the mid-1860s the government had reached an impasse in a period of depression. British policies of free trade had ended Canada's preferential position in the British market. The American Civil War was over and on the southern border was a powerful military machine under an anti-British government. In 1866 the United States permitted the Reciprocity Treaty of 1854 to lapse, resulting in a loss of markets to Canadians. At the same

time the Fenians threatened to raid Canada, Assiniboia and
British Columbia.

Faced by these many problems, Macdonald and Brown
agreed to form a coalition, permitting, they hoped, the creation
of a more functional system of government and also the annexation of the west, which would strengthen Canada's economy.
Following a series of conferences, the British government
passed the British North America Act establishing the Dominion of Canada on 1 July 1867. The new Dominion originally
consisted of the four provinces of Ontario, Quebec, Nova Scotia and New Brunswick.

Clause 146 of the BNA Act stated:

It shall be lawful for the Queen ... on Addresses from the House of
Parliament of Canada, and from the Houses of the respective Legisla-
tures of the colonies or Provinces of Newfoundland, Prince Edward
Island, and British Columbia, to admit those Colonies or Provinces, or
any of them into the Union and on an Address from the Houses of
Parliament of Canada to admit Rupert's Land and the North-western
Territory, or either of them, into the Union, on such terms and condi-
tions in each case as are in the Address expressed.

The Canadian government moved quickly to implement this
clause. Within four years all of western Canada was part of the
Dominion, and in 1873 Prince Edward Island became a province. Only Newfoundland, which did not join until 1949, and
the Arctic Islands were not included in Canada by 1873.

The Deed of Surrender

Before Canada could take over Rupert's Land it had to be
surrendered by the Hudson's Bay Company. Because the British government had granted the charter, it too became indirectly involved. Britain was sympathetic towards Canada's
ambitions, but by the Rupert's Land Act of 1868 it placed the
onus on the Dominion for making a settlement with the company. The governor and committee of the company, though
they had agreed in principle to concede unproductive fur lands
in the fertile south, refused to surrender its claims until the
terms of settlement had been agreed upon, and the British government supported their position.

A Canadian delegation negotiated in London over the winter

and in March 1869 an agreement was reached in the "Deed of Surrender." In return for the land, the Canadian government agreed to pay the sum of £300,000, as well as pay for the telegraph construction material stored at York Factory. The company would retain a stated acreage around each of its 120 forts or posts, varying from 5 to 3,000 acres (2 to 1200 ha) a total of 45,000 acres (18,000 ha). For fifty years the company was to receive one-twentieth of the surveyed land in the "Fertile Belt," which was defined as that region west to the Rocky Mountains, south of the North Saskatchewan River and east to Lake Winnipeg and Lake of the Woods: the company eventually received 7 million acres (2.8 million ha) in this belt. The company was to retain the right to trade, and in the north remained unchallenged.

Dissension in Rupert's Land

For as long as the people of Rupert's Land could remember they had been dependent on the Hudson's Bay Company. Now the company's control was to end, but nothing in the Deed of Surrender or the BNA Act made reference to the future of the company's employees or the settlers, the Metis or the Indians. Over the years the company had built an organization of loyal servants and officers to whom had been distributed 40 per cent of the profits. Following the reorganization in 1863, the officers feared that this arrangement would end and for several years the chief factors and chief traders negotiated for a clarification of their status as shareholders. Whereas employees of all ranks had formerly felt secure in their relationships with the old company, they had no confidence in the new organization and a spirit of discontent spread throughout the posts. The Deed Poll of 1871 now ended the practice of shared ownership but the commissioned gentlemen were promised a share of the profits and a minimum salary; however, they would have no share of the profits from land sales. In fact, they received very little. In 1887 no further commissioned officers were to be appointed, and in 1893 profit-sharing rights and the designations chief trader and chief factor were withdrawn, replaced by salaried employees. The era of the old Hudson's Bay Company had ended.

During the 1860s the settlers, Metis and Indians were suffering from a series of natural misfortunes. There were years of drought when crops were far below normal. In 1867 and 1868 one of the worst grasshopper plagues in history destroyed what little crops there were. The buffalo was being decimated and the annual buffalo drive, though it covered ever-greater territory, obtained decreasing supplies of meat and hides. Many people were hungry, in spite of relief sent from Canada, the United States and Britain and from the Hudson's Bay Company.

The company, Metis and Indians had established a system of coexistence in which each group maintained its independence but co-operated in their mutual interests. With the company's decline and reorganization, one of the major participants was withdrawing and the established pattern threatened to disintegrate. The proposed sale of the Hudson's Bay territories to Canada threatened the land rights of Indians and Metis, who held no legal title of their own. In addition, new "foreign" elements were entering the land. Indians and Metis had looked with suspicion on the Palliser and Hind expeditions, while the Catholics in Red River were concerned about the increasing number of Protestant Canadians as well as the activities of the Toronto-based businessmen led by William Kennedy. Westerners were aware of the growing propaganda in eastern newspapers for annexation. In 1868 Metis and Indians became alarmed when English-speaking surveyors arrived in Red River to chart a road to Lake Superior, for this route would obviously encourage more settlers from Canada. When surveyors began to survey and stake vacant land in Red River, the opposition became resistance. A group of threatening Metis forced the surveyors to leave their work near the settlements, but they moved to the unsettled regions of the south.

The fate of Assiniboia was apparently to be left to later Canadian policies and politicians. It was British territory, but while the company was surrendering its claims and until Canada accepted the terms of surrender in 1869, the legal authority was in doubt. The colony felt insecure and abandoned.

There were 11,500 people in Assiniboia of whom 5,700 were French Metis. They formed a strong "nationalistic" community that was suspicious of the English-speaking Metis, Britons,

Scots, Americans and Canadians.

The local government appointed by the Hudson's Bay Company consisted of a governor and a council to assist him. After 1853 this council included representatives from the main religious denominations as well as English- and French-speaking Metis. The latter repeatedly petitioned for a bilingual council but without success. Actually, the council's jurisdiction extended only fifty miles (80 km) from the junction of the Red and Assiniboine rivers and it could not interfere with policies of the Hudson's Bay Company. Upon the surrender of the charter, the council's authority was unclear. In the approaching crisis it proved to be impotent and quietly disbanded.

Although the Metis were a closely knit community, they lacked a strong leader to consolidate their demands. Louis Riel appeared to fill this need.

Louis Riel

Louis Riel was born in St. Boniface in 1844, the first of eleven children. His father had been a Metis leader and his mother was French Canadian. Louis grew up among the Metis and at the age of fourteen he was selected to attend the Sulpician College at Montreal where he was noted for being proud, quick tempered and a good scholar. At the age of twenty-one he decided not to enter the church and began a career as a lawyer. When the law no longer appealed to him, he wandered through Canada and the United States before returning to St. Boniface in 1868, where he found that many changes had occurred in ten years. Across the river was the nucleus of a town called Winnipeg, occupied by newcomers who had little sympathy for the old system.

After a few months in Assiniboia, the young, passionate and loquacious Riel was organizing the Metis to stop the surveyors. Shortly afterwards, in October 1869 when the Metis met for the annual buffalo hunt, he was appointed secretary of the executive. This executive group now proclaimed itself a "National Committee" and began to organize the people. They proclaimed their opposition to annexation by Canada and their determination to protect the lives and security of the Metis. Riel repeatedly stated his loyalty to the Queen of England and, at the same time, his opposition to unilateral annexation by Canada. On 2 December 1869 he quietly took over Fort Garry and established his headquarters there.

Meanwhile, the Canadian government had appointed William McDougall as provisional lieutenant governor of the newly acquired Rupert's Land and North-West Territories. He travelled via the United States to make an official declaration of transfer in Assiniboia, but when he arrived at the border he was stopped by a group of Metis acting under instructions from the "National Committee of the Metis of Red River" and was told he could not to enter the territory without a permit from the committee. McDougall withdrew and returned to Canada.

The people of Red River were generally sympathetic to Riel's demand that only mutual negotiation not simple annexation must precede union with Canada. They were, however, divided in their attitudes towards Riel. The established English-speaking community, including Metis, were either indifferent or doubtful. Even some French-speaking citizens were not convinced that his policies were correct. The recently arrived Canadians were strongly opposed. To gain the support of these people Riel invited various parishes to elect representatives to a forty-member convention, from which a provisional government of English- and French-speaking representatives was selected, with Riel as president. The government drew up a bill of rights and prepared to send a delegation to Ottawa to present its demands.

The confusion in Red River was watched with interest by the United States. A strong drive began in Minnesota for the annexation of Red River. This threat from the United States as well as McDougall's rebuff disturbed John A. Macdonald, who refused to pay the Hudson's Bay Company for the transfer of territory until the unrest was quietened, and sent two commissioners, Rev. J. B. Thibault and Charles de Salaberry, to explain the Canadian viewpoint. Riel informed them that Red River already had a government and would only deal with officials authorized by the Canadian government to negotiate terms.

The Canadian government now sent Donald A. Smith as special commissioner to Fort Garry, to assess the situation and pacify the Assiniboians. Smith had served the Hudson's Bay Company in Labrador for twenty years and was eventually to become a member of parliament and one of Canada's leading financiers.

Meanwhile, the antagonistic, aggressive Schultz and his Canadian followers refused to accept the authority of the provisional government and a number of them were jailed. Smith arrived during this brief period of tension and was himself temporarily taken into custody.

In January 1870 Smith convinced Riel to permit the election of a convention of twenty English and twenty French representatives. The convention established a new provisional government which, after some dissension, chose Riel as president. This government reaffirmed the decision to send a delegation to Ottawa and modified its bill of rights. Among the demands were: provincial status for Rupert's Land with rights similar to other provinces, representation in both houses of parliament, a bilingual lieutenant governor, responsible government, special land grants to the Metis, a railway from Lake Superior to Red River, and amnesty for all members of the provisional government. Later Riel added a suggestion that the new province be called Manitoba.

Besides Riel, another man who had considerable influence with the Metis was Alexandre Taché, bishop of St. Boniface since 1854. Unfortunately, at this critical time he was absent on a mission to Rome. En route he had warned the Canadian government of the unrest among the Metis and had protested against the appointment of the English-speaking McDougall. Later he opposed the sending of a military expedition. Taché convinced Riel to request, without the consent of the provisional government, separate schools similar to those of Quebec.

A number of the imprisoned Canadians escaped and began to organize resistance. A few weeks later the provisional government released the remainder of the prisoners, but this did not stop the movement for counterrevolution. On 18 February 1870 a small force attempted to seize Fort Garry, was captured without bloodshed and imprisoned. Among the prisoners was Thomas Scott, an earlier escapee, who now became a belligerent, vocal leader of the prisoners, threatening the jailers and denouncing the Metis. Riel was a special target for his violent threats. On 3 March the Metis demanded that Scott be tried. He was found guilty of treason against the provisional government and executed by a firing squad.

The repercussions of this drastic step persist today. How legitimate was the provisional government? It was not recognized by the Hudson's Bay Company nor by the Canadian government; but had either of these legal authority over Red River in this period of transition? For years Ontario had been receiving reports from Schultz and his followers, supported by the widely read, biased *Nor'Wester*, that the majority of the people wanted freedom from the company and union with Canada. The Canada First party in Ontario claimed that Scott was executed by the French Catholics because he was a Protestant. A great wave of indignation swept through Ontario, fanned by Canada First and the visiting Schultz. To citizens of Ontario the uprising became a dramatic protest by a small rabid group of unstable Metis; whereas Quebec supported Riel against such accusations, seeing him instead as a leader protecting the French-speaking Catholic citizens of Assinboia from the pressures of Ontario-oriented Protestants. The latent antagonism between the two provinces was stirred.

Riel believed that Scott's execution would deflate the threatened revolt against the provisional government, bring peace and order, and strengthen his position in negotiations with Canada. Riel's error in judgement undid much of his constructive work and left a legacy that would eventually lead to his own execution.

The Manitoba Act

The western delegation had two difficult tasks in Ottawa: to explain the actions of the provisional government and to negotiate terms for union. In the reaction against Scott's death, two of the delegates were arrested for a short time, but negotiations did open. Manitoba was to be accepted into Confederation as a province. Because Red River was the only settled area of any size in the North-West Territories, the new "postage-stamp province" was little larger than Assiniboia, extending only as far north as the southern end of Lake Winnipeg.

By the terms of the Manitoba Act of 12 May 1870, Canada would pay $27.27 per head for a population of 15,000, plus

$0.80 per head annual subsidy until the population reached 400,000; the federal government would have the powers of jurisdiction specified in the BNA Act as well as control of public lands. Furthermore, 1.4 million acres (560,000 ha) of land would be set aside for Metis settlements, each person, including children, entitled to 240 acres (96 ha). The act made no mention of schools. When these terms were accepted, the North-West Territories were transferred to the Dominion of Canada on 15 July 1870.

Red River was one of numerous problems faced by John A. Macdonald as he tried to weld a nation together. During negotiations, Ontario demanded that a military force be sent to the colony and the rebels crushed. Quebec opposed such action. Although amnesty had been implied, the Canadian government evaded a decision, claiming that since it did not yet control Manitoba, such a step was the prerogative of the British government. After some delay a military force under Col. G. J. Wolseley was dispatched on the understanding that it was only a peace-keeping mission and not punitive. It would give security to the inhabitants of Red River and would assure the Indians that order would be maintained; it was to supervise the installation of government in Manitoba, and it would also demonstrate British interest in the region to the Americans. The force was composed of 400 Imperial regular troops and 800 Canadian militiamen from Quebec and Ontario.

Organizing Manitoba

The Metis believed that the change to provincial status would be peaceful and expected no recriminations. But as the military force approached, rumours of retribution grew. When the troops were within sight of the fort, Riel's friends convinced him to flee into the countryside with some of his associates. Their fears were well founded: many of the Canadian militia joined the discontented Canadians of the colony in persecuting and bullying the Metis and some were killed and injured, but Riel could not be found.

Lieutenant Governor Adams G. Archibald arrived after the troops with instructions to grant amnesty, and gradually peace was restored. Archibald undertook to organize the province on a bilingual basis. A census showed 11,963 population: 558 Indians, 5,757 French Metis, 4,083 English-speaking Metis, and 1,565 whites of whom 747 were native born and 294 were born in eastern Canada. Government officials were appointed, and the province was divided into twenty-four electoral districts. After the first election on 1 December 1870, the new legislature adopted moderate policies and chose a Legislative Council that included French and Scottish Metis. The first session was bilingual. Shortly afterwards four members were elected to the federal government.

The settlement was threatened at this time by an invasion of Fenians from the south assisted by W. B. O'Donoghue, a Metis. When there was some fear that the Metis might support the raiders, from his hiding place Riel advised them to assist the authorities and oppose the invasion; the danger was quickly defused, and Imperial troops were withdrawn after only a short service.

As surveyors began to mark out the land for new settlers, the Metis discovered that, despite promises, under the new government they still had no legal claims to the land they occupied, and they demanded that their original farms and homes be guaranteed to them. The government of Canada was dilatory in recognizing these claims. Not until 1873 were survey allotments made. The following year the government issued each family either entitlements of 160 acres (64 ha) or scrip entitling the holder to 160 acres. Two years later only scrip was issued. The value of the scrip was little appreciated by the Metis who were unfamiliar with legal forms or with private ownership of small parcels of land in the midst of plenty. Unscrupulous speculators obtained the scrip for a few dollars or some whisky. Many disillusioned Metis left for the free country of the Saskatchewan Valley or for the open lands in the United States.

The hidden Riel was still a problem and an influence. In 1873, without being seen in public, he was elected by acclamation to the House of Commons. He travelled east under an assumed name but did not dare to appear in the House and remained in Montreal. In 1874 he was re-elected. In Ottawa he managed to sign his name on the register without being recognized, but again he was afraid to face the House, from which he was subsequently expelled.

His fears were not unfounded. A companion, Ambroise Lépine, had been found guilty for the Scott trial and was sentenced to death, though his sentence was commuted by Governor General Lord Dufferin to two years' imprisonment and forfeiture of his political rights. Prime Minister Alexander Mackenzie introduced a bill granting amnesty to all persons connected with the Manitoba troubles except Lépine, O'Donoghue and Riel, who were banished for five more years. Thus Riel became a wanderer in the United States where in 1878 he took out citizenship papers. The efforts of Canadian officials to get rid of him had apparently succeeded.

If Riel's activities had ended at this time he would have earned an honoured but minor niche in Canadian history. His execution of Thomas Scott was an unfortunate outcome of the tensions, fears and frustrations of this period of indecision, though it was turned to inflammatory effect by the anti-Catholic Orangemen of Ontario. Riel's leadership had resulted in the establishment of Manitoba province and responsible government. Had it not been for his influence, Red River could conceivably have been annexed to the United States. Undoubtedly it would have remained a restless small corner of the North-West Territories, which would struggle for recognition by the federal government for thirty more years. Riel was not forgotten by the Metis, who would shortly call for his leadership in another time of crisis.

The North-West Territories

Section 146 of the BNA Act implies that the admission of colonies or provinces into Canada would be by joint agreement of the provincial legislatures and the federal parliament. However, "Rupert's Land and the North-western Territory" would be admitted upon an address to the queen from the Canadian parliament. This implies that the territories, including Assiniboia, could be annexed by unilateral action; there is no mention of their representation in parliament. As we have seen, this procedure caused the initial protests at Red River resulting in the Manitoba Act. The remainder of the territories were annexed by Canada and their form of government was established by Ottawa. One of the reasons for the present "alienation of the west" and protests by native Indians and Metis has its roots in these unilateral and autocratic actions by the federal government.

In 1869 the Canadian government passed "an Act for the Temporary Government of Rupert's Land and the North-western Territory" after it obtained the land from the Hudson's Bay Company (at that time including Assiniboia), providing for the appointment of a lieutenant governor to administer the lands under instructions from Ottawa. This "temporary" act was renewed in 1871 and 1873.

The large expanse of the North-West Territories had very few people. There were small settlements in Edmonton and near the Prince Albert mission, as well as trading posts and a few missions scattered as far as the Yukon. Each of these might have a population of from 3 to 40 men and their families. The census estimated the total population at 40,000, of whom three-quarters were Indians, probably 9,500 were French- or English-speaking Metis and just over 1,000 were whites.

In spite of the troubles at Red River the federal goverment remained apathetic towards the territories. The temporary government act had stipulated that a lieutenant governor and council would be located in Winnipeg, and Adams G. Archibald was appointed lieutenant governor of both Manitoba and the territories. Although he submitted lists of proposed members for the council, not until December 1872 were eleven men appointed. They received no indemnity for their service.

Although Archibald had organized the government and appointed officials, he had little actual power and was mainly the recipient of requests, complaints, suggestions and general information from missionaries, traders, Metis and settlers. From these many reports he forwarded suggestions to Ottawa, but little attention was given to the needs and aspirations of the people scattered across the wilderness. The federal government established prohibition in the territories, organized the North West Mounted Police and introduced a federal Department of the Interior.

When Alexander Mackenzie became prime minister, he brought in the North-West Territories Act of 1875. The territories council was to consist of five members who would receive remuneration, but in 1876 only three were selected. One important clause stated that when an area of 1,000 square miles (2600 km²) had a population of 1,000 adults, it could elect a member to the council. The centre of administration was moved from Winnipeg to Fort Peel and then to Battleford, which was expected to be on the proposed railway line and the parallel telegraph line. After the decision to transfer the railway to a southern route, the capital was moved to Regina in 1882.

British Columbia's Dilemma

At this time the British Empire was entering its most prestigious era: colonies large and small, rich and poor, were scattered throughout the world. One of the most isolated was British Columbia. A proud member of the Empire, it had developed a strong sense of unity and an advanced system of government, but its economic connections with Britain were minimal. The early fur trade ties with Canada had faded and communication lines were across the Pacific, not eastward across the mountains and plains. For Britain, there was little economic advantage to be gained from the colony but it did have a vital strategic value. It was the only British colony in the Pacific north of Hong Kong and as such was an important base from which to check the expanding powers of Russia and the United States in the north Pacific. But sentimental ties and the presence of a few naval vessels did little to alleviate the colony's growing problems.

The union of Vancouver Island and British Columbia had not ended the depression. The booming population of the gold rush days had brought expanded trade and shipping and had encouraged the construction of buildings and roads. Now many people had left the colony but roadbuilding debts and other costs of government remained. Customs duties, land sales and road tolls had been the government's main sources of revenue, but these had all drastically diminished. The colony was isolated from markets and most goods were produced for local consumption. Although the United States was the main foreign market, exports were handicapped by the high tariff policies of that country. Except for coal used by naval and merchant steamers, exports of lumber, salmon and furs differed little from pre–gold rush days.

In this predicament three alternatives were proposed. British Columbia could remain an isolated British colony and hope for future growth. It could join—be annexed by—the United States. A vociferous annexationist group in British Columbia obtained just over one hundred names on a petition of support.

The third choice was to join the newly formed Dominion of Canada, but this met strong opposition. Governor Frederick Seymour opposed union and was supported by his executive and other government officials who feared the loss of their positions. The colonial leader of this group was Dr. J. S. Helmcken. He believed that the distance to Canada was too great for successful union and that, with its small population, British Columbia would have little influence on national problems, being forced instead to adjust its policies to those of Canada and see its industries suffer from eastern competition. Furthermore, because British policy was to withdraw its troops from Canada, British Columbia would be left defenceless.

On the other hand, there were some influential pro-Confederationists like newspaper editors Amor de Cosmos and John Robson. At this time the government of the colony consisted of a governor appointed by the crown, an Executive Council of five, nominally appointed by the queen but in reality by the governor, and a Legislative Council of whom thirteen were appointed and eight elected. Both de Cosmos and Robson used their newspapers to demand responsible government under a fully elected assembly. From the time they arrived in British Columbia, these men had opposed the established government led by the authoritative James Douglas and officials such as Judge Begbie. Their opposition continued against Governor Seymour. Later both would be elected to the Legislative Assembly and in turn become premiers of the province.

Given the council's opposition, there was little pressure in British Columbia to join Confederation. The British government also showed little enthusiasm prior to 1867, but after the Dominion was formed and Rupert's Land annexed, the British attitude changed. Possibly the American purchase of Alaska and the threat of American annexation, which could end British influence in the north Pacific, was a factor. With improved steamship services and the expansion of European interests in Asia, an "all-red route" across North America to the Orient was a possibility—but only if British Columbia remained in the Empire. In 1869 when Governor Seymour died, the British government appointed Anthony Musgrave as governor with instructions to encourage union with Canada.

The Province of British Columbia

Under Musgrave's leadership union was soon debated in the Legislative Council, which sent a delegation of three to Ottawa with a list of proposed terms. The delegates crossed the United States by train in the first year that this was possible. The experience must have influenced their attitude towards the possibilities of transcontinental transportation. The delegates were warmly received in Ottawa and within a month the terms of union were agreed upon. The Canadian parliament passed the British Columbia Act and the Imperial government, accepting the address to the queen, passed an order-in-council admitting British Columbia as a Canadian province. The colony officially became a province on 20 July 1871.

The terms of union were exceedingly generous; in fact, some provinces felt they were too generous. Canada assumed all of British Columbia's debts, paid an annual subsidy of $35,000 and an annual grant of eighty cents a head for the estimated population of 60,000. (In fact, the province's 1871 census established the figure as 36,247, of whom only 10,589 were non-Indian.) An additional eighty cents a head would be paid annually until the population reached 400,000, the allowable maximum. Canada would provide a fortnightly mail service by steamer to San Francisco. Pensions would be paid by Canada to any government officials who lost their positions because of the transition. British Columbia's federal representation was to be three in the Senate and six in the House of Commons. The Dominion government undertook to begin within two years and complete within ten years a railway connecting existing lines to the Pacific seaboard; the provincial government was to convey to the Dominion government up to twenty miles (32 km) of public lands on each side of the railway in return for $100,000 per annum. The Dominion also guaranteed the interest on a maximum of $500,000 for the construction of a graving dock at Esquimalt. The federal government would be in charge of Indian affairs. In all other matters, the original BNA Act would prevail.

The first lieutenant governor of the province was Joseph W. Trutch, who had lived there since 1858 and had been one of the Confederation delegates. The problem of responsible government was left to his council: soon after it ratified the terms of union, an act was passed abolishing the Legislative Council and establishing an elected Legislative Assembly of twenty-five from twelve unequally represented electoral districts.

Faced with economic depression, British Columbia had been bribed to enter Confederation. Having few historical or traditional ties to Canada, the province has always retained a sense of being a unique unit isolated behind the mountains. As Dr. Helmcken said, "B.C. is in, but not of Canada." Within a few years grievances disrupted the federal-provincial relationship. Railways remained an irritating ulcer, beginning with the early construction delays and indecisions, right up to the modern dispute over expansion of the British Columbia Railway and closure of other lines; freight rate and capacity problems were never resolved. As early opponents had warned, tariff policies were suspected of being favourable to eastern industrialists. Faraway Ottawa seemed callous in its unilateral protection of western fisheries. Federal immigration policies nullified the efforts of provincial politicians to set restrictions. In spite of these continuing problems, strengthened through two major wars, the people of British Columbia gradually accepted their position as a significant unit in a larger federation.

Century of Discovery

The century ending with the formation of the province of British Columbia had seen amazing changes in North America. In 1771 Quebec was a small colony along the St. Lawrence, and the land to the west as far as the Mississippi River was Indian reserve. The New England colonies were still British. The north Pacific was completely unexplored except by a few Russian fur traders in the Aleutian Islands. The Arctic Islands were unknown, and the Hudson's Bay Company was still confined to the Hudson Bay coast. The land north and west of Lake Superior was Indian territory, where buffalo roamed unrestricted in great herds and few animals were hunted; where lone pedlars from Montreal were rediscovering the early French trade routes.

In 1871 white settlements extended across the continent, and the Indians had become dependent on imported supplies. Travel routes were well established. A transcontinental railway was promised which would require a labour force, establish new travel routes, and spawn new communities and industries. Newcomers would fill the open spaces. These changes would end the freedom of the Indians, finally decimate the buffalo and displace fur trading as the major occupation.

Chapter Five

COMING OF THE RAILWAY
(1871 – 1885)

The Homesteads

T HE opening of the west to settlement had been the basic objective in the annexation by Canada. The Dominion Lands Act of 1872 established the system of land subdivision for Manitoba and the territories. A base line was set at 49° latitude and a base meridian just west of Winnipeg. From this latter line the country was divided vertically into "ranges" numbered from the east, with allowances made regularly for the earth's curvature. Each range was divided into square townships, numbered consecutively from the international boundary. A township contained thirty-six sections of one square mile (2.6 km²) east-west beginning in the southeast corner (see diagram). Road allowances of one chain fifty links were surveyed between all townships and sections. Originally allowances were to be made for existing farms which were usually long with a narrow frontage on a river or lake, but in many cases these were ignored.

The Hudson's Bay Company was to have one-twentieth of the land in the fertile belt, described as two sections in every fifth township, and one and three-quarters in all other townships—section 8 and three-quarters of section 26. Sections 11 and 29 throughout the prairies were set aside as education endowments: part of this land would provide school sites and the rest would be leased or sold for building and maintenance funds. All other even-numbered sections were for homesteads,

Township 43 Range 3

31	32	33	34	35	36
30	School 29	28	27	HBC 26	25
19	20	21	22	23	24
18	17	16	15	14	13
7	HBC 8	9	10	School 11	12
6	5	4	3	2	1

Township 42 Range 4

Township 42 Range 2

Township 41 Range 3

Typical prairie township: sixteen even-numbered sections were available for free homestead grants and sixteen odd-numbered sections were reserved for the CPR or as Dominion lands and sold.

and the odd-numbered were public lands to be disposed of only by sale. Later, when the Canadian Pacific Railway agreement was signed, all the odd-numbered sections in townships four deep on both sides of the rail line were turned over to the railway. Heads of families and persons age twenty-one (later eighteen) were entitled to a free homestead of one-quarter section for a nominal registration fee of ten dollars, on condition that they do a specified amount of improvement. After the surveys were completed, Dominion public lands might be purchased from the federal government for one dollar an acre (0.4 ha), with a limit of 640 acres (almost 260 ha) per person.

New Settlements

The 1870s saw considerable movement of people in the territories. The promise of a railway brought new settlers from Ontario and the British Isles; they spread along the proposed railway route, at that time expected to head towards the Yellowhead Pass. The first settlers in Manitoba tended to homestead sections having trees and water but as these became filled they went to the outer surveyed lands.

Many Metis, disillusioned by the land settlement in Manitoba, moved northwest to the Saskatchewan River valley. As they settled, often near missions such as Batoche and Duck Lake, they occupied fertile river frontage in the old way. Community councils were formed, similar to those established for the buffalo hunt.

A number of Metis settled in and around Prince Albert where the first important white settlement in the North Saskatchewan country was to grow up around a Presbyterian mission established in 1866 by Rev. James Nisbet. Eight years later Battleford became the headquarters for the surveyors of the telegraph line. Other communities along the Winnipeg-Edmonton route expanded, such as Fort Pitt, Fort La Corne and Fort Carlton. Edmonton became the distribution centre serving the north and west for both land carriers and steamshipping.

During these years the multicultural characteristic of the prairies took root. Between 1874 and 1878 the first large group of 6,000 German-speaking Mennonites came from Russia and received eight complete townships in southern Manitoba, becoming the first to establish a permanent agricultural settlement in the prairies without direct access to water.

In 1872 Sigtryggur Jonasson, an Icelander, emigrated to Canada in search of land suited to his starving countrymen. Three years later, after a disappointing winter in Ontario, his group of Icelanders established Gimli on the western shore of Lake Winnipeg. In spite of a severe winter and a smallpox epidemic the following year, the surviving settlers stayed on and their colony of New Iceland became a centre for new arrivals. It had its own local council and ran its own affairs until it was absorbed by the new District of Keewatin in 1876. Gimli became the model for numerous other Icelandic settlements that were established in other parts of Canada and the United States.

The federal government pointed to the large French-speaking population in the west as an inducement to Québécois who had been emigrating in increasing numbers to the neighbouring states. An 1874 order-in-council set aside land for repatriated French Canadians. Nearly 2,000 came from the New England states between 1875 and 1878; after that the numbers were negligible.

Population growth was slow compared to that of the neighbouring American states, because of the lack of efficient transportation east of Winnipeg and the long overland trek west of Winnipeg. Nevertheless, growth was steady and businesses sprang up to meet demands. In 1881 Manitoba extended its eastern boundary to Ontario and expanded 160 miles (256 km) north and 100 miles (160 km) west. In keeping with the regulations of the North-West Territories Act, the electoral district of Lorne (which included Prince Albert, the largest town in the territories) elected the first member to the North-West Territories council in 1881. In 1876 the District of Keewatin had been established east and north of Manitoba with a separate government whose council met at Winnipeg. In 1882, portions of the North-West Territories were designated as the districts of Assiniboia, Saskatchewan, Alberta and Athabasca, still administered by a central government. The administrative foundation for the expected era of settlement was in place.

River Steamers

Steamboats were used on eastern rivers early in the 1800s and by 1850 they were the main traffic bearers on the larger river systems. Cities along the St. Lawrence, Hudson and Mississippi systems became dependent on water traffic. On the Pacific coast, the Hudson's Bay Company steamer *Beaver* arrived at Fort Vancouver from England in 1836 and began half a century of service to coastal communities.

Northern rivers such as the St. Lawrence and the Mississippi north of St. Paul were closed for part of the year by ice, but the open season was one of great activity. The main transportation routes of the fur traders had followed the rivers to the far west; now, with increasing population and the demand for more goods, it was logical that steamboats be used on the western rivers, too.

Lumber was available for shipbuilding but the heavy, awkward machinery had to be imported overland. Most rivers were frozen for a large part of the year, which meant not only a cessation of revenue but also the problem of safe storage for the vessels.

The Saskatchewan River, which appears to be a natural waterway, had special problems. In many places the water was shallow. At times, after heavy rains or during the spring runoff, the river was a rushing torrent. Every spring the currents would change the channels, and navigation was difficult in the unpredictable waters. Before the Saskatchewan enters Lake Winnipeg it drops quickly for three miles (4.8 km) through the Grand Rapids. Since it was impossible for one steamboat to navigate the entire river, several boats plied different sections and goods were portaged from one to the other. Stern-wheelers were found to be more practical than side-wheelers on the rivers of western Canada because they could be brought closer to shore.

The first steamer to reach Fort Garry from the south was the *Anson Northrup* (later named the *Pioneer*) in 1859. The Hudson's Bay Company bought her and later built the *International* in 1862 at Fort Garry. For a number of years, in co-operation with Norman W. Kittson's company below the border, the company maintained a monopoly of the Red-Assiniboine river traffic. In 1871 it decided to phase out York boats in favour of steamboats. The *Chief Commissioner*, a steamer built at Fort Garry in 1871–72, was used on Lake Winnipeg. As the southern routes became more used, York Factory ceased to be the important import centre.

In 1873 the company assembled a steamer above Grand Rapids to serve the Saskatchewan Valley, but she was wrecked on rocks soon after and was replaced by the new *Northcote* which travelled to Fort Carlton. The S.S. *Northcote* was 150 feet (45 m) long and 28.5 feet (8.55 m) wide, her registered tonnage 290.63 (263.65 t). Well loaded she drew 40 inches (1 m) of water. The following year she reached Edmonton carrying goods that had left Fort Garry only thirty-four days before. Three years later the company constructed a tramway around Grand Rapids for the transshipment of goods, and steamboat service on the North Saskatchewan expanded. In 1882 the Hudson's Bay Company sold its steamers to one of a number of steamship companies by then operating in the region.

The proposed construction of the Canadian Pacific Railway threatened steamboat traffic; in fact, contracts for the telegraph line between Red River and Edmonton had been granted soon after the first steamers were used on the Saskatchewan. In 1881 steamboats stopped carrying on the Assiniboine; meanwhile, the decision of the railway to adopt a southern route extended the steamers' life on the northern rivers. In 1880 the federal government improved navigation through the Saskatchewan's rapids by removing rocks and building canals, thus permitting heavier cargoes and also lessening the navigation dangers of autumn low waters.

In 1885 the *Northcote* was called upon to assist in putting down the North-West Rebellion in what has been called "Canada's first naval battle." At Medicine Hat she was loaded with ammunition, provisions and men for the relief of Battleford, but was delayed when she grounded on shoals. At Batoche she was supposed to act as a gunboat and came under rebel fire. When the Metis cut her cables and broke the smokestack, she drifted downriver and out of the battle zone. The *Northcote* carried some wounded to hospital in Saskatchewan along with the captured Riel. Other vessels were also used for transport during the crisis, and at the end of the campaign troops returned to Winnipeg by steamboat down the Saskatchewan and through Lake Winnipeg.

The story of steamboats on the Saskatchewan River is not one of great success. Battered by rocks, caught on shoals or beaten by winter ice, they were abandoned one by one along the river. The completion of the railway from Calgary to Edmonton in 1891 finished the stern-wheelers. A few vessels continued to carry local traffic until 1954 when, except for a few excursion boats, the era of steam on the Saskatchewan ended.

Before steamboats arrived on the Mackenzie River system, goods were hauled overland 100 miles (160 km) from Edmonton to Athabasca Landing on the Athabasca River. Over the years the old trail had become a cart road for freighting and for mail stages that ran twice a week all year. At Athabasca Landing the Hudson's Bay Company built scows which floated down the river and over a few minor rapids to the rapids at Fort McMurray. The scows were usually broken up for lumber at this point on the route and the crews hiked back to pick up new ones. After portaging goods around the rapids, crews took a waiting set of scows to Fort Smith on the Great Slave River where another portage was necessary before the route to the Arctic was reached. Some York boats were used but could only be returned by arduous tracking against the current.

In 1883 the company built the *Grahame* at Fort Chipewyan on Lake Athabasca. The engines, boilers and other metal parts were transported overland from Edmonton to Athabasca Landing and floated down the river by barge. In 1885 the *Wrigley* became the first steam vessel to cross the Arctic Circle when she travelled to the mouth of the Mackenzie. Steamers came into common use on various Mackenzie River tributaries, especially on the Peace where they went as far as Hudson's Hope. Tramways were built around rapids to connect steamship lines.

In 1912 the Canadian Northern Railway reached Athabasca Landing, eliminating the old stage route from Edmonton. Four years later, the Edmonton, Dunvegan and British Columbia Railway reached Peace River Landing. From this time on, steamboats declined on the Athabasca River, but those on the Mackenzie continued for many years. The arrival of all-season highways and airlines eventually displaced steamers as the major method of inland transport.

During the construction of the Canadian Pacific Railway, the *Skuzzy* was built at Yale on the Fraser River. In her first attempt to pass upriver through Hell's Gate rapids on the Fraser in 1882, she failed. Her second effort succeeded because her engines were assisted by over a hundred Chinese labourers, who pulled on ropes through rings fastened to the canyon walls. The *Skuzzy* was one of a number of steamboats working on the upper Fraser and its tributaries.

As in the 1850s railway boom in Canada West, when schemes were proposed to connect almost every town to major outlets, steamer routes in the west reflected a similar enthusiasm for building connecting links. Wherever there was a stretch of navigable water on a river or lake, the steamboat became a common sight. Because of the difficulties of road-building in mountainous country, British Columbia had more inland steamers on short runs than did any other region of Canada. Upon the completion of an American railway near the border as well as the Canadian Pacific farther north, steamboats were introduced into the lakes of the Columbia River system in 1885. Regular routes served the Okanagan, Arrow and Kootenay lakes from the railheads. After a decade of activity, steamboat traffic was curtailed by the arrival of the southern branch of the Canadian Pacific Railway and U.S. branch lines from the south. Nevertheless, the lake steamers continued to be the main transportation service connecting railways to isolated settlements and they opened the fruit lands in the valleys. By the 1930s highways were beginning to parallel the lakeshores. The steamers tried vainly to compete but by the mid-1950s the era of the lake steamer was finished.

The natural water route into the Yukon Territory is the Yukon River which empties into the Bering Sea. By 1871 the American vessel *Yukon* was serving the river; later she was used by the Hudson's Bay Company when it moved from Fort Yukon in Alaska to Fort Reliance. Several American vessels served the river making calls as far inland as Fort Selkirk, and during the gold rush they were the major source of supplies for Dawson City.

In 1899 the White Pass and Yukon Railway was built from

Skagway to Lake Bennett and Whitehorse by an English company, opening an all-year supply route, but its capacity and range was limited. Steamboats remained the major bulk carriers until World War II when the threat of Japan forced the construction of the Alaska Highway and the staging route of airfields from Edmonton. The coming of all-weather trucks and airplanes marked the end of the steamboats. The last vessel left Dawson on 26 August 1955. Within a short time even the rafts carrying lumber had disappeared. People moved their homes from the rivers to the new highways and in 1953 the capital was moved from Dawson to Whitehorse. The colourful era of inland transportation in Canada had ended. All that remains today of this great period are a few commemorative plaques, vessels refurbished as museums or restaurants, and a few steamboats employed in mundane dredging or summer touring.

Waterways will remain important for cheap bulk transport. An obvious example is the significance of the Great Lakes route to the western grain trade. In recent years, the feasibility of tanker traffic across the Arctic has been studied intensively. The Berger Report (1977), on the proposed Mackenzie Valley natural gas pipeline, states that barges will be a major transportation method for oil research and pipeline construction in the north.

Indians Own the Land

As early as 1763, George III had issued a proclamation which recognized that the land belonged to the Indians; it stated that they were not to be dispossessed of their lands without their consent. The Hudson's Bay Company never questioned that the land belonged to the Indians and, until it relinquished its charter, recognized that its employees lived and traded on the prairies only with the native peoples' sanction. Each tribal group controlled a traditional area suited to its lifestyle, but the territory was community controlled and personal possession of land was an alien concept.

Unlike the nomadic prairie Indians who wandered over large areas, the Indians of British Columbia, especially on the coast, were settled in comparatively small but densely populated areas. Smaller corporate entities—tribes or clans—controlled a defined area of land through the inheritance of hunting and fishing rights. Thus these people had a kind of land entitlement not shared by prairie peoples.

The early traders adjusted their practices to the neighbouring natives, for success in obtaining and transporting furs depended on their co-operation. The traders commonly made some gesture of payment in return for permission to establish a trading post, agricultural lands or mines.

Early Indian Agreements

As early as 1778 John Meares at Nootka on Vancouver Island wrote, "[Chief] Maquilla not only readily consented to grant us a spot of ground in his territory, whereon a house might be built for the accommodation of the people we intended to leave there. . . . In return for his kindness and to insure a continuance of it, the chief was presented with a pair of pistols. . . . [His kinsman] Callicum was also gratified with suitable presents."

In 1817 the Earl of Selkirk made an agreement with five Salteaux, Assiniboine and Cree chiefs (who signed by affixing their animal totems) granting to George III land along the Red River from Lake Winnipeg to Grand Forks, and along the Assiniboine to Portage la Prairie, two miles back from the rivers and six miles around white settlements. (The Indians understood two miles to be the greatest distance at which a horse can be seen on level prairie.) In return each nation was to receive 100 pounds of good merchantable tobacco annually.

James Douglas continued in the far west the policy of purchasing land entitlement from the natives. For land in present-day Victoria and its environs he paid £150.3.4, much of it in goods as is shown by the payment of 371 blankets and a cap to the 122 men of the Songhees band. Similar agreements were made with other tribal groups on Vancouver Island, by which certain lands within the surrendered area were reserved for their use. Douglas, supported by the colonial office, thus recognized that the native peoples had ownership of the land which could be terminated only by mutual agreement. After 1858, when he was no longer chief factor, neither his Legislative Assembly nor the British government could agree on the

responsibility for land payment; but Governor Douglas continued to negotiate the establishment of residential reserves.

The Indian Treaties

When Canada took over the North-West Territories it inherited the responsibility of dealing with the Indians. The tribes of
the west were hunters who moved freely through the land limited only by the territorial claims of their neighbours. In the
Blackfoot country white people were still not welcome. But, as
we have seen, infiltration of white traders had changed the
habits of the native peoples. Blankets, guns, knives and other
goods had become necessities. Nevertheless, many of the
ancient social customs remained.

Other insidious influences besides trade goods affected the
Indians. European diseases spread quickly—measles,
diphtheria and scarlet fever exacted heavy tolls. Most dreaded
of all was smallpox. Samuel Hearne wrote that a smallpox
epidemic in 1780–81 killed nine-tenths of the Chipewyan
between Hudson Bay and Great Bear Lake. Periodically, as in
1837 and as late as 1870, the smallpox plague swept from one
tribe to another wiping out entire villages throughout the west.

The lifestyle of the prairie Indians was dependent on the
buffalo. With the advent of guns and horses, hunting had
become easier and often only the choicest meat—the tongue
and hump, for example—was kept; the rest of the carcass was
left for animal predators or to rot. Then the demand for pemmican grew as traders and settlers arrived, and the American
railway builders needed meat to feed their work crews. The
American buffalo hunters apparently killed 10 million migrating buffalo in 1871–75 alone, taking only the skins. In Canada
there was also an increasing demand for meat and hides. As
the indiscriminate slaughter and waste decimated the herds,
Metis hunters were forced to travel farther from their bases
each year. In 1880 there were still some small herds, mostly in
the United States. Five years later only a few scattered animals
were to be found.

The plains Indians were now travelling farther. They met
their needs by taking furs and hides north to the trading posts
on the North Saskatchewan River or south to the American

Fort Benton. The border meant no more to these people than it had to the buffalo.

The Hudson's Bay Company policy had been to restrict and often forbid the sale of liquor to Indians. When its charter was sold, these restrictions were gone and, in spite of federal regulations establishing prohibition in the territories, whisky was being traded—most commonly in the isolated south where Americans established posts such as Fort Whoop-Up near present-day Lethbridge, Alberta, and made alcohol and rifles readily available. By 1880 the Indians were in desperate straits. Their natural means of livelihood, the buffalo, was destroyed, their lands were being occupied, and their numbers were declining.

The Canadian government recognized that if white settlements were to be established in the west, some accommodation must be made with the Indians regarding the division and ownership of land. Therefore a series of seven treaties were negotiated, though it is questionable whether the Indians, having no experience of individual land ownership, interpreted the agreements in the same way as the cosigners. In their poverty-stricken condition and under pressure from government, they had, in fact, little choice. Nor could the government of that time foresee future developments and problems. Officials were of the opinion that traditional cultures would disappear and that individuals would become assimilated—an illusion that was to persist for many years.

Treaties 1 and 2 (1871) covered the territory in and near Manitoba. Treaty 3 (1873), which was for the area between Lake Superior and Lake of the Woods, prepared the way for the roads and railways necessary to move settlers westwards. Treaty 4 (1874) concerned the Qu'Appelle-Assiniboine Valley and the area to the west. Treaty 5 (1875) extended from The Pas north of Lake Winnipeg to the Nelson River. Treaty 6 (1876), signed at Fort Carlton, included all the fertile belt to the Rocky Mountains. Treaty 7 (1877), the Blackfoot treaty, completed the coverage from Lake Superior to the Rocky Mountains.

Although there were variations, the treaties all accomplished the following: the Indians relinquished claim to their territories from Lake Superior to the foothills of the Rocky Mountains except for certain specified land allotments, usually one section (260 ha) for each family of five. This land could not be sold without government consent and would be situated where the Indians were in the habit of living; thus many small reserves were created instead of a few large ones. In return for surrendering their land, Indians retained the right to hunt and fish in these territories except where the land was occupied. The government would make a small cash payment of twelve dollars plus a perpetual annual payment of five dollars per head to each Indian man, woman and child, with special gifts and salaries for chiefs and head men. The people would receive agricultural implements, seeds and cattle to help them establish self-sufficient agricultural communities. The treaties also provided for schools and medical care on the reserves. All treaties prohibited the sale of alcohol on reserves.

The treaties prepared the way for western settlement and railway construction with almost no confrontations between Indians and whites. Nevertheless, before 1883 Lieutenant Governor Edgar Dewdney, as Indian commissioner, arranged to have bands living along the border and near the proposed railway route moved onto reserves established farther north. The land question was less urgent in the more northerly regions but eventually other treaties were signed. Treaty 9 (1905) covered northern Ontario. Treaties 8 (1899), 10 (1906) and 11 (1921) included all the territories of the Mackenzie River drainage basin. A large area of land in the far north as well as most of British Columbia were still not covered by federal agreements.

When Treaty 11 was signed, there were nearly 4,000 natives in the North-West Territories and only 653 "others" which included Metis, nonstatus Indians and whites. In the forty years 1941 to 1981 the population more than tripled, from 12,000 to 43,000. The 1971 federal census showed a population of 34,805, of which 7,180 were Indians, 11,400 Inuit and an estimated 1,500 Metis. The 15,000 white people, most of whom were transients, reflected the spread of mining activity into the Mackenzie basin and nearby Arctic waters.

In the mountains of British Columbia the Indians were divided into many smaller seminomadic groups and the problem of Indian lands was more complex. After 1871 when Douglas retired and Indian affairs came under the control of Joseph Trutch, later lieutenant governor, the Indians were no longer seen as important participants in the fur trade but as impediments to mining and settlement. As white settlement spread on the mainland, the newcomers simply took the land they wanted, and the government, probably because of lack of funds, restricted the natives without recompense to allocated reserves of varying size. Further, the government was not prevented from several times cutting back these reserves. Periodically there were minor uprisings against white penetration, as when Indians threatened gold miners on the Fraser River, or when a survey crew was killed in Bute Inlet in 1864. Usually the visit of a naval vessel soon cooled any restlessness along the coast, and the appearance of government officials temporarily resolved the problems of the interior.

When British Columbia entered Confederation in 1871, the administration of Indian affairs became a federal responsibility, but because land resources were under provincial jurisdiction, there was bickering for many years between the two levels. The province refused to make land available for additional reserves or to co-operate in administration. Eventually compromises were reached; more reserves were established and earlier ones enlarged. By 1892 the reserves numbered 778, averaging less than a thousand acres (400 ha) each. The provincial government's autocratic and obscure policies for designating suitable reserve land—often the poorest available—and its refusal to agree to a specific acreage per family led to many Indian protests, but little attention was given to their claims. As in other parts of North America, diseases exacted a heavy toll so that in the twenty years following 1871 the Indian population of the province was estimated to have decreased by 10,000 to a low of 25,000. It was another twenty years before the numbers began to increase.

Before Confederation the Indian population declined throughout the west and did not start to recover until the 1930s; some people foretold eventual extinction or at least assimilation. The free hunting groups could not adjust to the limitations of a settled agricultural life in spite of government pressures. Without sufficient food, proper clothing and proper health care—inadequate even on the reserves—and lacking skills for a white man's society, they suffered malnutrition and disease.

Education was provided by government and mission schools but, given their non-Indian staff and textbooks containing irrelevant material in a strange language, these institutions were unsuited to Indian experience and contributed little to Indian well-being. The Indians continued to be restless even after the failure of the uprising of 1885. Many left the confining reservations for the cities, but they were unprepared and untrained for city life and many were caught in a syndrome of urban poverty.

The North West Mounted Police

When Capt. W. F. Butler travelled from Fort Garry to Rocky Mountain House and made his report on the "Great Lone Land" to the Canadian government in 1870, he pointed out the confusion resulting from the withdrawal of the Hudson's Bay Company and the absence of any new law-making machinery in the territories. He recommended the establishment of a police force and some form of judicial authority.

Police control was originally a provincial responsibility and the idea of a federal police force was new. John A. Macdonald finally accepted that, in spite of the costs, a law-enforcing body was necessary. Canadians were aware of the gun-fighting, the lawlessness, and the bloody clashes with Indians on the American western frontier. Largely because of the policies of the Hudson's Bay Company, Indians in Canada were not as aggressively resentful of the white intruders; now a police force would reassure both the Indians and settlers that Canada intended to maintain order. It could be used to stop the infiltration of lawless American traders. A federal force would also demonstrate to the United States that Canada intended to hold the western territories.

The government realized that the Americans would not favour a military force along their border, especially after the British had ostentatiously withdrawn their troops from Canada in 1871. Similarly, they might criticize the name "Mounted Rifles" or the appointment of officers with military titles. On 23 May 1873, the North West Mounted Police Act was passed. A planned force of 150 men was increased within a year to 300. More than a police force, all the officers were justices of the peace and the commissioner had the powers of a magistrate. Thus they would be able to hear criminal cases and mete out quick punishment.

Six weeks after the act was passed, a group of American wolf hunters, claiming they were looking for some stolen horses, massacred a camp of Assiniboines in the Cypress Hills. This was the most violent of several similar incidents and merely accentuated the need for rapid action. One hundred and fifty recruits from the eastern provinces were dispatched during the cold of October and November over the Dawson Trail to Winnipeg. Here they were issued red jackets: from the earliest times British invading armies had worn red; now it was a reminder of the good relationships that had existed between Britain and the Indians in the early wars against the French and Americans, and it symbolized the far-reaching powers of the British Empire (always mapped in red) and its reputation for law and order. The recruits drilled through the winter in Winnipeg and in May were joined by a second contingent of 150 men.

During the summer 275 men struggled on the "Great March" westward, parallelling the southern border. When they started, the participants were raw recruits who had little knowledge of military affairs or of the land they were to penetrate, and their march took much longer than the expeditions of experienced plainsmen. Sometimes stretching for ten miles (16 km), the expedition included Red River carts, wagons, cattle, farm machinery, horses and weapons including two small field guns. Carts broke down, water was often scarce in temperatures over 90° F (32° C), a plague of grasshoppers descended upon them—as well as flies and vicious mosquitoes, dysentery broke out, and horses often wandered away. By the end of summer the experience had brought about adjustments; the movement was better organized, and the raw volunteers had become seasoned veterans prepared for duties. One division was sent to Edmonton, finally arriving in November. Another division was sent to Swan River in northern Manitoba.

The main body continued westward until September but could not find Fort Whoop-Up. A small group was sent to Fort Benton for supplies, where they recruited the Metis Jerry Potts who was to be their most famous guide for twenty years. He soon found Fort Whoop-Up but the place was abandoned. The force built and wintered in Fort Macleod, named after the assistant commissioner. In 1875 Macleod met an assembly of Blackfoot, Bloods and Peigans: Chief Crowfoot (a Blackfoot) welcomed the introduction of law and order on their behalf. This was typical of the respect and expectations that the Indians were to hold for the force as it extended its control.

In the following years new forts were established—Fort Walsh (after Insp. J. M. Walsh), Fort Calgary and Fort Saskatchewan. In 1876 Sitting Bull and his Sioux fled into Canada after wiping out the American army force under General Custer. The Mounties immediately confronted them and warned Sitting Bull that he could stay in Canada only if there was no trouble. The Canadian government, however, did not want the warlike Sioux to settle in Canada lest they stir up the Blackfoot, and refused help and food supplies to the hungry refugees, who returned after a short time to the United States.

The NWMP grew in size and established posts in isolated areas. It wiped out the whisky trade and brought a sense of security to the new settlers of the west. The Indians appreciated the protection from marauding American whisky runners and came to believe that the Mounties applied equal justice to natives and whites. In 1878 the headquarters were moved from Fort Macleod to Fort Walsh, and five years later to Regina. In 1904 the name was changed to the Royal North West Mounted Police and in 1920 it became the Royal Canadian Mounted Police.

The Pacific Scandal

When British Columbia entered Confederation, the federal government had promised to build a railway to the Pacific within ten years. The idea of a transcontinental railway was not new. Orators and writers had been forecasting it for thirty years, and the United States had achieved theirs with the completion of the Union Pacific in 1869.

During the Canadian railway boom in the 1850s, many speculators, with loans, land grants and other incentives from various levels of government, had accumulated large profits, though it is true that many also went bankrupt. The promise of railways into the west offered new opportunities to eastern railway promoters.

As new immigrants arrived in Ontario, they found a shortage of land for settlement and an impenetrable wilderness blocking their westward movement. Many were diverted to the United States where lines of communication were better established. Ontario farmers and industrialists were suffering from the loss of British markets following the introduction of free trade and the repeal of navigation laws, as well as the loss of American markets as a result of that country's tariffs.

To all these sectors, a populated west promised unlimited business opportunities. Thus, as early as 1858, the Grits under George Brown had made the annexation of the northwest a plank in their party platform, and when John A. Macdonald promised a transcontinental railway, he was generally supported. The main criticisms were for the ten-year limit and the high costs that this would entail. During the entire history of construction, costs would be the most controversial and urgent problem. How could three and a half million people finance such an immense undertaking?

The railway would have to be built by a private company with government assistance, mainly in the form of land grants—a method commonly used in earlier railway construction. Macdonald was determined that it should be an all-Canadian road: from the various groups considered as contractors, he favoured a syndicate led by Sir Hugh Allan, probably the richest man in Canada. Macdonald apparently did not know that Allan was working with a group of Americans, the most controversial of whom was Jay Cooke, a financier who controlled the Northern Pacific Railway. Cooke hoped to connect the new Canadian railway with his own lines south of Winnipeg and thus postpone indefinitely construction north of the Great Lakes, giving him control of the traffic into western Canada. During the federal election of 1872, in order to ensure their contract, Allan's group supplied over $300,000 to the victorious Conservative candidates.

In the following year the Liberals produced proof in the House of Commons of the Americans' influence in the Conservative victory, climaxing their accusations by quoting the damning telegram from Macdonald to the Americans' representative: "I must have another ten thousand ... do not fail me." When it became obvious that this "Pacific Scandal" would result in his defeat in the House, Macdonald resigned.

The ensuing election gave the Liberals under Alexander Mackenzie an overwhelming majority of sixty seats. Mackenzie was a hard-working, religious Scotsman, a former stonemason. As Macdonald's opponent, he had criticized the ten-year limit for building the railway, but unable to abrogate the agreement with British Columbia, he was forced to make a start: he was not enthusiastic and construction was inevitably delayed.

The Surveys

The first step towards construction of the railway to the Pacific coast was the selection of a route. The engineer-in-chief for almost a decade was Sandford Fleming, who had been chief engineer for the Intercolonial Railway to the Maritimes. He is famous for the concept of standard time belts and promoted the construction of the Pacific cable which would be an "all-red route" for communication within the British Empire.

Fleming selected leaders to conduct surveys of the many possible routes. In 1871 he personally travelled across the continent from Winnipeg by the old Carlton Trail, the Yellowhead Pass, and the Thompson and Fraser rivers to New Westminster. Thereafter he supported the Yellowhead Pass for the railway route. It was commonly believed that the line would start at Selkirk, north of Winnipeg, head northwest over the narrows of Lake Manitoba, then join the Carlton Trail to Edmonton and the Yellowhead.

Another major decision was the selection of a terminus on the Pacific coast. Numerous passes as far north as Pine Pass at 55° latitude were inspected. Ten routes from the Yellowhead to the coast and seven possible inlets were studied. The terminus narrowed to two choices—Victoria on Vancouver Island or Burrard Inlet on the mainland. The former route would cross the Cariboo district and reach the ocean through a narrow canyon to Bute Inlet; bridges would be built across the islands to take the line to Vancouver Island and south to Esquimalt. The alternative route would follow the North Thompson, Thompson and Fraser rivers to the head of Burrard Inlet. This route would revive such towns as Kamloops, Hope and New Westminster and was strongly supported by mainlanders.

The old rivalry between New Westminster and Victoria

reached new heights. In 1873, just before the Pacific Scandal, a sod-turning ceremony in Esquimalt presumably marked the beginning of the railway to that city. Five thousand tons of rail were shipped to Nanaimo and Esquimalt, where they rusted for four years and no construction started. Ironically, neither of the two rival cities was to be the terminus.

The Liberal Era

The depression that began in Britain, the United States and Canada in 1873 continued throughout the term of Mackenzie's Liberal government. Canada was faced with falling prices, business failures, unemployment and declining trade. Immigration dropped. In Liberal Ontario, where the depression hit industry, party dissidents who disagreed with Mackenzie grew in number, for party loyalty in those days was not as strong as it would later become.

In such times, Mackenzie did not intend to incur a large national debt from the transcontinental railway. His solution was to build short rail lines between connecting waterways; as money became available, additional trackage would be constructed. This implied a building program extending over many years. During his term of office the surveys were almost completed and some short lines constructed. In 1875 a ceremonial sod was turned at Fort William to denote the beginning of the railway to Winnipeg. This line would be built from both ends (it was eight years before the two lines met), and in 1877 the locomotive "Countess of Dufferin" was unloaded from a barge at Winnipeg to herald the beginning of construction east and west from that city. The government-contracted route from Winnipeg to Pembina on the U.S. border was built and in 1878 it connected with the St. Paul and Manitoba Railway. Winnipeg finally had rail connection to the outside.

British Columbia was increasingly exasperated by the surveying delays and the uncertainty of the route. There was talk of secession from the Dominion. In 1874 the province appealed directly to the colonial secretary, Lord Carnarvon, and in an attempt at appeasement, Governor General Lord Dufferin and his wife made a lengthy visit, travelling throughout the province. Lord Carnarvon suggested revised terms: the railway from

Esquimalt to Nanaimo would be completed as soon as practical, surveys on the mainland would be pushed, a telegraph line would be built immediately, and when the surveys were completed the government would spend $2 million a year for construction in British Columbia. In return, the province would accept 31 December 1890 as the deadline for the completion of the railway. Mackenzie added a rider that the terms would be adopted only if they meant no increase in taxes. When the Senate refused to pass the bill accepting the the Carnarvon Terms, talk of withdrawal revived in British Columbia.

In 1878, just before the federal election, Mackenzie announced that the western terminus would be Burrard Inlet and, as a token of intention, he had the rusting rails moved from Esquimalt to Yale. This gesture gained him no seats in B.C. which voted solidly Conservative.

Mackenzie's out-going Liberal government had several accomplishments to its credit, including the establishment of the Supreme Court of Canada and the introduction of the secret ballot. It had almost completed the railway surveys and had built some short lines. It had not solved the problems of the depression.

The CPR Charter

After two subdued years in opposition, John A. Macdonald began to revive his party. He adopted an appealing slogan, "National Policy," which supported a high tariff to restrict American imports and revive industry. In its broadest sense, the slogan also implied: a vigorous immigration policy to populate the west and to develop agriculture, which would assist eastern industries; completion of the Pacific railway which would assist British Columbia, prairie farmers and, especially, the industrial centres of Ontario and Quebec. Macdonald is recognized as one of Canada's greatest prime ministers partly because of the vision expressed in his National Policy of a nation united from coast to coast under a central government. He could not foresee that the heterogeneity of Canada would result in a federal system in which central government powers would be challenged by regional interests. The depression years, the personality of Macdonald, and

National Policy resulted in a stunning defeat for the Liberals: the Conservative majority in 1878 was sixty-eight seats.

Macdonald intended that private enterprise would build the railway, but it took time to find a group with enough capital. Meanwhile, in British Columbia a government contract was issued to the American Andrew Onderdonk, who was to build the line between Port Moody and Kamloops. Onderdonk proved to be a wise choice, for he was a capable, driving organizer.

A railway syndicate was formed under the leadership of George Stephen, president of the Bank of Montreal, R. B. Angus, manager of the Bank of Montreal, Donald A. Smith, former governor of the Hudson's Bay Company, and James J. Hill (who shortly withdrew to build his own Great Northern Railway). These men and their associates raised financial support in Canada, the United States, Britain, France and Germany.

In February 1881 the Canadian Pacific Railway Company was awarded a charter under the CPR Act. By the official terms, the railway received a subsidy of $25 million and 25 million acres (10 million ha) of prairie land (which was to be tax free for twenty years) in alternate mile-square (2.6-km^2) sections to a depth of twenty-four sections on either side of the railway. Building materials would be free of import duties. Stations and other railway property would be free of taxation forever. The government would turn over the completed lines as well as those for which contracts had been let, on their completion. These included the Port Moody–Kamloops section, the Fort William–Selkirk lines, and the Pembina branch. The most controversial clause, especially for Manitoba, said that for twenty years no other line could be built south of the CPR or within fifteen miles (24 km) of the border. In return, the company promised to complete the road within ten years.

Little construction was carried out in the first year: the company had to be organized; rails and other materials and equipment were ordered. The government promised to complete the line from Fort William by 1882, thus opening a route for supplies. Some final surveys had to be made, and funds had to be raised. In May, James J. Hill made the startling announcement that the line would be built on a southern route towards Kicking Horse Pass.

In January 1882 the CPR hired William Cornelius Van Horne as general manager. Experienced in American railway building, Van Horne brought tremendous energy and enthusiasm to the construction of the CPR. Under his direction the formerly sluggish progress became an organized and rapid drive.

Construction proceeded in three sections. The eastern section, connecting with leased eastern lines at Callander, Ontario, would follow the north shore of Lake Superior to Fort William and Winnipeg. The prairie section would drive in an almost straight line from Winnipeg to Kicking Horse Pass. From here, by a route not yet established, the railway would be projected to meet the Onderdonk section.

Track laying on the prairies presented no special problems; even so, the rate of construction was unprecedented. In 1882, 417 miles (667 km) were completed. In British Columbia, Onderdonk was building the railway in sections. In the first year little track laying was done while a series of tunnels was driven through the hard rock north of Yale. Workmen suspended on ropes down the precipitous wall of the Fraser Canyon blasted toeholds in the rock; the loss of life in such mountain sections was great. Supplies were transported over the old Cariboo Road or on the *Skuzzy*. Onderdonk's great problem was a shortage of labour: he imported men from San Francisco and the east but they were not enough, so he followed the example of the American railway builders and brought in large numbers of Chinese, from California and China. Estimates of the number of Chinese who worked on the railway vary greatly—from 6,500 to about 12,000; certainly without their massive contribution the western section would not have been built.

Southern Cities

The sudden change of route to the south meant a decline in the hopes and expectations along the old Winnipeg-Edmonton trade route. The railway would instead pass through Indian country almost uninhabited by white people. Every eight or nine miles (13 or 14 km) along the new track settlements grew, some little more than section houses, some villages built around grain elevators, and a few important cities.

With the restoration of law and order by the North West Mounted Police, the movement of people to the west recovered, especially after the railway was projected. Winnipeg became the dominant commercial centre and was incorporated as a city in 1873. Between 1875 and 1880 its population more than doubled to 8,000. Independent businessmen as well as branches of eastern mercantile and manufacturing establishments moved into the city. There were commercial enterprises of every variety: retail stores, wholesale houses to serve the western towns, lumber mills, flour mills, metal works, clothing factories, as well as private banks and branches of the powerful eastern banks. The *Manitoba Free Press* began publication in 1872, the first of several newspapers.

Winnipeg was the junction of routes from the United States, the Dawson Trail, the Assiniboine settlements, the Carlton Trail and Hudson Bay. It was the provincial capital and the seat of government for the District of Keewatin. Railway construction proceeded in several directions. After the railway connection was completed to American railways in 1878, Winnipeg became a distribution point for immigrants as well as railway supplies. In that year the first wheat was exported via the southern line.

The year 1880 saw the beginning of a great real estate boom in Winnipeg and its story is an extreme example of the surges and collapses that were to hit other towns. People were pouring into the city and building was escalating. For almost three years land prices soared. A lot selling for $1,000 might be resold for $10,000 within a week. In a few months tens of thousands of dollars could be made. Real estate salesmen, land promoters, loan and investment companies, and banks all contributed to the enthusiasm. Capital poured into the city from the east, from the United States and from Britain.

At the end of 1882 the boom collapsed as quickly as it had grown, partly due to a great flood of the Assiniboine and Red rivers which destroyed many of the new buildings. The city had been the heart of railway construction, but the activity had now moved to the end of rail west and east. By 1883 many stores were overstocked and many firms were bankrupt. Wages and prices declined. These disasters caused the capital flow to dry up, and eastern banks instructed their branches to tighten credit. The Manitoba government was forced to pass the Exemption Act of 1884 which ensured that neither machinery nor buildings nor land up to 160 acres (64 ha) could be seized for debt. The repercussions of this collapse were long-term: immigration was drastically reduced as the bad news spread; British investors became dubious about Canadian investments, which probably handicapped the hard-pressed CPR; certainly provincial and city credit suffered for many years.

Meanwhile the CPR was planning its route—at first through Selkirk, twenty miles (32 km) north of Winnipeg, and north-west to the narrows of Lake Manitoba; but Winnipeg petitioned strongly for a change of route through that city, offering $300,000 towards construction of a railway bridge across the Red River to Winnipeg. This was not enough to convince the CPR. Later, in 1881, the CPR agreed to enter Winnipeg and to locate its workshops there if the city would grant another bonus of $200,000 plus land for a station and exempt CPR property from civic taxation in perpetuity. The line was first built through Selkirk, but later a shorter direct line was con-structed through Winnipeg and Selkirk collapsed.

As the CPR extended its track westward, land along the railway sold quickly. Speculators attempted to forecast the railway route and went ahead to buy up land where depots might be located. The railway, however, maintained secrecy about its route and adopted a policy of selecting sites where land could be obtained cheaply. Thus numerous settlements that expected to become cities on the main line found them-selves by-passed and their land almost worthless. Early Bran-don, Regina, Calgary and Port Moody are examples of manipu-lation by the CPR: depots located away from established settlements.

In 1882 Edgar Dewdney, lieutenant governor of the North-West Territories, decided to move the capital to Regina, on a site by Wascana or Pile of Bones Creek at the possible crossing place of the railway. The name was selected by Princess Louise—the wife of Governor General Lord Lorne and daughter of Queen Victoria. The headquarters of the North West Mounted Police would also be located there, and soon real estate agents were selling lots near the new government buildings. The CPR, however, established its station two miles (3.2 km) east where it controlled the land.

As the railway progressed, many Indians watched its advance with trepidation. The Cree chief Piapot had his tepees erected on the railway right-of-way but policemen knocked them down and the Indians withdrew. Later the Blackfoot chief Crowfoot refused to allow the railway to pass through his lands, but was persuaded to back down by the much-respected Father Albert Lacombe; Dewdney allotted other land in exchange for the right-of-way through the reserve.

Calgary, in the heart of the Blackfoot country, was close to the junction of the Elbow and Bow rivers, near the Old North Trail between Fort Benton and Edmonton. A few miles to the west were Catholic and Methodist missions, and American traders had established a trading post near the river fork. Close by the first cattle ranches had begun. The site first gained attention when the North West Mounted Police established Fort Calgary in 1875 on the east bank of the Elbow River. A settlement, originally called Elbow, began to grow around the police post and by 1881 the population was about seventy-five. News of the railway's approach brought more people and speculation, but again the CPR selected its own site, on the west bank of the Elbow. In 1884 Calgary was officially proclaimed a town and grew quickly to incorporation as a city ten years later.

The year 1883 was a successful one for the railroad. In January the Lake Superior section had a gap of 600 miles (960 km), the prairie section had reached Swift Current, and the western section was a series of short lines. By the end of the year, there were still large gaps in the east, the prairie section had passed Calgary, and in the west the gaps were closing.

When Kicking Horse Pass in the Rockies was arbitrarily selected, many skeptics believed that no pass would be found west of it through the Selkirk Mountains. For three years the stubborn Maj. A. B. Rogers searched the wild country until in 1882 he discovered a practical route through Rogers Pass. Spectacular and difficult, this pass enabled the railway to use a shorter route than one following the Columbia River around the Big Bend.

In 1884 construction was proceeding at a rapid rate west of Calgary towards Kicking Horse Pass. In this section the CPR laid 600 feet (180 m) in less than five minutes, a record for hand-laid track which still stands. By the end of the year the track was through the pass and had reached Donald on the Columbia River. At the same time it was possible to take the railway from Port Moody to Sicamous, east of Kamloops.

Unrest in the West

In Manitoba there was growing opposition to the monopoly of the CPR and an increasing demand for provincial control of public lands. The unrest intensified after the serious floods, crop failures and record-low crop prices in 1882. News of these disasters led to a decrease in immigration and the collapse of the land boom. The depression just starting would last until 1896.

The sudden letdown after the years of optimism caused growing discontent. Bitter criticism of the CPR was indirectly an expression of western opposition to the financial establishment in Ontario and the policies of the federal government. The CPR monopoly was blamed for the high freight rates. The railway controlled some of the best land, which it was holding undeveloped for speculative purposes. The CPR was blamed for preventing the construction of a railway to Hudson Bay (even though in its day the Hudson's Bay Company had diverted most of its traffic from the bay to the more economical route through Minnesota). One of Riel's last petitions included a request for a railway to Hudson Bay, which would give western farmers direct access to European markets.

The Manitoba government was demanding control of its resources, especially land, and an end to the CPR monopoly; and it was pressing for more provincial rights. The farmers resented the burden of debts owed to eastern financial interests. They resented, too, the federal tariff policies which protected eastern industries whose costs, because of the limited market, were high, and which also increased the costs of imported machinery. The same eastern commercial and financial interests had advertised the west as a land of opportunity, had encouraged immigration, and had exploited the land; but they had not described the hardships and risks. Manitobans believed that Ontario controlled and dominated the federal government, and that the government's financial policies, tariff rates and support of the CPR were evidence of indifference to western problems.

In the territories, responsible government and provincial status were demanded in place of the autocratic rule of Lieutenant Governor Dewdney. In spite of warnings from many influential people, Ottawa paid little attention to the complaints, though it did grant some concessions, modifying land regulations, for instance, and permitting elected representatives on the North-West Territories council. A convention of the Manitoba and North-West Farmers Union in Winnipeg in 1883 petitioned Ottawa for various reforms, including a limitation on immigration. As a result, a federal committee was appointed to study the problems, but no action was taken.

The wild buffalo were gone, and the traditions and lifestyle of the Indian people had been disrupted. They were now expected to restrict their wanderings to agricultural reserves and adopt the ways of the white farmer. The government had promised to assist in this transition with equipment, education and health care, as well as a food supply to carry them through a short period of adjustment, but it was impossible to make such a revolutionary change in a few years. Thousands of hungry Cree and Blackfoot gathered at Fort Walsh for relief supplies. In an attempt to force them away from the border and into northern reserves, authorities closed Fort Walsh. The hunger did not go away.

In 1883–84 the government, following a policy of financial restraint, cut food supplies and educational grants. Petitions by the Indians to the police and government officials brought no response. As the resentment increased, the police found that the respect and obedience they had built up was declining. Two Cree chiefs, Big Bear, who would not sign Treaty 6, and Poundmaker, were joined by many of the discontent to protest conditions. Neither leader believed that force could succeed, but they found it increasingly difficult to restrain their followers.

The conditions of Red River in 1870 were being repeated along the Saskatchewan Valley. The society and livelihood of the natives and Metis were being threatened by the influx of unsympathetic aliens. The Metis were again a forgotten people, having neither the influence of the whites nor the treaties of the Indians. Many of them had come from Red River and they wanted a similar grant of land or scrip. They took responsibility for running their own isolated communities, but the lengthening railway, the decline of the buffalo and the expanding surveys made them increasingly insecure. Petitions sent to Ottawa received only vague replies.

After the 1883 convention in Winnipeg of the Manitoba and North-West Farmers Union, combined meetings of whites and Metis were held in several places. The outstanding Metis was Gabriel Dumont, a famous buffalo hunter who had natural military ability, but he lacked the executive ability or political experience to become a successful or inspiring leader. In the spring of 1884, a general meeting of whites and Metis resolved to send a delegation to confer with Riel in Montana, who was persuaded to return to Canada to co-ordinate the various protest movements. He held several meetings of consolidated groups and was initially accepted. When nothing came of their repeated petitions, the Metis grew more aggressive while the white settlers, English-speaking Metis and Roman Catholic priests, who hoped for peaceful constitutional change, began to withdraw their support. In March 1885 Riel seized some arms near Batoche and cut the telegraph lines to centres south and west. As he had done in 1869, Riel established a provisional government of Metis, expecting that such a step would again force the federal government into negotiations; but he did not recognize that conditions had changed. On the earlier occasion there had been the legitimate claim that there was no authorized government, but now the land was part of Canada. More significantly, Riel did not appreciate the great changes that had been brought about in the territories by the railway.

The North-West Rebellion

Three days after Riel's provisional government was proclaimed, John A. Macdonald appointed Maj. Gen. Frederick Dobson Middleton to lead a body of militia to Red River. Meanwhile, Supt. L. N. F. Crozier had strengthened the North West Mounted Police forces on the North Saskatchewan. Hearing that a meeting of Metis was to be held at Duck Lake, he sent a small force to secure a quantity of arms stored at a trading post there, but the police were met by a large force of Metis and withdrew. A larger detachment was again met by the Metis, led by Dumont with Riel present, and shooting began. Twelve police were killed before the force withdrew. Meanwhile, Big Bear's Crees, stirred by the Metis opposition, were raiding for supplies and eventually seized Fort Pitt. Settlers fled to the forts and towns. Near Battleford, Poundmaker's Crees were looting the countryside.

Rapid countermoves were necessary. Van Horne offered to transport the militia on his railway and, in spite of the fact that four sections totalling eight-five miles (136 km) were incomplete, the troops from Ottawa were in Winnipeg in eight days, in contrast to the one hundred days it took in 1869. By mid-April three forces were moving northwards from Qu'Appelle, Swift Current and Calgary (see Map 8). At Fish Creek, Middleton's forces were checked by the Metis, and at Cut Knife Creek Lt. Col. William Dillon Otter's force was stopped by Poundmaker. The climax came at the four-day battle of Batoche. Dumont fled to the United States and Riel surrendered. The Indians were scattered and Poundmaker and Big Bear were taken prisoners. It had taken 8,000 men to quell the North-West—or Saskatchewan—Rebellion, at a cost of 200 lives and $6 million.

Riel continues to be a focal point around which racial, religious and political animosities rage. He apparently was opposed to violence, prayed daily, claimed to have visions, and believed in his mission to establish a Catholic Metis nation; yet, in his last days, he broke from the Catholic Church. He came to Canada to lead a protest movement, not a rebellion. Macdonald's government, much as it might have wished to do otherwise, was forced for political reasons to bring him to trial in Regina in 1885. Refusing to plead insanity in his own defence, he was found guilty of treason by a totally Protestant, Anglo-Saxon six-man jury; impressed by his pleas on behalf of the Metis, they recommended mercy. But in spite of numerous petitions, Macdonald realized that if he pardoned Riel, he would lose his support in Ontario. Riel was hanged nine days after the Canadian Pacific Railway was completed. Eight other Metis were executed and twenty-one imprisoned, as were

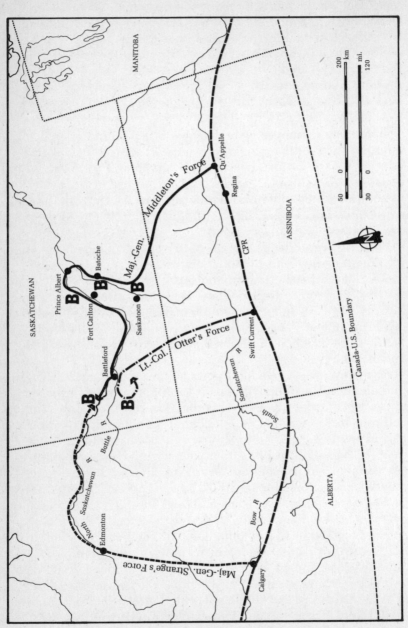

MAP 8: THE NORTHWEST REBELLION, 1885

twenty-three Indians including Big Bear and Poundmaker.

The insurrection was a major disaster for the Metis, not only because of the immediate persecutions and the loss of established homes and farms but also because it destroyed the political cohesiveness of the group. Some who had not joined the rebellion were granted scrip, given up for a pittance, and many wandered towards the Peace River and other outskirts of civilization. Their pride and autonomy would not be re-asserted for many years. The starving Indians had had little to lose, and their actions did gain some recognition of their plight.

Riel remains a controversial figure in Canadian history, interpreted afresh by writers and playwrights. His execution deepened the chasm between English-Protestant Ontario and French-Catholic Quebec. In the latter province, the actions of Macdonald's Conservative government still have repercussions: except for the brief interlude of the John Diefenbaker sweep, Conservative politicians have been unable to overcome the memory of Riel's betrayal.

In recent years, resentment against unsympathetic control by Ottawa has grown in the west. The native peoples and the Metis have organized themselves against continuing discrimination at both the provincial and federal levels. Such developments have resulted in a more sympathetic attitude towards Riel. Although a few die-hards see him as a traitor justly hanged, to many people he is the first western leader who demanded justice, recognition and self-government denied by an autocratic, eastern-oriented federal government. The North-West uprising was more than the local protest of a few malcontents; rather, it was the culmination of efforts by the early free-roaming prairie peoples to check the overpowering pressures of agricultural settlement which coincided with the railway and the introduction of new large-scale farming techniques.

Craigellachie

The cost of the Canadian Pacific Railway was enormous. Throughout the entire history of construction there was a frantic search for new funds. Sometimes the government granted supplementary subsidies; other money was raised, often at high cost, through heavy loans or the sale of stocks and bonds.

At one critical point, when George Stephen successfully manoeuvred a loan in Britain, he cabled to Donald Smith a traditional rallying cry of the Scottish clans, "Stand fast, Craigellachie." Stephen, Smith, Angus and Van Horne, despite the threat of personal bankruptcy, gambled their fortunes on the success of the railway.

In spite of their efforts, the shortage of money remained critical. In 1885 the government refused to lend another $5 million and the railway appeared to be doomed before completion. At this crucial time the CPR successfully moved the troops putting down the North-West Rebellion, revealing the value of the railway, and parliament passed the loan. British interests were also impressed, and whereas they had previously been wary of investing in the railway, they now accepted a bond issue of $35 million.

On 7 November 1885 the two lines from east and west met in Eagle Pass west of present-day Revelstoke. A brief ceremony marked the driving of the last spike at a point named, significantly, Craigellachie. Because of the financial problems of the railway, the spike was "just as good an iron one as those between Montreal and Vancouver," not the customary gold. In the following year the first transcontinental train reached Port Moody from Montreal.

Van Horne had never been satisfied with Port Moody as a terminus and believed that the location should be farther west by the deeper waters of Burrard Inlet. Here were two small lumbering settlements, Hastings and Granville, the latter known as "Gastown" after "Gassy" Jack Deighton, the owner of the hotel. Van Horne drove a hard bargain. The landowners of Granville were forced to donate one-third of their lots to the railway. The provincial government granted 6,000 acres (2400 ha), including most of the centre of the present city of Vancouver and almost the entire southern waterfront of the inlet. The western terminus of the railway became incorporated as the City of Vancouver in 1886, and in the following year the first passenger train arrived in the city.

Eighteen years after Confederation, Macdonald's vision of a Canada connected from sea to sea had been realized. Built to expand the commercial empire of Ontario and Quebec, the railway was to open new lands for settlement and speculation, for new markets and raw materials. With law and order, Canadian control had been established. Along the railway, boom towns were burgeoning.

At the time of Confederation, eastern expansionists viewed the west as Ontario's "Manifest Destiny," where an English-speaking, largely Protestant, provincial annex would arise. The early Ontario arrivals into Assiniboia carried this vision, but fifteen years later the attitude had changed. The people of the west had struggled through droughts and depressions, they had met the geographical challenges of the wilderness, and they had developed a society and identity of their own. They were westerners, with their own problems and ambitions, and they were resentful of the power and influence of central Canada and the federal government. Settlers were discontented over the distribution of land, the monopoly of the CPR, the high costs of supplies and the high interest rates. Westerners felt they were being manipulated by the railway, eastern financiers and the federal government, and so they demanded greater participation in government and an extension of local authority. Repeated pleas to Ottawa were ignored, put off through referral to ineffectual committees, or resulted in only minor concessions. The unhappy Metis and Indians were in more desperate circumstances than before the Riel uprising, for they were scattered, decimated by diseases, hungry, poverty-stricken and unsettled.

The railway opened the west in following years to a flood of newcomers, and westerners became increasingly vociferous in their demands for change. Western alienation a century later was a continuation of these protests of the 1880s.

Chapter Six

FILLING THE LAND
(1885 – 1914)

Heavy immigration was expected to follow the railway. In 1882, 25,000 new people arrived in the prairies and in the following year 100,000, but after these two encouraging years immigration tapered off and became erratic. Reports of drought, early frosts, floods and grasshopper plagues discouraged prospective settlers. Many recent arrivals left western Canada for the United States. The North-West Rebellion, with its threat of Indian troubles, turned away many other would-be immigrants. Furthermore, the depression that had started in 1873 and was relieved briefly during the construction period was to continue until 1896.

Nevertheless, growth was steady. Settlers followed the surveyors into the outer regions. The North Saskatchewan Valley continued to attract homesteaders, who added to the considerable Metis population. Following the railways a chain of settlements stretched in a long narrow line to Calgary. The increasing population encouraged the building of branch lines both north and south of the main line, and by 1890 lines had begun from Regina to Prince Albert and from Calgary to Edmonton.

Although the majority of newcomers continued to be English-speaking, many Europeans arrived, and for some of them reserve lands were set aside. In 1885 the philanthropic Count Paul O. d'Esterhazy organized a colony of Hungarians, and in succeeding years small groups of Germans, Rumanians,

Czechs, Scandinavians and Finns arrived. Although the numbers were low, they were the nuclei for larger groups to follow.

Ranching

The American railroads hastened the cattle ranching of Wyoming and Montana by making available the highly profitable markets of eastern United States and Britain. By the early 1870s, the overflow of this movement spread into the Canadian foothills, coinciding with the arrival of the North West Mounted Police who provided security from Indian depredations as well as creating a limited local market. With the passing of the buffalo, the establishment of Indian reserves required large quantities of meat for the starving people.

By 1880, with the railroad approaching the Rockies, eastern capitalists as well as a number of English gentlemen saw the opportunities not only of making profitable investments but also of establishing themselves as landed gentry on large estates worked by employed labour. An order-in-council in 1881 permitted leases of 100,000 acres (40 000 ha) for a term of twenty-one years at the rate of $10 per 1,000 acres (400 ha) per year. The withdrawal of land from public domain and allotment to private interests was expected to deter squatters and homesteaders on the ranchland, but they arrived with the railway. The cattlemen formed a strong alliance for the management and regulation of their industry. Supported by wealthy industrialists in the east, they were able to check temporarily the challenge of the settlers, but eventually their numbers exerted too much pressure. The opposition Liberal Party was supported by opponents of the ranchers and was able to exert pressure on the government, which announced in 1892 that the lease system would end in four years but leaseholders might purchase one-tenth of their lease for $1.25 per acre (0.4 ha). The same year that the lease system ended, the anticattlemen's Liberal Party came into power and the ranchers' political power steadily declined.

Because the last years of the nineteenth century had above-average rainfall, the arid region described by Palliser seemed to be a myth. Agricultural practices had been improved by the tillage methods of "dry-land farming" used in the United

States. But later years would prove the hazards of the region both to ranchers and farmers. The extraordinarily cold winter of 1906–7 killed thousands of cattle, and the drought years of the 1920s and 1930s forced many farmers to leave. Ranching survived, and with the introduction of government irrigation works in the fertile belts, crop growing in wheat, barley and sugar beets remains a major industry of the region.

Wheat and Manitoba

The majority of Manitobans were French-speaking at the time of the Manitoba Act, which recognized a bilingual province. In spite of the efforts of local French leaders and the support of Quebec, however, only a limited number of new French immigrants arrived, and within a short time Manitoba was predominantly English-speaking. The minority groups—French, Icelandic and Mennonite—tended to cluster in their own communities. The growing population, recorded in 1881 at 65,954, resulted in the expansion of boundaries east, west and north. By this time the possibilities of wheat growing had been recognized. Many new steel machines, such as the mechanical drill, steel plows, the self-binding reaper, mowers and the steam thresher, made cultivation more efficient. Horses or oxen still provided most of the power. The introduction of earlier-ripening Red Fife wheat lessened the dangers of frost and rust. Railways provided transportation to new markets.

The larger wheat harvests demanded improvements in storing and shipping methods. Trackside elevators were built by the railways and by private companies which often had agreements with the railways; new special cars were constructed for the handling of grain, and expanding settlements got new branch lines. In spite of these improvements, there was always a shortage of storage capacity and of transportation facilities to handle the wheat before winter closed the Great Lakes system.

Discontent grew with the continuing depression. In the United States farmers were organizing and the movement spread to Canada. In 1883 the Farmers Co-operative and Protective Union of Manitoba met in Brandon and later in Winnipeg; unfortunately, their organizational efforts occurred during the North-West Rebellion, and when some extremists began to talk of secession, many moderates withdrew, causing the movement to collapse. It had drafted a "Bill of Rights" which listed the grievances of the province and farmers. Among its demands were "Better Terms" and "Provincial Rights," including provincial control of public lands, the withholding of land from speculators, the end of the CPR monopoly, and the right of the provincial government to charter railways.,

Provincial Rights

The movement for provincial rights had begun in Ontario when it opposed Macdonald's attempts to establish a strong central government which could disallow provincial legislation. Ontario successfully challenged several of these disallowances and thus weakened the powers of Ottawa.

The first dispute arose over the Ontario-Manitoba boundary: the federal government claimed that the boundary as established in 1881 for Manitoba was near Fort William, but Ontario claimed as far west as the northwest angle of Lake of the Woods. In 1884 the Judicial Committee of the Privy Council favoured Ontario and thus established the present boundary.

Throughout the west farmers, merchants and politicians were strongly opposed to the monopoly clause in the CPR charter. They claimed that the railway, without competition, was charging excessive freight rates and was also adding to costs through its control of grain elevators. The outcry intensified in 1883 when the railway raised its freight rates. The government of Manitoba undertook to challenge the monopoly clause by issuing its own railway charters. The test came with the provincial chartering of the Northern Pacific and Manitoba Railway, which would be built in two sections from Winnipeg west to Portage la Prairie and south to the American Northern Pacific. When this line attempted to cross the Canadian Pacific tracks, it was stopped by an injunction and the dispute was referred to the Supreme Court of Canada, which in 1889 ruled that the legislature of Manitoba indeed had the power to charter railways within the limits of "Old Manitoba." The first step against monopoly had been successful.

The premier of Manitoba from 1878 to 1887 was John Norquay, a descendant of an old Red River Scottish-Metis family.

In 1886 his efforts to obtain provincial control of public lands failed, but he did win "better terms" when the annual federal grant to the province was increased.

Norquay had been brought up in an atmosphere of French-English partnership and attempted to continue a policy of mutual consultation in his government rather than party rule. Nevertheless, the increasing preponderance of English-speaking people in the province lessened the influence of the French. From 1883, the large Ontario faction helped form the Liberal Party which, five years later, came to power under the leadership of Thomas Greenway, marking the introduction of party government and the decline of French influence in Manitoba.

The Manitoba Schools Question

The Manitoba Act stated that the school system should guarantee the rights of French-speaking Roman Catholics, though no legal system of separate schools was established. Most French attended Catholic schools, while most other religious and ethnic groups attended Protestant-run schools which were less denominational. Encouraged by the English majority in the province, in 1890 the Liberal government of Manitoba, firmly backed by the Ontario Protestants, made English the only official language, changed the educational system to follow that of Ontario, but made no provision for separate schools. Macdonald hesitated to apply disallowance, yet the Conservatives were pledged to guard French educational rights in Manitoba. The Ottawa Liberals supported their Manitoba colleagues. Macdonald promised remedial legislation to establish separate schools but took no action. This vacillating attitude added to the opposition to the Conservatives that had been growing in French Canada since the execution of Riel.

The federal Conservatives had been in power for nineteen years and John A. Macdonald was old and tired. Under his leadership the party won the election of 1891, but Macdonald died in June of that year. There was no strong Conservative successor, and in the next five years four prime ministers attempted to hold the Conservatives together. Under the last of them, Charles Tupper, the main issue was the remedial bill to settle the Manitoba Schools question, but party dissension caused the bill to be withdrawn.

The election of 1896 ended the era of John A. Macdonald and introduced the age of Wilfrid Laurier. The Conservatives had grown old in office while the Liberals were led by the young, attractive and eloquent Laurier, who had surrounded himself with a group of outstanding political leaders.

Two election issues were significant for the west. The Liberals proposed freer trade and reciprocity as opposed to the protectionist tariffs of Macdonald's earlier National Policy. Second, the government's indecision on the Manitoba Schools question split the Conservative Party and accentuated religious differences and the problem of provincial rights.

The new government was immediately faced with the contentious schools question. Emphasizing the need for co-operation and compromise, Laurier arranged discussions between the federal and Manitoba governments. From these a compromise was reached: (1) the nondenominational nature of the Manitoba schools would remain; (2) any religion could be taught by any denomination at the end of the day and under specific conditions, and (3) where a certain number of pupils spoke French, a bilingual teacher could be employed. Although this was not satisfactory to the Catholic bishops, their protests were eventually quelled by a papal legate, and the Manitoba Schools question lost its immediate political importance.

In passing it must be noted that the problem of French rights in Manitoba continued to fester until 13 December 1979 when the Supreme Court of Canada declared that the denial of bilingualism in government was unconstitutional, being contrary to the Manitoba Act of 1870. The Manitoba government was thus faced with the enormous task of translating all laws since 1890 into French. In the Constitution Act of 1982 only Manitoba, Quebec and New Brunswick were recognized as officially bilingual.

The policy of compromise shown by the Liberals in the Manitoba Schools question was applied to other problems. Even before the election Laurier had modified his position on free trade and reciprocity and had supported a policy of limited tariffs for revenue purposes but not for protection. Thus the Liberals made little change in existing policies of maintaining support for Canada's industrial community. One important principle for the west was that of preferential tariffs, designed to favour those countries, especially Britain and the Empire, that gave Canada favourable rates, which considerably helped western grain exports.

Pacific Province

Within a month of the arrival of the first train in Vancouver, the *Abyssinia* from Yokohama berthed at the CPR docks. On board was a full complement of first class passengers and a cargo of mail, tea and silk. Along with two other vessels, she had been chartered by the railway to establish its transportation route to the Orient. In 1891, Canadian Pacific Steamships began its own steamship line with the beautiful *Empresses*— the *India, China, Japan* and, later, the *Empress of Canada*. Sandford Fleming's dream of an "all-red route" from Britain to Asia was complete.

Railway construction brought thousands of workers to British Columbia. With the railway in place, the population was augmented by immigrants. Vancouver's population was growing by over one thousand a year, and new communities were being established along the railway and in the interior valleys. New and old industries, supported by distant capitalists, prospered. Lumber mills increased their output and canneries spread along the coast. On Vancouver Island coal mining expanded, and in the Kootenays the discovery of gold, silver and copper introduced a new mining boom. Lumber, fish and minerals were exported to South America, Australia, China, Britain and the Pacific American ports. These exports along with Asiatic imports and services to coastal communities were making Vancouver a major shipping centre.

In contrast to the boisterousness of Vancouver, Victoria remained quietly conservative. It became the stopping place for the great ocean liners; and some local goods, such as flour and wheat, were shipped out. One of the most important industries for many years was the seal hunt, and at one time Victoria's sealing fleet numbered sixty-five vessels. Nearby, the drydock at Esquimalt naval base was almost complete. Except for one in Singapore, it would be the only drydock on the Pacific capable of handling the largest ships.

In federal elections British Columbia steadfastly voted Conservative. In provincial matters, however, there were no political parties and premiers lasted only as long as they could maintain the uncertain support of the members of the legislature. Because a wide variety of sectional interests were represented, loyalties were precarious and premiers were defeated only to be later reinstated. In the first thirty years there were fifteen changes of ministry. The members of the legislature were wealthy men profiting from the new industrial expansion. Although divided on many issues, they generally supported measures that encouraged new industries—railway contracts, timber leases, mineral claims, roadbuilding and export trade. This was an era of speculation, in which government believed in a future of continuous growth based on unlimited resources.

The New Canadians

Laurier's accession roughly corresponded to the end of the depression. New methods of farming resulted in more dependable crops. In 1892 William Saunders developed Marquis wheat, which ripened seven days faster than Red Fife and also gave a larger yield. It effectively pushed settlement northwards two hundred miles (320 km). (Later experiments were to introduce even faster-ripening varieties.) The improved world conditions encouraged grain exports, which in turn resulted in an expansion of grain elevators and shipping. A network of branch railway lines spread like a spider's web across the prairies, bringing new life to isolated communities.

As, in earlier times, news of crop failures had discouraged immigrants, so news of success encouraged many restless and dissatisfied Europeans to come to Canada. An aggressive immigration program was spearheaded by Clifford Sifton, the federal minister of the interior. His methods have been compared to a "medicine show," for they were flamboyant and spectacular. Tens of thousands of pamphlets, posters and advertisements were sent to Europe and the United States describing the opportunities, the free homestead policy and the special transportation rates. Canadian immigration agents were sent out as well, and European and American journalists were given expense-paid trips to Canada. In about three years the results of the propaganda began to be seen, and each year thereafter thousands of immigrants arrived from the United States, the British Isles and continental Europe.

At this time Austria-Hungary was a large disintegrating empire in Central Europe, in reality a collection of impoverished ethnic states under the rule of an alien autocracy. From this empire came many racial groups escaping oppression and hoping to improve their miserable peasant lives. More Hungarians joined relatives already in Canada; and now others came—Croatians, Czechs, Slovaks, Germans, Poles and Rumanians. Some stayed in eastern Canada, many went to the industrialized cities, but most pressed into the west. Often they settled in groups, and the names of many western towns and districts reflect these early communities.

Swedes had been in Canada from the time Lord Selkirk brought them to Red River, but now a large number spread across the prairies. Danes settled on the prairies and in fewer numbers along the coast of British Columbia. Norwegians trace their presence in the west from the nineteenth century when a group was employed by the Hudson's Bay Company to build a winter road near Norway House. Actual settlement began in 1887 when a group remained in southern Manitoba. Today most are in the prairies, but many gravitated to the forests, fisheries and mines of the west coast which is similar to their homeland. Germans had been in Nova Scotia since 1750 and had spread to Ontario. Now large numbers came from various parts of Europe and settled across the country. Today they form the third largest ethnic group in Canada.

There were people of almost every creed—Roman Catholics, Greek and Russian Orthodox, Presbyterians, Anglicans, Methodists, Lutherans, Sikhs, Moslems, Buddhists, Mennonites and Jews. They came from the aristocratic families of Britain, the serfdoms of eastern Europe and the overcrowded regions of Asia. All brought skills and traditions which were to mould Canada into a distinctive multicultural nation. From every ethnic group came individuals who became leaders of social, scientific, artistic, athletic and political life. The following selections illustrate some of the problems and achievements typical of ethnic groups in the west.

Oriental Exclusion

Chinese were found at first only on the west coast, but after the railway was completed, some began to move eastward. Chinese Canadians are one of the oldest western ethnic groups and contributed to Canada's Pacific Rim ties.

The first recorded immigrants were labourers imported by John Meares to Nootka, later taken to Mexico by the Spanish during the Nootka crisis. Over fifty years later a few Chinese merchants established themselves in the new city of Victoria where they were accepted as businessmen.

The first large influx of Chinese occurred during the Fraser River gold rush, most coming via California where they had participated in the earlier gold rush and were therefore experienced in all methods of placer mining. Whereas white miners were inclined to be impatient, moving from place to place in search of richer strikes, the Chinese persevered, successfully working bars that others had disregarded or abandoned, as well as prospecting for new discoveries. They tended to remain apart from the whites but worked in groups for efficient exploitation of their mines. Many were transients who returned to their homeland with their gold, but most remained in the colony to continue mining, work as labourers, establish garden farms or expand the businesses they had started.

The second great influx occurred during the construction of the Canadian Pacific Railway. When it was finished, like the miners many workers returned home but most stayed in the province. Serious unemployment followed the layoff of railway workers, and many whites turned against the Chinese: because they would accept lower wages and living standards, they were accused of taking jobs away from others; xenophobic rumour and propaganda fuelled the opposition. In British Columbia, many occupations were closed to Chinese and municipal contracts often forbade the use of Chinese labour. In 1877, during a strike at the Nanaimo coal mines, violence erupted when the Chinese continued to work. In Vancouver, which boomed as a railway terminus, anti-Chinese feeling led to strong demands for the removal of new arrivals, and in February 1887 an anti-Chinese meeting precipitated a mob attack on the city's Chinatown and destruction of most of the homes. Many people left the city for neighbouring communities but some remained to form the nucleus of a new Chinatown. Although many worked in canneries, they were not permitted to fish commercially. As years passed they continued labouring, some went into domestic service, while others opened businesses which became the foundations for successful modern enterprises.

Public opinion and pressure by labour unions forced governments to take action. In 1883 the mines were demanding that Orientals be excluded from immigration and from employment. Provincial exclusion acts were passed but all were disallowed by the federal government which hoped to expand trade with China. In 1885 the Dominion Franchise Act excluded any person of Chinese descent from voting and levied a head tax of $50 on every new immigrant—raised to $100 in 1900 and to $500 in 1905. Yet these restrictions had little effect and Chinese continued to come to the province.

Around the turn of the century, while anti-Chinese sentiment was intense, two more Asiatic groups arrived on the west coast: Japanese began immigrating about 1896 and East Indians a decade later. The Canadian government could not attempt to restrict Japanese immigration since its policies were limited by the Anglo-Japanese Alliance. The Japanese government, unlike the Chinese, was sensitive about its emigrant citizens, and any action against them might cause a deterioration of the Alliance. Some lessening of Canadian tensions was achieved by a "gentlemen's agreement" in 1907, by which Japan agreed to limit emigration.

The regulation of East Indian immigration also presented a special problem for the exclusion forces. East Indians had the same British citizenship rights as Canadians, so to handicap these immigrants the Canadian government in 1908 passed the "continuous passage" legislation, which demanded that all immigrants arrive directly from their native country. A challenge to this legislation failed in what is known as the *Komagata Maru* incident. The *Komagata Maru* was a Japanese ship, with a Japanese crew, chartered by an Indian businessman. She sailed from Hong Kong and picked up passengers in Singapore and Yokohama, most of them originally from India. The vessel was met in Vancouver by an angry crowd which refused to permit passengers to land. After they had waited in the harbour two months, a court decision upheld the illegality of this indirect immigration and the ship was forced to leave with her passengers.

Anti-Asian animosity now took in the Japanese and East Indians, and the demand for "Oriental Exclusion" became more strident. In 1907 a mob swept through Vancouver's Oriental section, destroying Chinese property, but it was repelled by the Japanese. William Lyon Mackenzie King, then deputy minister in the Department of Labour, was sent to investigate the riots and awarded compensation to the Chinese. In 1913 another riot broke out in Nanaimo where Chinese were being used as strikebreakers in the mines. In 1914 Premier Richard McBride stated the typical attitude of British Columbia politicians when he said, "We realize that Western and Oriental civilizations are so different that there could never be an amalgamation of the two."

After World War I, Oriental immigration into Canada was almost closed for many years. The continuous passage legislation handicapped the East Indians, and federal exclusion acts were passed against the Chinese in the 1920s. The Anglo-Japanese Alliance ended in 1922 and Canada was able to pass restrictive legislation against the Japanese, though in 1928 an agreement was made with Japan limiting immigration to 150 annually.

The Jews

Jews have been in Canada since early British occupation. They first came to British Columbia during the gold rush, and in the ensuing years became leaders in the colony and province. The first great influx of Jewish immigrants occurred after 1880 as a result of the pogroms in Russia and Rumania. Jewish-Canadian communities helped many of them to settle on farms in western Canada, but the majority were urban or village people without farming experience: although some remained on the land, most migrated to the cities. Later waves of immigrants arrived during the period of Nazi persecution and also from the unsettled East European countries such as Poland after the Second World War. As a culture with a long history of persecution and forced to live in ghettos, the Jews have tended to form strong communities in urban areas, producing leaders in all professions, in commerce and industry, politics and the arts.

The Doukhobors

Spread across Canada are over 100,000 people of Russian origin, not only from Russia proper but also from neighbouring countries which were once part of the Russian empire. About two-thirds of them are urban dwellers.

The Doukhobors (literally "spirit-wrestlers") were a Russian religious sect who believed in communal living, opposed state authority and structured religion and, being antimilitary, refused to serve in the army. For these reasons they were moved from one part of Russia to another, until the 1890s when their refusal to accept military service led to extreme persecution. With the support of Count Leo Tolstoy, sympathizers of the sect searched for another location.

In 1899 a third of the Doukhobors—7,000—emigrated to Canada, the largest contingent of immigrants to arrive at one time. The Dominion government promised them exemption from military service, assisted their passage and granted them three large blocks of land in what is now Saskatchewan—two in the Yorkton and Swan River areas and one in the neighbourhood of Saskatoon and Blaine Lake. Two of these blocks, by arrangement with the Canadian Pacific Railway, were continuous. The Doukhobors established communal living in small villages. To obtain funds, designated members were sent out each year to earn cash which was turned in to the community.

At first their villages were isolated but within five or six years new railways entered their lands, neighbouring settlements grew and nearby homesteads were occupied. Many of the young people adopted some of the habits, such as dress, that they encountered on their forays outside. Some drifted away to seek a different lifestyle. Thus beset by outside influences, the sect became divided among those individuals who acquired their own farms or entered commerce and the professions, and those who maintained the old way of life in the community.

Two federal regulations met with strong opposition from the Doukhobors—that their lands be registered under individual names, as outlined in the Dominion Lands Acts, and that all marriages, births and deaths be registered. Later the requirement of compulsory education was also opposed. When the Doukhobors refused to register land individually, the government began to reclaim sections.

Fearing the loss of land and disintegration from outside pressures, between 1908 and 1913, 6,000 or about two-thirds of the members moved to British Columbia, where with community funds they obtained 5,700 acres (2300 ha) near Grand Forks, Castlegar and Brilliant where they established settlements. In the following years they expanded and reorganized, and entered into various agricultural industries, such as food processing and lumber production. Thus in many ways their attitudes and activities changed, becoming similar to their neighbours'. There remained, however, a hard core of fanatics, the Sons of Freedom, who opposed most change. This minority group would continue to oppose authority, military service and compulsory education, periodically expressing its displeasure by burning buildings such as schools and by holding nude demonstrations. In recent years these extremists have been opposed by governments as well as their own leaders, but they still intermittently demonstrate against government regulations and modifications of their faith.

The Mennonites

The Mennonites were a German religious sect which adhered to the New Testament as their guide to faith and life. They were opposed to violence and would not take part in wars; as a result, they were often persecuted and moved from place to place, one group eventually settling in south Russia. Traditionally, they were an agricultural people who stayed in their own communities and were little involved in wider political activities. Near the end of the nineteenth century, as international tensions were growing throughout Europe, they sensed new threats to their religious and economic life. In the early 1870s, over 7,000 Mennonites left Russia, some to join settlements in Ontario while many founded settlements in Manitoba and the territories. In their isolated communities, they organized a system of government which made land allotments and established churches and schools. During and after the two World Wars, about 45,000 more Russian Mennonites migrated to Canada. They have tended to concentrate in pockets throughout Canada from Ontario to the Fraser Valley. Today there are 80,000 baptized members in more than 500 congregations.

During World War I there was a violent reaction in Canada against things German, and laws were passed to eliminate the German language in all public and private schools. The Mennonites continued to maintain their own schools, but the Canadian government built new schools and appointed trustees and teachers, which the Mennonites ignored. The Manitoba and Saskatchewan governments made attendance at public schools compulsory in 1920 and began to jail parents and preachers who were opposed. Many Mennonites migrated, a large number of them to Mexico. Eventually the remaining Mennonites were forced to submit to the pressures and accept the public school nonsectarian program. Over the years compromises have been made and a number of Mennonite schools have been established where instruction is in English but German may be taught for part of the day. More significant has been the training of Mennonites to become qualified teachers, able to pass on their culture while bringing an awareness of the outside world.

Through the years Canadian Mennonites have evolved into twelve autonomous conferences which, while differing in some practices, remain united in their basic beliefs and deal with each other through the Mennonite Central Committee (Canada) with headquarters in Winnipeg. In a changing society thousands of Mennonites have moved from the original rural agricultural settlements to urban centres. Many participate in business, education and the professions. They have maintained their belief in helping each other and have encouraged the preservation of their cultural values; at the same time they have shown a willingness to meld into Canadian society and to contribute their resources towards a culturally rich nation.

The Ukrainians

The majority of early Ukrainian immigrants came to Canada from Galicia and Bukovina, two provinces under the Austro-Hungarian Empire, the first group arriving in 1895. The years 1911–14 were the period of greatest influx, though there were later waves in 1926–31 and after 1946.

The first arrivals had lived as little more than serfs in Europe and their early years in Canada were difficult for they had very little money. Their homes, as those of many other newcomers, had walls of sod or uneven logs chinked with moss, sod roofs and mud floors. Gradually, as they harvested their first crops and worked as wage labourers, the roofs became straw thatch like those in their homeland. By hard work, within a few years these early homes had given way to frame buildings. The Ukrainians first settled on the prairies, gradually occupying homesteads between Winnipeg and Edmonton. Today about one-tenth of the prairie population is of Ukrainian descent.

The Ukrainians adapted to Canadian ways and encouraged their children to attend public schools, agricultural colleges and universities. They readily adopted new improvements and became prosperous farmers. Many of the arrivals after 1946, displaced by the war, were skilled workers, highly educated professionals or artists. Since that time they have become more urbanized, the largest concentrations being in Winnipeg, Toronto, Edmonton and Vancouver.

Agricultural Associations

Farming communities often organized local agricultural societies through which farmers could meet, compare progress and arrange fairs. In the 1890s, encouraged by government, farmers' institutes were established. Such organizations were active in protesting against the monopoly of the railway and the eastern-controlled grain elevators. The farmers suspected that the monopolistic grain companies charged excessive rates, did not grade the grain fairly and did not give correct weight. Pressed for money, the farmers accepted low prices, and speculators held the grain until the price rose later in the year. The growers believed that the CPR worked in conjunction with the elevator companies.

When the CPR announced in 1897 that it would not permit farmers to load individual cars but would accept grain only from the elevators, a wave of protest arose. The resulting report of the Royal Grain Commission of 1899 was followed by the Dominion Act, usually called the Manitoba Grain Act of 1900, which also applied to the territories: the grain trade west of Fort William was to be federally supervised by a commissioner at Winnipeg with weightmasters at selected receiving points, and farmers were permitted to load grain directly onto railway cars.

In the same year the Winnipeg Grain Exchange was established. Two years later the Territorial Grain Growers and the Manitoba Grain Growers associations were organized. When the provinces of Alberta and Saskatchewan were created, the territorial association divided into the United Farmers of Alberta and the Saskatchewan Grain Growers Association. All these associations worked together and in 1906 encouraged the formation of the Grain Growers' Grain Company, a co-operative association. When it applied for a seat in the Winnipeg Grain Exchange, it was refused because of the opposition of private grain merchants to co-operative principles. Pressure from the Manitoba government, which recognized the importance of agricultural votes, resulted in acceptance by the Exchange on condition that some of the co-operative aspects of the association be modified.

Encouraged by the success of their grain company, the Saskatchewan farmers, with provincial government encouragement, formed the Saskatchewan Co-operative Elevator Company in 1911. Two years later the Alberta Farmers Co-operative Company was developed. The marketing associations dominated the sale of grain and considered amalgamation so that in 1916 the Grain Growers' Grain Company and the Alberta Farmers Co-op merged to form the United Grain Growers. The success of these organizations encouraged the growth of other co-operatives in other agricultural fields, such as livestock, dairy and poultry.

Parallel with the movement for grain distribution co-operatives grew a consumer co-operative movement, fostered by immigrants from north European countries having co-operative organizations. The number of co-operative retail outlets increased rapidly in the first twenty years of the twentieth century.

At first these organizations were not political, though farmers in general were in sympathy with the Liberal policy of low tariffs. Not until the end of World War I did the farmers support active political participation in an effort to improve their conditions.

Alberta and Saskatchewan

Legislation in 1875 had provided for the implementation of representative government in the North-West Territories. An area not exceeding 1,000 square miles (2600 km²) containing not less than 1,000 British subjects would be entitled to elect a member to join the appointed councillors. In 1881 the first member was elected and the number increased rapidly with settlement until by 1886 there were fourteen elected and six appointed councillors sitting in Regina.

Major changes were made over the next two years. In 1887 the first North-West Territories members were elected to the House of Commons and in 1888 two senators were appointed. That year also saw the installation of a territorial Legislative Assembly with twenty-two elected representatives, assisted by three appointed advisory members from the legal profession who had no vote. The lieutenant governor acted as the representative of the Dominion government which still controlled revenue in the form of grants. The Conservative federal government agreed to the demand for responsible government and control of finances in 1891: membership in the assembly was by election only and was increased to twenty-six; it selected its own executive and was given control over the spending of a portion of the federal grant. With increased power, the territorial government assisted improvements in agriculture and education in methods of field cultivation and animal husbandry. In an era of prosperity the territories were preparing for provincial status.

The dominant figure in the new Executive Council was F. W. G. Haultain, who was a vigorous proponent of self-gov-

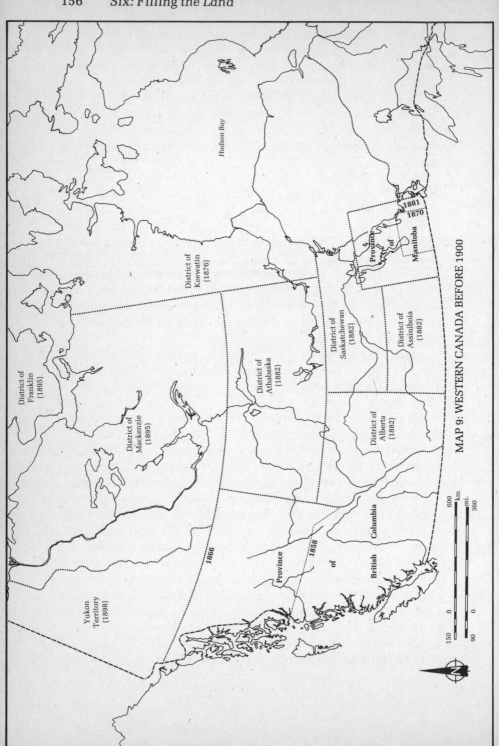

MAP 9: WESTERN CANADA BEFORE 1900

District of Franklin (1895)

District of Mackenzie (1895)

District of Keewatin (1876)

Yukon Territory (1898)

Hudson Bay

District of Athabaska (1882)

District of Saskatchewan (1882)

District of Assiniboia (1882)

District of Alberta (1882)

Province of Manitoba

1881
1870

Province of British Columbia

1866

1858

km
600
mi.
360

0
150
0
90

ernment in the territories but was opposed to the influence of French Canadians and Roman Catholics. In 1892 he curtailed the use of French in recording the proceedings of the assembly and reduced the power of separate school districts. When the North-West Territories Act was amended in 1897, full responsible government was granted and Haultain formed the first administration.

In 1905 the Alberta Act and the Saskatchewan Act established two new provinces under the general terms of the British North America Act. These were federal acts and not the result of negotiations between colonies, as had been the case with Manitoba and, especially, British Columbia. That the action was unilateral would later become another minor factor in the grievances of Alberta and Saskatchewan against the federal government.

The Dominion government believed that for the good of the whole country the free homesteading policy should continue, and therefore retained control of public lands. A form of compensation was offered: a fund, estimated at $1.50 per acre (0.4 ha) for 25 million acres (10 million ha), was established for each province, totalling $37.5 million. Annual payments would range from one to three per cent based on population growth. This formula was also applied to Manitoba in 1908. Over the years the terms were modified by several federal-provincial conferences, but it was not until 1930 that the natural resources were turned over to the three provincial governments.

Haultain had been a Conservative supporter and had bitterly opposed the Liberals, who won again in 1904 under Wilfrid Laurier. Haultain had struggled for responsible government and provincial status, had opposed splitting the territories into two provinces, had wanted control of natural resources and was against separate schools. But another federal requirement in the granting of provincial status was that the system of separate schools be maintained. Influenced by the Liberal government, the lieutenant governor therefore selected Walter Scott as Saskatchewan's first premier until the first provincial election in 1905, in which Scott's Liberal Party was successful against Haultain's Provincial Rights Party.

After the separation of Alberta and Saskatchewan, the

remainder of the North-West Territories was returned to "colonial status," by which authority remained in the hands of the federal government. For sixty years progress was slow towards responsible government.

The Yukon

After the Fraser River gold rush, miners continued to probe the northern rivers of British Columbia and into the Yukon; at the same time miners were active in Alaska. In 1887 the federal government organized a research expedition into this almost unknown country. Dr. George Mercer Dawson and Richard George McConnell, geologists, accompanied by William Ogilvie, a surveyor, spent over four months in the region, covering over a thousand miles (1600 km). Their report detailed the geology, flora, climate, agricultural possibilities, navigable rivers, and the fur trade. Three years later Ogilvie returned with a United States geological survey to establish the international boundary on the Yukon River, at this time the main traffic route and location of the Yukon centre, Forty Mile.

In 1894 the North West Mounted Police sent Insp. Charles Constantine to survey the territory, and the following year a detachment of twenty-four was posted to Forty Mile to undertake the work of magistrates, gold commissioner, land agent and collector of customs.

In 1896 George Carmack and two Indian companions, "Skookum Jim" and "Tagish Charlie," found gold on Bonanza Creek, a tributary of the Klondike River, precipitating in the next three years another great gold rush of miners from all over the world. Some made the 1,500-mile (2400-km) trip up the Yukon River, a few tried to reach the mines through northern British Columbia or from the Mackenzie River, but most came by steamboat to Skagway, Alaska. From the coast they began the arduous crossing of either the Chilkoot Pass or the White Pass over the St. Elias Mountains to the water route to the Yukon River. The North West Mounted Police opened a post at Skagway and at the international boundary in the passes, to assert the authority of the Canadian government in the Yukon and keep a record of the newcomers as they arrived from American territory along the coast. Anyone entering the country was required to possess a year's worth of supplies, or roughly 1,500 pounds (680 kg), to get them through the hardships ahead, or be turned back. The police kept a record of every improvised vessel that left Lake Bennett on the far side of the passes: when the ice broke in May 1897, 800 boats and rafts were ready to make the trip down the Yukon to the new gold centre at Dawson.

The sudden rush of miners resulted in the building of the White Pass and Yukon Railway, at that time the continent's northernmost railway. It was a major feat of engineering, not only for its conquest of the difficult terrain but also for the speed of its construction. Two lines began from the coast at Skagway and inland at Whitehorse, joining at Carcross in 1900. Today its spectacular route is a significant supply artery as well as a major visitor attraction.

Because of the sudden population increase, the Yukon was made a separate territory in 1898. The federal government appointed a commissioner, and a partially elected Legislative Council was responsible for local affairs such as education, roads and welfare; the federal government retained control of mining and policing. In 1902 the Yukon sent its first elected member to the House of Commons. Unfortunately, the people left as fast as they had arrived: at the height of the rush, Dawson City's population alone was 25,000; by 1921 the total territorial population was only 4,000. After 1940, with the opening of the Alaska Highway and airlines, the Yukon was accessible to the outside. Tourists, mainly Americans en route to Alaska, are a major source of revenue, 70 per cent of them arriving by the Alaska Highway. The discoveries of rich lead-zinc deposits, the prospect of untapped mineral resources and the proposed Alaska Highway natural gas pipeline have all augmented the older fur trade economy. By 1980 the population was over 26,000.

The Alaska Boundary

The 1825 treaty between Russia and Britain had stated that the eastern boundary of the Alaska Panhandle should "follow the summit of the mountains situated parallel to the coast," yet that "the British possessions shall be formed by a line parallel to the windings of the coast which shall never exceed the distance of ten marine leagues." The phrase "parallel to the windings of the coast" was interpreted by the British to mean parallel to the outside coast while the Americans claimed the line would parallel the head of the inlets, making the British territory landlocked, without direct access to the ocean. Negotiations begun in 1884 clarified little, but then the sudden influx of miners made agreement imperative.

The British and Americans agreed to a commission of three "impartial" judges from each disputant. The Americans, under the jingoistic President Theodore Roosevelt, were known to be biased, but Britain was anxious to maintain good relations with the United States and the resulting award in 1903 of a compromise line which largely supported the American claim was considered by many Canadians to be a betrayal by Britain. The decision completed the land boundary between the United States and Canada.

Since the mainland of British Columbia extends from 49° to 60° latitude, the Alaska boundary decision meant that only the southern half of the province had direct outlet to the sea, but in 1903 northern British Columbia was still a wilderness and the boundary line seemed of little importance. By midcentury, when mines, forest industries, railways and roads were opening the north, the loss of the coastline handicapped development not only in British Columbia but also in the Yukon. Furthermore, the northern provincial salmon rivers had their outlets in American territory, and fishing rights along the coast are one facet of the continuing Canadian-American fisheries dispute. Negotiations for transportation facilities through the Panhandle have had little success in the face of American disinterest.

Union Organization

Accompanying the spread of the industrial revolution from Britain to the United States was the union movement demanding better working conditions. Immigrants from both countries influenced the growth of unionism in Canada.

The first Canadian unions began early in the nineteenth century in New Brunswick and Nova Scotia and by midcentury there were numerous unions of skilled workers in the Maritimes, Quebec and Ontario. At first they were individual local craft units such as printers, tailors, carpenters and shoemakers. The bakers in Victoria were probably the first to unionize in the west when they formed a society for their protection in 1859. It was in the central provinces that the locals began to consolidate; the strongest unions were in Toronto which became the headquarters of the first national unions. During the 1860s and 1870s there were already a number of international unions, and as Canadian unions increased they were often affiliated with their American counterparts.

The Trades Union Act of 1873, which clarified the legal status of unions, gave encouragement to the movement. In the 1880s, during increased industrialization and the expansion of railways and the building trades, union activity spread across the country. Labour councils were formed in most cities. The Toronto Trades and Labour Council was formed in 1881 and shortly afterwards became the Trades and Labour Congress (TLC) of Canada. Trades and labour councils were formed in Winnipeg (1887), Victoria and Vancouver (1889), New Westminster (1890), Nanaimo (1891), Rossland (1897), Calgary (1901), Kamloops and Dawson City (1902), and Regina (1907). In 1890 the first member from British Columbia attended the TLC convention and eight years later the North-West Territories were represented. It was the influence of the British Columbia member that caused the organization to seek the exclusion of Chinese. The strength of the TLC caused the federal government to introduce a number of reforms and in 1900 to create the federal Department of Labour. Western delegates condemned the TLC for not organizing workers outside the skilled crafts. In 1911 the British Columbia Federation of Labour was formed, at first as a craft union, but it came to support industrial rather than craft unions. A short time later the Alberta Federation of Labour was formed.

British Columbia has been a leader in militant unionism. By the 1870s, the struggles between employers and workers, especially in the mining industry, were becoming critical. The most belligerent actions involved a series of miners' strikes on Vancouver Island: in 1877 a strike was broken by the militia, backed up by a British naval vessel; in 1883 an attempt to stop employment of Chinese failed, as did another in 1903. One of the most bitter struggles began in 1911 when 4,000 miners walked out in Nanaimo and the company used nonunion and Oriental labourers to continue production. Provincial police and soldiers were brought in as riots broke out and property was damaged. Over 200 miners were jailed. After two years, the workers finally returned with little gained. Miners also struck in other western towns—in 1895 and 1901 in Rossland, in 1906 in Lethbridge and 1911 in Crowsnest Pass.

During the early 1900s the union movement continued to grow and strikes were common. West coast fishermen opposed the granting of fishing licences to Japanese. In 1901–2 nation-wide strikes tied up the transcontinental railways. In 1906 the militia was called out during a street railway strike in Winnipeg.

The TLC did not take political action though it did influence political attitudes. Some locals, such as those in Winnipeg and Vancouver, supported socialist or labour candidates who ran as independents, but in only a few cases were they successful.

In 1914 the prairies had basically an agricultural economy and in the rural districts there was little need for employee unions. The growing union movement was strongest in the industrialized cities and in the primary industries of mining, fishing and forest products, as well as rail transportation, which all depended on a capitalist/working-class system of production.

In 1914, a deputation of Edmonton unemployed demanded work at 30 cents an hour plus meals and clean beds. Farm labourers and hired men, who were paid $25 to $35 a month plus board, were in seasonal demand, and the average wage for factory workers in Saskatchewan was $10.80 a week.

In March of that year a British Columbia labour commission submitted a report that upheld the right of workers to strike without penalty but also supported the right of other men to work during a strike. Conditions and aspirations of the time are indicated by the following selections from its recommendations: sanitary conditions in bakeries and barber shops should be improved; regulations should be made regarding the voltage and height of overhead electric wires; there should be government supervision of first aid in logging and mining camps; a workmen's compensation board should be established; all factories should close at noon on Saturdays; white female help should not be employed by Chinese; textbooks in public schools should be free; only British citizens should be employed in government or public works.

Railway Expansion

The great flood of immigrants soon occupied the lands adjoining the main line of the Canadian Pacific Railway and newcomers were forced to settle farther and farther away. Branch lines to supply these communities and to permit export of their grain were in wide demand. By 1900 there was a shortage of rail lines and grain facilities. Between 1905 and 1915 wheat acreage in the prairie provinces increased from 3,941,000 acres (1 595 000 ha) to 11,745,000 acres (4 753 000 ha).

The CPR was active in building branches both north and south of its main line, completing lines from Regina to Prince Albert in 1890, from Calgary to Edmonton in 1891, and from Calgary to Fort Macleod in 1892. In 1896 the CPR sought federal assistance for a rail line from Lethbridge through the Crowsnest Pass to the developing gold, silver, lead and zinc mines near Nelson in southeastern British Columbia. If the CPR did not serve this area, American lines would. By the Crowsnest agreement of 1897, extended by the Railway Act of 1925, the company, in return for a cash subsidy of $11,000 per mile (1.6 km) to a maximum of $3,630,000, agreed to reduce freight rates between ten and twenty per cent on certain specified commodities inbound to the prairies and by three per cent on grain and flour outbound to the Lakehead. The 1899 rates for grain and flour quoted at one-half cent a ton per mile were still in effect in 1982.

This agreement has been a source of dispute to the present day. Although the railways claim huge losses, the farmers contend that full freight rates would put them out of business because, in a competitive market, they would have no way to pass on the increased costs. It has been claimed that one of the reasons for the shortage of cars to carry grain to Churchill, the west coast or the Lakehead is that the railways are using their

cars for profitable products such as potash and coal. Some
westerners support a modification of the rates, suggesting that
the relatively cheap movement of feed grain encourages competitive meat and livestock industries in the east. Secondary
industries suffer because it is actually cheaper to ship the raw
material east and to return the finished product. Thus there has
been disagreement not only between federal and provincial
governments but also between the western provincial governments themselves: while Alberta, with its diversified economy,
favours some changes, agrarian Saskatchewan has been
strongly opposed.

The federal Department of Transport released a report on
rail freight rates which set the railways' 1981–82 loss on grain
shipments of 30.4 million tonnes as a result of the "Crow rate"
at $644.1 million. Farmers paid only 18.7 per cent of that cost.
The report recommended that the federal government subsi-
dize both the railways and farmers for moving grain, allowing
the Crow rate to rise: the largest subsidy would go to the railways at first, then over the years proportionally more to the
farmers. At the same time farmers would pay increasing rates
so that by 1991–92 they would be paying 39 per cent of the
cost. The expense to the federal government over ten years
would be $8.9 billion, about five times its previous subsidies,
in order to reimburse the railways for operating and upgrading
costs while protecting the farmers from the full impact of
higher shipping rates. The effect of the report is yet unknown.

When the Supreme Court of Canada found against the Canadian Pacific Railway monopoly clause in Manitoba in 1889, the
company agreed to surrender its claims in return for a federal
guarantee of the interest on a $15-million bond issue. This
judgement, given the great demand for new rail lines, resulted
in numerous applications to provincial governments for
charters. Many projects never began construction while others
collapsed after a few kilometres were built. The federal government discontinued its railway land grants, making its last grant
in 1894, and the new policy became official during the Liberal
administration by the Dominion Lands Act of 1908. However,
federal construction aid continued in the form of financial
grants and guarantees.

American railways, such as the Union Pacific and the Great

Northern, projected lines northwards across the border into the prairies and British Columbia. By making informal agreements with these railways not to duplicate lines and by setting rates, the CPR was able to prevent a freight rate war and to maintain its monopoly along its prairie lines.

Memories of the old fur trade route to Hudson Bay remained and prairie organizations continued to demand a railway to the bay. In 1884 the federal government authorized a land grant of 12,800 acres (5180 ha) in Manitoba and the territories for the Winnipeg and Hudson Bay Railway and Steamship Company. Expeditions were dispatched in 1885, 1897 and 1903 to study routes. In 1900 the Canadian Northern Railway acquired the earlier charter and between 1910 and 1913 had built past The Pas. The war interrupted construction and interest languished afterwards. When the National Progressive Party revived the subject in the House of Commons in the '20s, Mackenzie King, needing their support against the Conservatives, agreed to complete the railway. The link between The Pas and Churchill was completed in 1931. The railway never became the great grain outlet that had been envisioned, but it was to help mining development in northern Manitoba.

Several charters were granted for railways projected to open the land north of Edmonton, into the Peace River country. In 1910 the Edmonton, Dunvegan and British Columbia line was built as far north as Lesser Slave Lake and in 1916 to Grande Prairie. Although rail construction was erratic, several lines eventually reached Dawson Creek in 1931. Three of these lines, the Edmonton, Dunvegan and British Columbia, the Central Canada Railway and the Alberta Great Waterways Railway, were combined in 1929 as the Northern Alberta Railway, operated as a joint venture by the Canadian Pacific and the Canadian National Railways.

The Canadian Northern Railway

William Mackenzie and Donald Mann, two Ontario-born railway contractors, in 1895 acquired the charter of the Lake Manitoba Railway and Canal Company and, with the aid of a bond guarantee from the Manitoba government, completed a railway northwest to Dauphin. Then they negotiated running rights and acquired charters from other railways. In 1899 their Canadian Northern Railway was incorporated by federal statute. Three years later the two men made a leasing agreement with the R. P. Roblin government: they received bond guarantees for a railway to the Lakehead on condition that Manitoba controlled its rates. Its lower wheat rates made it competitive with the CPR.

In 1905 when the provinces of Saskatchewan and Alberta were formed, the Canadian Northern, with provincial and federal aid, began to expand northwest from Dauphin. Its route led through Saskatoon, North Battleford and Edmonton towards the Yellowhead Pass. The federal government guaranteed its bonds to the extent of $13,000 a mile (1.6 km) in the Manitoba to Edmonton section and gave permission to build and acquire lines in Ontario, thus establishing the basis for a transcontinental railway.

The Yukon gold rush had spawned a number of railway projects in northern British Columbia, but although several charters were granted, nothing was built. After Premier Richard McBride established a positive railway policy, in 1910 Mackenzie and Mann incorporated the Canadian Northern Pacific Railway Company to build from the Yellowhead Pass to the coast with a line to Vancouver Island. The provincial government guaranteed construction bonds to a maximum of $35,000 per mile and granted free right-of-way through crown lands and exemption from provincial taxes until 1924.

The route from the Yellowhead followed the North Thompson, Thompson and Fraser rivers. Because the Canadian Pacific was already built along the latter two, the Canadian Northern was forced to take the opposite, more difficult banks. The last spike was driven on 23 January 1915. The temporary western terminal was Port Mann, a few miles upriver from New Westminster, but Mackenzie and Mann were planning to reach Vancouver, difficult because of the large CPR holdings. A deal with the city allowed them to fill in a large area of mud flats at the head of False Creek for their terminus, and in October the first train from eastern Canada reached Vancouver.

Mackenzie and Mann had completed a second transcontinental but the costs, especially in British Columbia, had exceeded their estimates and the railway went bankrupt. In

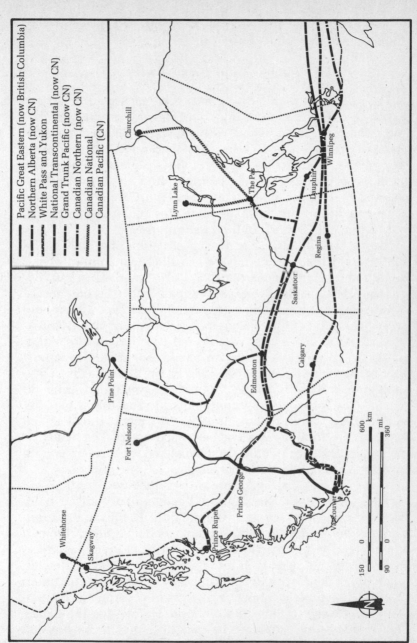

MAP 10: MAJOR RAILWAY LINES

Pacific Great Eastern (now British Columbia)
Northern Alberta (now CN)
White Pass and Yukon
National Transcontinental (now CN)
Grand Trunk Pacific (now CN)
Canadian Northern (now CN)
Canadian National
Canadian Pacific (CN)

1917 the federal government took over the railway and its liabilities.

The Grand Trunk Pacific Railway

The Grand Trunk Railway had been chartered in 1851. Although it was the most important railway serving Ontario and Quebec it seldom paid any dividends. In 1900 it appointed the dynamic American Charles Melville Hays as general manager to solve its financial difficulties. Hays came at a time when the flood of immigrants was pouring into Canada and wheat exports were rising dramatically, yet the Grand Trunk was benefiting little from the expanding west: much of its traffic was feeding the CPR or handling its surpluses.

Laurier was interested in the construction of a new transcontinental which he envisaged as an all-Canadian route opening the northern lands as the CPR had opened the south. By this time the Canadian Northern was planning to become transcontinental, but government attempts to arrange co-operation or amalgamation of the two companies failed: the Grand Trunk wanted to tap the western traffic but did not want to build across the unprofitable Canadian Shield. For political reasons Laurier required that both sections be built, and achieved a compromise. Federal acts in 1903 incorporated a government railway, the National Transcontinental, to run from Moncton to Winnipeg, and a private company, the Grand Trunk Pacific, to run from Winnipeg to a northern Pacific port. The bonds of the latter company would be guaranteed on principal and interest to a maximum based on mileage.

In the period 1905–14 the prairie provinces were enthusiastic about railway construction and actively encouraged both the Canadian Northern and Grand Trunk Pacific to build an extensive network of branch lines, guaranteeing the principal and interest on the companies' bonds. British Columbia, under Richard McBride, was even more enthusiastic. McBride owed much of his popularity to the number of railways he chartered in all sections of the province and made government investment in railways an effective platform. He assisted the Canadian Northern by extending its deadlines and increasing its grants. However, he felt that the demands of the Grand Trunk

Pacific were excessive and only after long acrimonious bargaining did the railway agree to begin construction from Prince Rupert.

The Grand Trunk Pacific was built in two sections—Prairie and Mountain. On the prairies the railway almost parallelled the Canadian Northern through the parklands from Winnipeg to the Yellowhead. From this pass the route followed the Fraser, Nechako, Bulkley and Skeena rivers to the newly planned city of Prince Rupert on Kaien Island. The last spike was driven near the Nechako River in April 1914, and shortly afterwards the first transcontinental reached Prince Rupert.

The Grand Trunk Pacific hoped to emulate the Canadian Pacific by establishing a trans-Pacific steamship service. It did establish an excellent fleet which, however, remained a coastal service.

Both the Canadian Northern and the Grand Trunk Pacific were overextended, nearing completion when the calamity of World War I struck. British capital dried up, along with expectations of increasing immigration. War demands created a shortage of track, construction materials and rolling stock. After a few years of struggle, by 1923 the Canadian government had taken them both over.

The Pacific Great Eastern Railway

In the twenty-five years prior to 1914, British Columbia issued about 300 railway charters, some for short lines, others for grandiose transcontinental projects. Few ever got started. Perhaps the most persistent schemes were for railways from the United States through New Westminster or Vancouver to the north—even to the Peace River or the Yukon. Although the Grand Trunk Pacific was supposed to open the north, it would not discourage a line that connected it to Vancouver from either Hazelton or Prince George.

The route commonly proposed went from Howe Sound northeast to the Fraser at Lillooet, then north to the Grand Trunk Pacific. In 1907 a number of charters were amalgamated and construction began from Newport (present-day Squamish). Five years later the McBride government granted a charter to the Pacific Great Eastern Railway to build north from Van-

couver through Prince George. The liberal terms were similar
to those granted to the Grand Trunk Pacific Railway: guarantees of bonds up to $35,000 a mile (1.6 km), free right-of-way
through crown lands, grants up to 100 feet (30 m) wide for the
railroad plus extra land for divisional points and townsites.
The company was to be exempt from taxation until 1926, was
to begin in 1912 and finish by 1 January 1915.

By the war, the company had difficulty borrowing money
and the government was forced to come to its aid while construction struggled ahead. In 1916 the victorious Liberals
inherited heavy debts and a railway that reached only from
Squamish to Clinton. In 1918 the province took over the railway and by 1921 the line extended sixteen miles (26 km)
beyond Quesnel. Here construction was stopped and the
unused rails north of the city were torn up and sold as scrap.

Prewar Survey

Conditions in western Canada in 1914 were far different
from those at the beginning of the century. The prime minister
of Canada was the Conservative Robert Borden who had
defeated Wilfrid Laurier in 1911. Although the most obvious
Liberal handicap had been reciprocity, there was, in truth, little difference in the tariff policies of the two parties. Although
much of the support for Borden, a Nova Scotia lawyer, had
come from the industrialists who opposed any reduction in the
protective tariffs, he also recognized that the prairie support for
the Liberal Party indicated the opposition of the agricultural
community to higher tariffs.

In 1912 the boundaries of Manitoba, as well as those of
Ontario and Quebec, were extended north: the western provincial borders had reached their final delineation. All four provinces had by this time established the party system of government. In Manitoba, the Conservative Rodmond P. Roblin had a
comfortable majority which was renewed in June 1914. In
Saskatchewan, the Liberal Walter Scott dominated the government. In Alberta another Liberal, Arthur L. Sifton, had been
elected in 1910 with a majority of ten. In British Columbia the
flamboyant Conservative Richard McBride was spending
money recklessly. McBride reflected the strong British atti-

tudes of the province in his unquestioning support of British policies and his backing of a Canadian navy. His opposition to Asian immigration and rights gained general support.

The great immigrant influx filled the fertile prairies. Over 440,000 homestead entries were made in the fifteen years preceding 1914. In 1913, the year of greatest immigration, there were 400,870 new arrivals and the beginning of 1914 seemed to promise that this figure would be surpassed. The census years 1901 and 1911 illustrate the rapid population growth of the west: Manitoba from 255,211 to 461,394; Saskatchewan from 91,279 to 492,432; Alberta from 73,022 to 374,295; British Columbia from 178,657 to 392,480. The total had almost tripled in ten years, from 598,169 to 1,720,601. In 1913 Winnipeg had become the fourth largest industrial city of Canada after Montreal, Toronto and Hamilton, with a population of over 296,000. Vancouver had 114,000, Calgary 75,000, Edmonton 65,000 and Regina 45,000. In the prairie provinces 65 per cent of the population was rural and in British Columbia 48 per cent.

The prevailing world recession resulted in many unemployed in Canada, yet despite this and a drought in southern Alberta and Saskatchewan, there was a spirit of optimism. Two new transcontinental railways and their branch lines were nearing completion. New northern railways were being planned towards the Peace River and Hudson Bay. Grain acreage in ten years had almost quadrupled. In 1913 Saskatchewan alone produced 112,369,000 bushels of wheat as well as other grain crops.

While the economy of Manitoba and Saskatchewan was still predominantly grain based, the Alberta economy was more diversified. Ranching was important. Coal mining was extensive and other minerals were being discovered. Albertans recognized the possibilities of natural gas and petroleum fields and a wild speculative spree followed the success of the Dingman oil well at Okotoks near Calgary on 7 October 1913. After this brief surge, the instability brought by war restrained further research and speculation for many years. In British Columbia production had a wide base: manufacturing led in values; agriculture, with a diversity of products, was second, followed by lumbering, mining and fishing.

Life was changing on many fronts as the result of twentieth-century innovations. Electric tramways were common in the cities. The increasing demand for electricity forced governments to consider developing hydroelectric power and to study possible dam sites. Telephones were ending the isolation of farms. Tractors and other machines were being used on larger farms, though smaller operations still depended on horses. Automobiles were beginning to appear, requiring new and improved roads. Airplane rides were a feature at exhibitions and fairs. Halls and theatres were showing cinematographs and motion pictures. With the spread of railways and steamship lines, comfortable holidays to the homeland were possible.

Growth was accompanied by many problems. The first 1914 session of the House of Commons included debate on: the Pelagic Sealing Treaty of 1911 by which Britain, the United States, Japan and Russia had agreed to limit the killing of sea otters and fur seals; the conservation of whales; railway construction, chartering and costs; provincial control of natural resources; immigration from Asia; the pollution of navigable rivers; old age pensions, and tariffs. How little Canadian problems have changed over seventy years!

Provincial governments were concerned with five major issues. Railway construction was enthusiastically supported. In the prairies the western grain growers were convinced that monopoly elements were responsible for low grain prices and were pressing strongly for more government supervision and socialization of the elevator system. There was a growing demand for prohibition and in some cases local option was in effect. Parallelling the movements in Britain and the United States was a vociferous demand for women's suffrage. Compulsory education from ages six to fourteen had strong support.

On 4 August 1914 Great Britain declared war on Germany and automatically Canada was at war. The patterns of Canadian life would be disrupted. Immigration, railway construction and prospecting were curtailed. On the other hand, many new and old industries expanded. The war was to bring new attitudes, new perspectives and a new recognition of Canada in the industrial world.

Chapter Seven

WAR AND RECOVERY

(1914 – 1931)

IRONICALLY, in the year that Canadians and Americans were celebrating a century of peace along their border, Canada was drawn into its first major war. When Britain declared war on Germany in 1914, Canada, as a member of the Empire, was at war. Robert Borden immediately assured the British government of the country's full co-operation.

The cost of the war in financial terms was immense and taxes were of necessity increased. Customs duties were raised and new taxes were placed on such items as coffee, sugar, liquor, tobacco and railway tickets. Stamps were required on cheques and postal rates were increased. To raise further revenues, and in an attempt to curb wartime profiteering, a mild business tax was introduced in 1916, followed by the personal income tax in 1917. Begun as a wartime expediency, the moderate income tax was retained and increased until today corporate and personal income taxes produce 60 per cent of government revenue. The most successful method of raising money was the sale of five series of Victory Loans, which covered 85 per cent of the total cost of war. Most were purchased domestically. They also constituted the largest element in the postwar national debt.

A nonrecoverable cost of war was the casualty rate, and for Canada it was particularly high. Canada provided over 600,000 soldiers in the course of the war. In addition, over 9,000 sailors enlisted in the Canadian navy and another body of Canadians made up a quarter of the British air services. The military forces comprised volunteers from all regions and from all levels of society. A total of 60,661 were killed, one in every ten Canadians who enlisted.

The Home Front

Probably as important as the sacrifices in money and men was the nation's contribution in equipment and supplies. Primary industries such as agriculture, mining and forestry expanded to meet the needs of war. Industrial plants were converted to war production and great quantities of munitions, airplanes, merchant ships and naval vessels poured from the factories. The result was a tremendous boost to the economy, and with large numbers of Canadians enlisted in the military forces and immigration curtailed, unemployment ended and union membership soared. During the war Canada's industrial output surpassed agricultural production for the first time, and the nation's economy was permanently transformed into an industrial one. Of the four western provinces, British Columbia gained most in industrial growth with its mines and forests being worked to capacity. Lumbering employed more people and produced more wealth than any other industry in Canada. The opening of the Panama Canal in 1914 enhanced the west coast shipping industry and established Vancouver as a major port.

Before the war Russia had been the greatest wheat exporting nation, but the German blockade, combined with internal disruption in Russia, cut off supplies to Europe. At the same time, much of the agricultural area of Europe was decimated by fighting armies. Large quantities of machinery and food supplies from North America were victims of German submarines.

To replace these losses, Canada made strenuous efforts to expand its grain production, especially in wheat. Farm acreage was doubled and much land of questionable value in normal times was put into production. The expected harvests in 1914 suffered from drought and early frosts. Similarly, the crops of 1916 and 1917 were affected by storms, drought and an epidemic of rust. Nevertheless, wheat output increased by 35 per cent and other grains by even more. The war established Canada as a major wheat exporting nation along with the United States and Australia. In 1917, the Canadian government appointed a board of grain commissioners to check price inflation, to regulate the grain trade and to set the price of wheat, which in 1918 was placed at $2.24½ per bushel for Canadian No. 1 Northern. With the end of the war the board was disbanded.

At first patriotic enthusiasm swept the country and the initial reports of Canadian heroism abroad were proudly received. But as the war dragged on and Canadian troops were involved in bloody battle after bloody battle—Ypres, Somme, Vimy Ridge, Passchendaele, Mons—early enthusiasm gave way to grim determination as people gathered to read the casualty list bulletins. There was hardly a family that did not mourn a father, son or brother, or suffer the haunting fear of the next list.

Economically, many individuals profited from wartime inflation. The workers in mines, forests and secondary industries, especially the war industries, earned higher hourly wages and had more work. The price of food rose and farmers shared in the higher prices. On the other hand, the apparent increase in wages was illusory, especially in the lowest income brackets, for the cost of living increased 50 per cent in the inflationary years between 1915 and 1919. Worker dissatisfaction was heightened by the fact that farmers and industrialists were not as affected by the new taxes. Unfortunately, the complexity of the war effort permitted some people to make enormous profits. This "profiteering" created indignation and protests, and every government was plagued with scandals connected to war contracts.

To conserve fuel, daylight-saving time was inaugurated. People were asked to reduce fuel consumption and to ration consumer goods. Thousands of home gardens permitted the export of more food products.

The war was tragic for many immigrant groups. Some of them, such as the Hutterites, Doukhobors and Mennonites, had come to Canada because of their pacifist beliefs. Many of the last left the country. Others remained to face the animosity of neighbours who had men serving overseas. The many Austro-Hungarians and Germans were divided among themselves.

Some were still loyal to Germany; others were torn between their new country and the homeland where many of their relatives still lived; still other families had been Canadian for over a generation. Yet to outsiders there was often no distinction between the newcomers and early settlers. Many had settled in communities where they had not been forced to speak English and where German-language schools had been organized. On 7 August 1914 the federal government passed an order-in-council stating: "Whereas there are many immigrants of German nationality quietly pursuing their usual avocation in various parts of Canada, it is desirable that they continue such avocations without interruption, therefore ... they should not be arrested, detained or interfered with unless there is reasonable ground to believe they are engaged in espionage." This moderate position could not endure long.

Dotted across the west were many towns and villages with German origins and names, some of which were changed in the hysteria of wartime. Most of the German-speaking population lived in Saskatchewan, where the 1911 census showed that almost one-quarter of the province or 110,000 people were of German background. There were also large numbers in Manitoba and Alberta, and a smaller group of 20,000 in British Columbia. Following the order-in-council, the federal government passed the Alien Enemies Act, which resulted in some people being deported and others interned. Still others were forced to register and to report their whereabouts at specified intervals. The enemy tongue was forbidden in schools and churches, though in a few communities having a high density of German Canadians the rule was relaxed. German-language newspapers were closed.

This double-pronged government effort at moderation and control did not erase prejudice. Many Germans and Austrians were refused employment and many were discharged. For self-preservation some changed their names to more Anglicized forms. Of the western provinces, British Columbia was the most virulently anti-German, and in Victoria a near riot resulted in the destruction of a hotel and several businesses carrying German names.

Canada was far from the scenes of war and, though submarine warfare was a problem for the east coast, western Canada had no fear of invasion except along the British Columbia coast. Under the Naval Service Act of 1910 establishing a Canadian navy, two outdated British cruisers had been bought and one, the *Rainbow*, was Canada's only naval vessel on the west coast. Then, at the beginning of the war, Richard McBride heard that two submarines were for sale in Seattle and purchased them for $1,050,000 with provincial funds. (For three days, until the Canadian government repaid the province, British Columbia had its own navy.)

The German Pacific fleet was rumoured to be off the west coast of the United States and there was speculation that it might raid the unprotected coastline of British Columbia, but fortunately, the fleet headed west. As a result of the Anglo-Japanese Alliance, Japan had entered the war on the side of the Allies, and the visit of the Japanese cruiser *Izuma* relieved the apprehensions of Victoria and Vancouver. The German Pacific fleet was eliminated early in the war by the British and Australian navies and the threat to the west coast disappeared. Technically, the Japanese fleet defended the northern Pacific until the United States entered the war in 1917.

Provincial and Federal Issues

During the war years elections were held in all four western provinces, in which the two Conservative governments were swept from office: in 1918 all four provinces had Liberal administrations. The Liberal successes were undoubtedly partly the result of campaign promises to inaugurate women's suffrage, prohibition and better schooling.

In Britain and the United States the suffragette movement, demanding women's rights and political equality, had become a strong, often militant force and spread throughout Canada, being especially strong in the west. The contributions of women to the war effort strengthened their claims for recognition. Related to the women's movement was the growth of temperance associations advocating the prohibition of alcohol. Women's suffrage was granted in the three prairie provinces in 1916 and in British Columbia in the following year. The federal government followed in 1918. Prohibition was adopted first in

Saskatchewan in 1917, shortly followed by the other western provinces.

When the first settlers came to the west whole families were required to work on the land, but as conditions became more stable, the value of education rose. Many children were dependent on home coaching or church schools. Increasingly, parents were demanding that governments provide efficient nondenominational schools. An increased emphasis on education strengthened the movement for compulsory education, and stricter measures were adopted against truancy between the ages of seven and fourteen.

The war years were also marked by stronger farm associations and greater union membership; their demands had little success at the time but would make a significant impact in postwar years.

The federal parliament, hastily recalled when war was declared, unanimously passed the War Measures Act giving the government extraordinary powers—right of censorship and control of all means of communication; the right to arrest, detain or deport aliens; control of all transportation services, all trading and manufacturing, and the power to appropriate or dispose of property. Steps were taken to increase the manufacture of agricultural implements and grain acreage, and to provide all the requirements of a military force, from clothes to machines.

At first men flocked to the recruiting stations, but as the war continued the rate of voluntary recruitment declined while the casualty lists lengthened. To maintain military strength, by 1916 the government was forced to consider conscription, knowing that there was strong opposition to it. French Canadians were traditionally opposed to Canada's involvement in British conflicts, but there was also strong opposition outside Quebec. Most farmers objected to leaving their fields or having their sons taken away when they were needed as workers. Labour unions were unanimous in their opposition. Various pacifist groups throughout the country were of course opposed, and there would be resentment against those whose applications for exemption were successful. Conscription would cause dissension—city people against farmers, English-speaking against French-speaking, soldiers against civilians.

In 1917 parliament passed the Military Voters Act and the Wartime Elections Act, granting the franchise to all Canadian men and women engaged in war service and denying it to conscientious objectors. People of alien enemy birth as well as any Europeans naturalized after 1902 and using a language of an alien country were disfranchised. The franchise was given to all women whose next-of-kin were soldiers. Soldiers were able to vote in a riding other than their home. The Conservatives judged that enlisted men, and women who had close ties to them, would favour a government that introduced conscription. When the franchise bills were introduced, a large body of English-speaking Liberals broke party ranks and supported Borden's government.

The Borden government had already been in office more than the statutory five years. Having passed the acts conducive to a proconscription vote, Borden now approached a number of Liberals to propose a coalition or Union Party. Laurier, harassed by the angry protests of Henri Bourassa in Quebec, refused to join the coalition and the Liberal Party became badly split along language lines.

In the election of December 1917, the Union Party won 153 seats, sweeping English-speaking Canada. Laurier's Liberals won only 3 of the 55 seats in the west but lost only 3 seats in Quebec. Since Canada had only slightly more than 60,000 recruits for the remainder of the war, the net value of the conscription policy is still a matter of dispute, for it left rifts that have not been forgotten. Almost thirty years later, the memories of 1917 were to haunt Mackenzie King in a similar crisis. Quebec has remained an almost insoluble problem for the Conservative Party, handicapped by memories of Riel and the Manitoba Schools question as well as conscription. Only once in this century, in 1958, has the federal party won a majority of seats in Quebec and even in the Conservative victory of 1979 it won only 2 seats in that province.

Canadian Autonomy

Two months after the Armistice of 11 November 1918, delegates met in Paris to sign formal peace treaties. Supported by the record of its war efforts, Canada took this occasion to press for recognition of its autonomy. Each dominion signed the Treaty of Versailles for itself under the British signature, making them all members of the League of Nations whose covenant was included in the treaty.

Two years later at the Imperial Conference, Prime Minister Arthur Meighen convinced Britain to abrogate the Anglo-Japanese Alliance, enabling Canada to reassess Japanese immigration, an issue of vital concern to British Columbia. British Columbia was also affected by the Halibut Fisheries Treaty with the United States governing the Pacific coast fisheries. This treaty was of nationwide significance, for it was the first treaty signed by Canada independently of Britain.

By the Statute of Westminster of 1931, the British parliament proclaimed that the dominions were "autonomous communities within the British Commonwealth." Canada requested that amendments to the BNA Act continue to be made by the British parliament, and that certain legal appeals be allowed from the Supreme Court of Canada to the Judicial Committee of the Privy Council. (This right of appeal was abolished in 1949 and the Supreme Court of Canada became the final court of appeal.) Although some modifications were made to allow Canada limited amendments to its constitution, the problem of "patriating the constitution" remained unsolved for fifty years until 1982, since provincial and federal governments could not agree on the division of powers.

In spite of its insistence on autonomy and an independent foreign policy, postwar Canada had little interest in external affairs. The federal government was determined to restore the national unity that had been threatened during the war years. Most Canadians agreed with this neutral attitude towards foreign affairs, having just completed a costly war in which they had no direct interest and now facing many readjustments. The people of a country expanding both in population and industrially had little time to become involved in the affairs of nations separated from them by two oceans.

Economic Expansion

The war had given great impetus to Canadian industrial growth and the momentum continued in the postwar years. By the end of the war, Canada had ceased to be predominantly an agricultural nation. The 1921 census placed the rural population at 4,436,041 and the urban at 4,352,442. Industrial production totalled $2,747,926,000 compared with agricultural production of $1,403,686,000.

The growth of large corporations made large capital investments possible. In Canada's early history the country had been built by British capital, but by the 1920s U.S. investments had surpassed British as Americans opened new subsidiaries and industries, beginning the domination of American capital in Canada.

Much of the economic development was in the primary industries. Pulp and paper became the largest industry in the country. Often related to pulp and paper, the production of hydroelectric power was a major industry in its own right. Mining expanded as discoveries produced new minerals required by an industrial world. The potential oil fields of Alberta had been forecast by the early Turner Valley discoveries and there was interest in Fort Norman in the Northwest Territories. Gas pipelines were being extended. The introduction of sugar beets near Lethbridge opened up a new industry for the west.

The dramatic expansion of primary industries spurred the secondary industries. Automobile production, highway and railway construction, airplane manufacturing and the production of a vast variety of consumer goods employed thousands of workers and led to subsidiary industries. As workers were drawn to industrial centres, more service industries were required and cities grew larger.

Although Canada had become an industrial nation, agriculture continued to be a major factor in the economy. While many of the primary industries and almost all of the secondary industries were located in Quebec and Ontario, they were dependent on the raw materials and the consumer markets of the agricultural west. Wheat production continued to dominate the prairie economy as the population and cultivated acreage increased. The wheat crop was the basis of railway success and encouraged the building of new lines. Wheat exports were responsible for large employment on the railways, in the cities and towns, and in the ports. The increasing urban-manufacturing life of Quebec and Ontario accentuated the differences between those provinces and the still predominantly agricultural west.

British Columbia was dependent on the industries of sea, mine and forest. Because of its growing dependence on the wheat export trade as well as on nearby markets for its own products, it was closely tied to the prairie provinces. And like them, B.C. was almost entirely dependent on manufactured goods from the east. Thus the four western provinces had common interests in the wheat trade, in opposing high railway rates, and in protesting the high cost of eastern goods, whose manufacture was assisted by high protective tariffs.

Changing Lifestyles

By the end of the 1920s lifestyles in many ways were similar to those of fifty years later. New sources of energy were being used, machines were replacing manpower and becoming technologically more efficient, and a variety of home appliances were relieving the homemaker. Most present-day conveniences, social patterns and varieties of entertainment were being experienced.

Telephones and electricity had been in use at the turn of the century; in the 1920s they had become part of every city home and were reaching the rural areas, ending their isolation. Kerosene lamps were disappearing. With electricity came many conveniences to make housekeeping easier—electric stoves, toasters, vacuum cleaners and washing machines. The ice wagons were gradually replaced by electric refrigerators. The growing demand for electricity resulted in hydroelectric dam construction and new factories specializing in electrical appliances. To encourage the sale of consumer goods, retail stores had introduced credit buying, by which goods could be paid for in monthly installments.

The first radio broadcasts in Canada took place in several cities in the early 1920s. The most important of the new electrical gadgets, it not only gave the country a sense of unity through coast-to-coast broadcasts but also brought isolated communities into the mainstream of Canadian life. By the end of the decade, the simple "crystal set" had been replaced by electric consoles; wind-up phonograph machines were disappearing; ornate moving-picture houses showed feature-length Hollywood films with sound (but not in colour).

The advent of gasoline-powered vehicles had a tremendous impact on work and transportation in the west. By the beginning of the century farmers had bought tractors and were experimenting with combines. Automobiles had been introduced but were few and unreliable until the improvements of the war years. During the 1920s they came into common use, revolutionizing family life. The machines were quite comfortable by earlier standards, for they were glass enclosed and had self-starters. The tires had inner tubes and standard equipment included irons for changing tires since patching holes was to be expected on the rough roads. In the automobile the family could escape from home for weekends or holidays. The proliferation of cars demanded better roads and speed limit legislation. Provincial governments were pressed into extending the highways. Dotted along the cement roads were service stations and motels catering to the new travel urge.

Even more revolutionary than the spread of the automobile was the development of air travel. J. D. McCurdy's *Silver Dart* made the first heavier-than-air flight in Canada only five years before World War I. Airplanes were still in the experimental stage—flimsy, unreliable and land based. At first the army could see little value in them except for observing enemy movements behind the lines. By the end of the war they were fast, manoeuvrable, and could land on ground, water or ship. In 1919 John Alcock and Arthur Whitten-Brown made the first trans-Atlantic flight from Newfoundland to Ireland in sixteen hours. In 1920 the Canadian government formed the Air Board, which established bases for forest fire patrols and surveys using surplus planes donated by the British and American governments. In that year it organized the first transcontinental flight from Halifax to Vancouver, accomplished in ten days with frequent stops, though actual flying time was forty-nine hours.

In the immediate postwar era, the Northwest Territories was still largely unknown and unmapped, containing scattered settlements of Indians and Inuit, Hudson's Bay Company posts and a few isolated mining camps. Transport was by canoe or sled and dog team. There were also, in the south, hundreds of demobilized air pilots and surplus war planes which could be picked up for about $3,000. From this combination of factors developed the bush pilots. With discarded air force planes, a minimum of flying instruments and a few landmarks, they flew through rain and snowstorms that made visibility almost impossible. There were no fuelling depots, no radio beams, no marked runways and no radar. The bush pilots flew "by the seat of their pants" into the uncharted wilderness and hoped to land on a "cow patch," a term applied to the first Edmonton airfield. Often machines broke down or propellers were broken by stumps or snowbanks, and were patched together in the bitter cold of the north for the desperate return journey. They carried medicine, supplies, machinery and passengers to the isolated outposts, which became dependent on their services. At first the bush pilots were individual adventurers, but within a few years commercial airlines, often with only a few planes, were making regular scheduled flights. Better planes carried heavy machinery to places inaccessible over land and made possible new mines in the north.

The increased use of the airplane demanded airfields, which at first were haphazard but by the 1930s existed right across the country. Larger commercial airlines prospered. The CPR had obtained a commercial licence for Canadian Pacific Airlines in 1919 and by 1942 it had amalgamated numerous small lines to provide regular service in northern Canada. Air Canada started in 1937 as Trans-Canada Air Lines (TCA) and began its first transcontinental service from Vancouver to Montreal in April 1939. The trip took fifteen hours west to east and three hours longer on the return.

Railway problems continued to plague the federal government. At the beginning of the war it controlled two national railways—the Intercolonial and the leased Grand Trunk Pacific—and in 1917 took over the Canadian Northern. By 1921 it had also taken over the Grand Trunk and Grand Trunk Pacific, whose difficulties had been further complicated by poor management. In 1923 these railways became the core of the Canadian National Railways, consolidated under the direction of British railwayman Henry Thornton.

The provinces were also embarrassed by railway policies

which had swollen their debts. In British Columbia construction of the Pacific Great Eastern was suspended. Alberta took over the Alberta and Great Waterways line. Manitoba and Saskatchewan were still seeking a railway to Hudson Bay.

Women as Persons

When in the early 1900s the women's suffrage movement became a powerful political force in Britain and the United States and spread to Canada, western Canadian women were aggressive in their demands for recognition. During the war years they had filled the absent men's jobs in farms and factories, as well as participating in relief organizations such as the Red Cross. When the war ended they expected to continue in the various occupations and responsibilities they had mastered. The 1920s expressed these new independent attitudes in things like freer styles of dress—partly encouraged by the introduction of new fabrics such as rayon for stockings; shortened hemlines and hair, and even smoking in public. Interest also developed in serious competitive sports, as was demonstrated by the era of the Edmonton Grads who dominated women's basketball from 1922 until their disbandment in 1940.

Many women's associations were formed to protect children, to provide home nursing and medical care, to improve sanitation and to better working conditions for women and children. Underlying all of these activities was a demand for equality and recognition not only in the business and professional world but also in politics. As noted, the provincial and municipal governments of the four western provinces granted women suffrage during the war years; in 1917 the federal government permitted a limited suffrage to women whose next-of-kin were enlisted men and in 1918 gave them the same voting rights as men. In this movement for equality the women of Alberta and British Columbia were leaders. In 1916 Emily Murphy of Edmonton became the first woman magistrate in the British Empire, and her appointment was followed by others. In 1916 Mary Ellen Smith was elected to the British Columbia legislature.

The year 1921 marked several "firsts" for women. From

Ontario Agnes McPhail was elected to the federal parliament. In British Columbiary Ellen Smith was appointed cabinet minister without portfolio, the first woman cabinet minister in the British Empire, followed a few months later by a similar appointment for Irene Marryat Parlby in Alberta. Not until 1952, when Tilly Ralston was made minister of education in British Columbia, was any woman in Canada given a cabinet portfolio.

British common law, which is also law in Canada, stated, "Women are persons in matters of pain or penalties, but are not persons in matters of rights or privileges." Thus section 23 of the BNA Act dealing with qualifications for membership in the Senate, in which four of the six headings begin with "he," taken with subsequent sections stating that "persons" may be appointed by the governor general to the Senate, implied that only men could be senators.

During the 1920s numerous women's groups made representations to the Canadian government to have this discriminating interpretation removed. Both Mackenzie King and Arthur Meighen made promises but no action was taken. In 1927 five Alberta women appealed to the Supreme Court of Canada: Nellie McClung, Irene Parlby, Louise McKinney, Henrietta Muir Edwards and Emily Murphy. They asked, in the "Person's Case," a simple question: "Does the word 'person' in section 24 of the British North America Act include female persons?" The women were shocked and disappointed when their appeal was denied. In a final effort they appealed to the Privy Council of England, which in 1929 announced its decision that "women are eligible to be summoned and may become Members of the Senate in Canada." The following year the federal government appointed two Ontario women to the Senate, but none of the "Famous Five."

The Protest Groups

The prevailing nostalgia for the 1920s envisages a country that was progressive, prosperous and optimistic. Although to many citizens this appeared true, many others were not content. They believed that drastic changes were needed in the democratic-free enterprise system to bring equality of opportunity and a fair distribution of wealth. This dissatisfaction found expression in three groups: the Socialist Party of Canada, the trade unions representing the working class, and the farmers.

In the immediate postwar years a repercussion of the Bolshevik revolution in Russia was the "Red Scare" in the United States, which saw communism as a worldwide threat. This fear spread to Canada where many people regarded socialism as synonymous with communism. Although there were extreme leftists in both the Socialist Party and the trade unions who were either communists or communist sympathizers, they were comparatively few. Yet their vociferousness created fears in established society. In fact, the Socialist Party was similar to the moderate socialists in Britain, supporting state control of natural resources and public utilities as well as an increase in welfare services. Its success in both federal and provincial elections was infinitesimal since it rarely elected more than one or two members. It produced some outstanding leaders whose sincerity and persistence influenced the policies of the dominant parties.

The unions were not as interested in a utopian future state as they were in improving present working conditions. In the immediate postwar years, as war industries closed and veterans returned, unemployment rose, to an estimated 17 per cent of the population in 1923. There was a demand for goods that had been restricted or unattainable and prices rose rapidly. Whereas union membership and wages had increased during the war years, now during high unemployment wages were falling far below the soaring cost of living.

From the time of the arrival of the United Empire Loyalists two hundred years ago Ontario has supported a strong British connection, and over the years the province has established a stable community with a conservative outlook. As secondary industry expanded, unions of skilled factory workers were formed similar to those in Britain. These early unions reflected conservative attitudes in their exclusion of unskilled labour and their opposition to radical ideas. The prewar west, on the other hand, especially British Columbia, was a newly settled land with an economy based on primary production in mining, logging and fishing. Much of the employment was in isolated camps or company towns in which homes and stores were employer owned. The workers were often imported from Britain or the United States, bringing with them new and radical ideas. The disproportionate influence of the employers in the camps and the workers' low wages against the high profits of the owner-capitalist or corporation were causes of continuous and bitter friction. B.C. workers formed unions, in spite of strong opposition from the employers, and some of them took in unskilled workers. They were more radical and less submissive to authority than the more conservative unions of the east, and strikes were frequent.

When the 1918 Trades and Labour Congress convention met in Toronto, it turned down every resolution from the more militant west. The following year the western unionists gathered at Calgary. Among their resolutions was one supporting the new Russian Soviet government and a demand that Allied troops be withdrawn from the Siberian invasion. The delegates supported the idea of a consolidated One Big Union (OBU), which would include all workers, skilled or unskilled, instead of trades members only as the eastern unions advocated. The westerners believed that their most effective weapon was the strike. If necessary, as a consolidated group, they would use the general strike, in which work in all industries and services was suspended.

While the OBU was meeting at Calgary, workers in Winnipeg's building and metal trades struck for better wages and working conditions. They were supported by the Winnipeg Trades and Labour Council which organized a vote on a general strike. The member unions voted overwhelmingly in favour and the general strike would last forty-two days. Although reports from the OBU convention must have had some influence, there was no actual connection between the two events. The long strike was supported by other western unions and in some cities, such as Vancouver, "sympathy" strikes were called.

The Winnipeg Strike was noteworthy because of the discipline of the workers. The strike committee kept firm control and discouraged demonstrations such as mass meetings which might lead to confrontations. Steps were taken to provide essential food and water to the citizens. In spite of this restraint, the strike aroused a barrage of vilification and propaganda from employers, governments and the press. It was depicted as an organized attempt to instigate a revolution similar to that of the Bolsheviks in Russia. The antistrike forces claimed that the troubles were caused by "aliens" and "foreigners" and demanded that the leaders be deported. Special police were employed and the federal government sent a force of RCMP to help them.

The climax came when a group of returned soldiers, against the orders of the strike leaders, staged a march. As had been feared, the marchers were confronted by police. Two men died and thirty were injured in the melee. The strike was broken and the workers returned with little gained. The Robson Committee Report found no evidence of a deep-laid plot for revolution nor any intention of the workers to use force. The report further stated that the causes of the strike were the high cost of living, long hours of work, low wages, poor working conditions and the unwillingness of employers to recognize the right of collective bargaining.

The failure of the strike was a setback for unionism. The radical OBU faded away. The general strike was recognized as a cumbersome and unpopular weapon that was ultimately ineffective (verified in 1926 by the nine-day general strike in Britain). Until 1939 labour unions steadily declined in numbers and influence, but the remaining core would become better organized and co-operate with American unions. They would also recognize the need for more active political participation. Several of the leaders of the Winnipeg Strike who were arrested and imprisoned later became influential leaders in government.

During the last two years of war, the federal government took over the pricing and marketing of wheat and in 1919, for one year, did it through a Canadian Wheat Board. During this time of expanding markets and high prices, western farmers were satisfied with the government's results. In the five years following the war, crops were poor, prices were low and the wartime markets were drastically reduced. To market their crops farmers began to establish "pools" in place of the earlier Wheat Board. The Alberta Wheat Pool began in 1923, Manitoba's and Saskatchewan's in 1924. The wheat pools were so successful that in following years farmers adopted the idea for other commodities.

Most farmers would never favour the commune system introduced in Russia: they were individual capitalists who owned their own land and tools, developed their farms through personal effort, and often employed labour. They had little in common with the labour unions, whose demand for higher wages meant higher wages to farm labourers and higher prices for equipment. On the other hand, farmers were also opposed to governments which they believed were subject to the pressures of eastern industrialists to support high tariff policies.

In 1916 the Canadian Council of Agriculture determined to bring political pressure on Ottawa by issuing a statement of aims called the "New National Policy." This was followed by the establishment of provincial political parties, and in 1919 the United Farmers of Ontario won the provincial election. In 1921, under the leadership of Henry Wise Wood, the United Farmers of Alberta became the government of that province.

Success in the provincial field encouraged the farmers to enter federal politics and to form the National Progressive Party (NPP) in Winnipeg in 1920. Its platform was basically the New National Policy: tariff reductions, aid to farmers, tax reforms including higher taxes on profits and income, co-operative methods of marketing and more public control of government through such measures as the referendum. Unfortunately, the NPP was divided on the question of party solidarity. The Albertans under Wood were opposed to it; others, led by Manitoban T. A. Crerar, envisioned a government in which all party members would vote as a bloc.

As the nation prepared for the election of 1921, the political scene was complicated by the presence of two new party leaders and a new third party attempting to unite the protesting labour and agricultural sectors. The Union government had continued after the war but ended in 1920 when Robert Borden retired because of poor health. His Conservative successor was Arthur Meighen, a successful trial lawyer before his election in 1908 and a member of Borden's cabinet. He was a very intelligent man, hard-working and sharp in debate, but he lacked the techniques of compromise essential to political leadership. As solicitor general during the Winnipeg Strike, he had brought in the federal police to quell what he considered to be a threat to Canadian unity.

Laurier had died in 1919 while the Liberal Party was still factionalized into those who supported and those who opposed the coalition government. The subsequent Liberal convention sought to revitalize the party and heal the split. It chose as new party leader William Lyon Mackenzie King, who had entered the House of Commons in 1908 and became Laurier's minister of labour. Defeated in both the 1911 and 1917 elections, he pursued his interests by mediating labour problems in the United States. In his absence from the country he had escaped the bitter party split over conscription and therefore was seen as a neutral leader.

Meighen and King were now firm opponents. Meighen's assurance and caustic debating technique were in direct contrast with King's apparently vague and rambling speech-making. King, however, had the ability to compromise, to organize people, to delegate authority and to plan political strategy. As a master politician, he was to dominate Canadian political life for thirty years.

The 1921 federal election revealed a country divided along regional, racial and economic lines. The Liberals formed a minority government with 65 seats from Quebec and 52 from Ontario and the Maritimes. The Conservatives dropped to 50 seats, mainly from Ontario, New Brunswick and British Columbia. The National Progressive Party showed surprising strength, taking 65 seats, including 24 in Ontario, 3 in British Columbia and 37 of a possible 43 in the prairie provinces.

Holding the balance of power in a minority government, the Progressives could have become the official opposition, but instead of leading an aggressive opposition with the Conservatives, they tended to support the Liberals who they believed were more sympathetic to their objectives. The wily King encouraged them in this attitude by his vague promises. Within two years of the election the NPP began to show signs of deterioration. In 1922 Crerar resigned as leader and was succeeded by Robert Forke, who wanted the NPP to act as a united opposition party; when this was opposed, mainly by the Alberta members, the party lost credibility and began to split into factions. They were divided in the vote on Liberal budget policies in 1924 and 1925.

Thomas A. Crerar was a Manitoba farm boy who became president of the Grain Growers' Company and was largely responsible for its organization and success. As a Liberal supporting Borden's coalition government, he was elected to the House of Commons at the age of forty-one in 1917 and became minister of agriculture. After the war he was not satisfied with King's proposals for tariff restrictions and joined the NPP, which chose him as leader in parliament. Crerar believed in party government so he left the divided NPP and returned to the Liberal Party where he became a cabinet minister under Mackenzie King. Later he was appointed to the Senate where he served until 1966. In a span of forty-nine years he served parliament for forty-four. When he died in 1975 at the age of ninety-eight, Prime Minister Trudeau described him as "a giant figure in the political development of Canada during the initial turbulent decades of this century."

In the 1925 election the Liberals were reduced to 101 seats while the Conservatives rose to 116, but with the support of the 24 Progressives, King was able to continue in office. Within a year the Liberal government was shaken by Conservative charges of irregularities in the Department of Customs. Knowing that the NPP would not support him on the imminent motion of censure, King asked Governor General Lord Byng to dissolve parliament so that an election might be held; but Byng refused and asked Meighen to form a government. The Progressives, however, would not support a Conservative government, and it was defeated three days after taking office.

In the ensuing election King successfully played down the scandal and maintained that the main issue was the unconstitutional action of the governor general. The election showed the Liberals with 116 seats to the Conservatives' 91. The NPP had dwindled to 13 plus 9 "Liberal-Progressives" who had indicated their sympathy with King.

From this time the NPP ceased to be a force in Canadian politics, but the experiment was to influence later developments. Mackenzie King had been forced to adjust his policies to lessen NPP opposition. To some of the Progressives and Independents, it became obvious that a successful third party must accept the parliamentary and cabinet system and act as a united party within that system. The labour members, led by J. S. Woodsworth, began to co-operate with the few Progressives in the House to form the nucleus of a combined labour-farm group. The foundations were laid for a new national party to challenge the old established parties.

The Optimistic 'Twenties

The first half of the 1920s had been a depressed and pessimistic period. Costs had risen while wages had remained low. Foreign trade had declined. Not only were wheat yields below average but the price of wheat had also fallen in a glutted market.

By 1925 the worst was over and for five years Canada enjoyed a boom period that has seldom been equalled. Factories were in full production and construction was expanding. Investments, especially by American corporations, were filtering into all phases of the economy. Lumbering, mining and fishing were setting production records. Unemployment was at a minimum. The stock markets were rising as speculation continued: people gambled on the future by heavy borrowing and by credit buying. There were bumper wheat crops from 1925 to 1929; but the market was lagging since other exporting countries were also having large harvests. The wheat pools carried over a million bushels in 1929.

The results of overexpansion and overconfidence began to show in 1929. The first serious warning came with the collapse of the wheat market. Less than a week later, on Tuesday, 29 October, came the great stock market crash. The 1920s, which had begun in confusion and unrest and had later been infected by a spirit of overoptimism, closed with the threat of dark days to come.

There were many lasting gains during the decade. The Hudson Bay Railway had reached Churchill in 1929 and the Alberta railways had reached the Peace River district. This was the great era of Peace River settlement. The region became famous when, at the Grain Exposition in Chicago, Herman Trelle of Wembley won the world championship for high-quality hard spring wheat for three years beginning in 1926. The

Peace River block, which the federal government had acquired
when the CPR was built, was returned to British Columbia.

Women served in the legislatures and the House of Commons and were eligible for the Senate. Prohibition had ended,
and between 1921 and 1924 the four western provinces and the
Yukon had established government-controlled liquor outlets.
Wheat pools had been established to market grain, and in British Columbia the government made membership in a fruit
growers' association compulsory. An old age pension act had
been passed in 1927 which paid twenty dollars a month to
British subjects resident in Canada for twenty years, of which
the federal government paid one-half to participating provinces. By 1934 all four western provinces were paying pensions.

Provincial Politics

Certain political trends began to be manifest in the western
provinces during the 1920s. The most obvious was increasing
mistrust of the old established Liberal and Conservative parties. They had originated in Ontario and Quebec and were
suspected of supporting policies advantageous to the east.
Located there were the financial centres to which farmers owed
money, the headquarters of the railways whose rates were
adjusted to favour the east, and the industrialists who favoured
high protective tariffs. Thus it behooved western Liberals and
Conservatives to act as provincial organizations and not as
affiliates of their federal counterparts. A member of a federal
political party might not be a member of the same provincial
party; in fact, a Liberal or Conservative federal member might
belong to an opposing provincial party. (An example of this
division occurred in May 1979 during simultaneous British
Columbia and federal elections, when the provincial Conservative leader accused the federal party of working against him to
gain the support of the provincial Social Credit in the federal
election.)

In spite of avowals of independence, the names Liberal and
Conservative were often a handicap to provincial parties and
encouraged the rise of third parties with new names. In contrast, apart from Quebec, only once did a third party control a

provincial government east of Manitoba—when the United Farmers of Ontario were victorious in 1919. Most successful third parties originated in the western provinces where their strategy was to concentrate on western problems.

Manitoba Politics

From its inception the province of Manitoba had been controlled by people of British descent, many of whom were from Ontario. At first political organizations were not strong and Premier John Norquay, though nominally Conservative, led a coalition of individuals who accepted him as a compromise premier. In 1888 the Liberals succeeded in electing Thomas Greenway. His government opposed bilingualism and was responsible for the controversial Manitoba Schools question. Laurier convinced Greenway to adopt a more moderate stance but lost the premier much of his support. The Conservatives had a vigorous leader in Hugh John Macdonald, the son of John A. Macdonald. By asserting the British character of the province and opposing the immigration of French and Europeans, he won the election of 1899. A few months later he retired in favour of the more moderate Roblin. During Roblin's term Manitoba almost doubled its population as Clifford Sifton's immigration policies brought thousands of central and eastern Europeans seeking land. Roblin succeeded in having the newcomers settled in the less desirable, more isolated lands to the north or in the poorer districts of Winnipeg. Nevertheless, he managed to gain the immigrant vote and by a close margin won the election of 1914 against the antiforeign Liberals.

In 1915 the revelation of government contracts awarded to party supporters forced a tired Roblin to resign, and in the resulting election the Liberals under Toby Norris made an almost clean sweep. In the antialien climate engendered by the war, Norris took steps to strengthen British influence and to force the assimilation of non-British groups by making English compulsory in public schools and by establishing a Civil Service Commission that hired on the results of competitive examinations which were a handicap to non-English-speaking applicants. Other reforms improved working conditions but Norris refused to recognize collective bargaining and thus prepared the way for postwar labour troubles.

During the war Norris's Liberals supported the federal Union government, but at the end of the war had reverted to the Liberals. Norris lost his majority largely because of the election of 12 United Farmer candidates and had to depend on the 11 Labour Party members to survive. It was at this time that the disastrous Winnipeg Strike occurred, which was blamed on non-British foreign agitators and served to strengthen the pro-British element. Outside the cities there was little sympathy for the strikers, and the government was criticized for not taking strong measures earlier.

In 1922 the United Farmers won a clear majority and convinced John Bracken to become their leader. Bracken was an Ontarian of British stock but had lived most of his life in Saskatchewan and Manitoba. He was a specialist in agricultural methods and had worked with both the provincial and federal departments of agriculture. He was recognized as an authority on dry farming. In 1912 he joined the College of Agriculture just opened in Saskatoon and in 1920 became principal of the Manitoba Agricultural College in Winnipeg. Bracken was not a believer in strong party government and supported a nonpartisan, co-operative approach. His government was in reality a coalition of farmers, labour and Conservatives. His support was strongest within the Winnipeg business sector and the farm communities, especially those of the anglophone southwest.

Manitoba had passed through the turbulent years of war, inflation, postwar labour unrest and antiforeign demonstrations. The people desired stability and economy and these Bracken promised. Bracken was a pragmatic individual with little imagination but he formed a well-administered, capable government. While protecting the British group from heavy taxation, he increased taxes generally and introduced a provincial income tax, reduced expenditures in health, education and welfare, but in 1928 did introduce the old age pension of twenty dollars a month for all citizens over seventy. Bracken was conservative, almost presbyterian, in his attitudes, and established a censorship board to regulate motion pictures. Accepting the fact that prohibition was not working, in 1923 he passed a Liquor Control Act setting up outlets for the sale of liquor, contributing substantially to provincial revenues.

Bracken promoted industry and encouraged forestry, mining, fishing and water power. He was responsible for the branch line of the Hudson Bay Railway to Flin Flon which made possible the opening of the copper and zinc mine in 1926. He always retained his interest in agricultural problems and was best with rural audiences. He strongly advocated provincial control of natural resources and was largely responsible for Mackenzie King's acceptance of this principle in 1930.

Although not spectacular, Bracken was a master provincial politician who exuded confidence. By holding his coalition together, he eliminated competition and governed Manitoba for twenty years.

Saskatchewan Politics

Before 1905 the government of the Territories was nonpartisan. The former premier of the Territories, F. W. G. Haultain, though a Conservative in federal interests, attempted to maintain a provincial party called the Provincial Rights Party, but in 1911 it merged with the federal Conservatives. When Walter Scott became the first premier of Saskatchewan in 1905, the federal and provincial Liberal Parties had close ties. His Liberal government was fully aware of the predominance of farm voters and co-operated with the province's agricultural organizations. The federal Liberals, too, appealed to farmers with their promise of reciprocity. The Liberals were also supported by the many new immigrants who, though unfamiliar with the Canadian democratic system, perceived that the Liberal Party had made possible their present independent status. As John G. Diefenbaker pungently stated, "It used to be said that social security was a monopoly of the Socialist party: the two were regarded as being synonymous in the same way that those who emigrated to Canada were told here that liberty and Liberalism were synonymous. They found that neither of these epitomies were well based in fact."

In agricultural Saskatchewan, labour was slow to organize and did not have the political influence that it had in the more industrial provinces. Scott did not ignore labour and passed the Factory Act in 1909 limiting hours and setting an employee minimum age, and two years later he established a bureau of labour and workmen's compensation. He also showed some sympathy for the native population.

The years 1910–12 were good years in Saskatchewan and in the 1911 federal election it supported the encumbent Laurier, electing only one Conservative. With the success of the Borden Conservatives, the provincial Liberal Party lost its alliance with the federal government.

In 1916 Walter Scott retired as premier and was succeeded by William Melville Martin, who had no difficulty in maintaining an overwhelming Liberal majority in 1917. Soon after this success, two events threatened his party. The Conservatives' discriminating Wartime Elections Act affected many German and Austro-Hungarian immigrants who had entered the province since 1902, disfranchising some of the Liberals' electoral base; and the formation of the federal Union government in support of conscription split the Liberals (though all federal members from Saskatchewan supported Borden). But since there was little organized opposition, Martin was able to overcome these problems and maintain control.

A demand for the separation of provincial and federal parties had resulted in the formation of the Non-Partisan League in 1916–17. Although unsuccessful in provincial elections, the League established the core of a later third party.

Although Saskatchewan farmers did not form a party, they were the most potent force in provincial politics, and officers of the agricultural associations were sometimes appointed to the cabinet. They were strong supporters of reciprocity, and when the Ottawa Liberals delayed augmenting it, the provincial Liberals retained the support of the agricultural community by dissociating themselves from the federal party. At the same time, they gained the sympathy of immigrants who had been hurt by the Wartime Elections Act and of labour which was opposed to conscription and inflationary prices.

Under Martin (1916–22) and Charles Avery Dunning (1922–26), the Liberals dominated the government. Dunning had been a member of the Saskatchewan Grain Growers Association and was a former manager of the Saskatchewan Co-operative Elevator Company. When he resigned from the provincial government to become federal minister of railways and canals, he was succeeded by J. G. Gardiner who made two fatal errors. He renewed connections with the federal Liberals, and he angered formerly supportive Catholics by forbidding the use of religious emblems and dress in schools. Saskatchewan had had a Liberal government for the twenty-four years since provincehood, but in the election of 1929 the party failed to retain its majority: the result was 28 Liberals, 24 Conservatives, 5 Progressives and 6 Independents. The last three parties united to form a coalition government which lasted for five years under the leadership of J. T. M. Anderson.

Alberta Politics

After Alberta was formed in 1905, the first election was a duel between Liberals and Conservatives. The Liberals under A. C. Rutherford swept the polls with 23 out of 25 seats and four years later repeated this success with 36 out of 41 seats. A number of scandals centring on railway contracts forced Rutherford to resign and he was succeeded in 1910 by Arthur Lewes Sifton. The election of 1913 reflected the loss of public confidence when Sifton won only 38 of 56 seats, and in 1917 when he was returned with a slightly reduced majority. Sifton had a dominating personality and held the provincial Liberal Party together with authority. When he left the party to enter federal politics, it began to disintegrate and never recovered.

The United Farmers of Alberta (UFA) was formed in 1909 to provide farmers with local recreational and educational facilities. Not until 1919 did the organization decide to enter politics, and by this decision it destroyed the provincial Liberal Party. The leader of the UFA, Henry Wise Wood, believed that government was controlled by the moneyed class through political parties, whereas his direct democracy theory would have individual occupational groups setting government policies through conventions. In 1921 the UFA won 38 out of the 59 provincial seats.

The elected UFA members, now in control of the government, attempted to apply their ideas within the established form of government. Although in theory their policies were determined by the conventions, in reality the decision-making power and responsibility remained within the cabinet. The practicalities of administration proved to be incompatible with Wood's idealistic conception. Although the UFA movement repeated its election successes in 1926 and in 1930, it was swept aside by a new visionary movement, Social Credit, in 1935.

British Columbia Politics

After the many years of confusing nonpartisan politics, British Columbians in 1903 welcomed the promise of stable government under the Conservative Richard McBride. The election had been close with the Conservatives winning only 22 seats against the Liberals' 17 and Socialists' 3, but with this clear majority McBride was able to act decisively. Supporting a policy of railway development and exclusion of Asian immigrants, and demanding "Better Terms" from Ottawa, the colourful, flamboyant McBride easily won the election of 1907. With only 4 opposition seats against him, the Liberals were powerless. His success in 1912 was even more emphatic, for no Liberals were elected and his only opposition was 2 seats for the Socialist Party of Canada.

The Labour and Socialist parties had been active in British Columbia before the turn of the century and in the years of minority governments their small number of elected members had been able to exert considerable influence. After the Conservative sweep, the Socialist-Labour influence became negligible, though in 1912 they were the official opposition. At this time the province was moving towards polarization of the Socialist and antisocialist parties. Conservative elements supported by the press generated strong antisocialist propaganda. But organized labour, with its own internal factions, and the Socialists could not overcome their differences, and the opportunity to challenge the established parties was lost; a socialist party was not to become a serious threat for twenty years, until the formation of the CCF.

The early war years were depressed for British Columbia. Lack of immigration reduced the sale of public lands, the price of copper and other metals was low, and a shortage of shipping injured the lumber and canned salmon industries. Municipalities cut their appropriations for public works. Labour was rebellious as unemployment increased. The government was criticized for its support of railways and the resulting growth of the public debt. There were political scandals and rumours of corruption. In 1915, McBride resigned as premier and became agent general for the new British Columbia House in London, where he died two years later. He was succeeded as premier by the colourless W. L. Bowser, who faced a discontented province.

The dissatisfaction in the province created a fertile field for a strong protest vote, but the Socialist supporters were in disarray and the Liberals had no members in the legislature. In 1916, completely reorganized under the leadership of H. C. Brewster, the Liberals surprisingly throttled their opposition, winning 37 out of the 46 seats. By this time war industries had been established in the province, unemployment had ended, wages and the cost of living were rising. The Liberals established a Department of Labour and a Minimum Wage Act to counter the increasing radicalism of labour and the socialists. When Brewster died in 1918 he was succeeded by "Honest John" Oliver. The new premier's emphasis on his background as a manual labourer and farmer was a refreshing change from the earlier politicians. He came to office when wartime demands were bringing prosperity to the province, but labour unions were complaining bitterly that wages were not matching inflation.

British Columbia has a long history of protest movements. The working class has been well organized and aggressive but in the early years had little political success. The elements of the left have been divided between those who favour the Labour Party controlled by the labour unions and the nonunion, anticapitalist Socialists who favour government control of key industries and resources. Because of the protest vote in the election of 1920, the Liberals won only 26 of the 47 seats. The Conservatives had 14 and Labour 4. Three years later a new protest party, the Provincial Party, united with discontented Conservatives, rural federal Progressives and others who were opposed to ties with the "old parties." Although this group had considerable support, they won only 3 seats and the party faded. With opposition split between the torn Conservatives and Labour-Socialists, Oliver's government was able to hang on until 1927, when he was succeeded by the uninspiring John Duncan MacLean. The following year a reunited Conservative Party under Simon Fraser Tolmie came to power.

Summary

The war had suddenly stopped the great inflow of immigrants whose numbers had reached unprecedented figures. After 1914 Canada entered fifteen turbulent years—war, inflation, labour unrest and eventually a few years of apparent prosperity which proved to be illusory. The population of the west continued to grow, but not as rapidly as in prewar years. In 1911 the four western provinces had 1.7 million people; in 1921, 2.5 million, and in 1931, 3 million.

Before 1914 the west was still in the process of development and organization as the empty lands filled up. The major sources of wealth were primary resources—crops (especially wheat), forests and mines. This early picture of western Canada as an isolated wilderness of prairie wheatlands and Cordilleran forests and mines has persisted in some parts of Canada and abroad to the present day. Yet by the 1920s new machines, revolutionary transportation, expanded education, scientific research and the discovery of new resources were transforming the west into more than a sparsely populated land of small, isolated communities. There was a spirit of optimism in the land and westerners no longer accepted their dependence on the east. They were developing attitudes and ambitions of their own and had their own visions of Canada. The region was approaching maturity and with it came a spirit of self-confidence and a desire for self-assertion and self-government. Numerous protest associations and movements as well as independent political parties demanded more recognition and more influence in the federal government. These protest groups were the foundations for more assertive and more powerful organizations in the depressed years ahead.

Chapter Eight

DEPRESSION AND WAR
(1930 – 1945)

Two themes dominate the history of the 1930s. In the international field, the collapse of the League of Nations accompanied by the rise in the Western world of militarism and dictatorships caused readjustments and realignments among the major powers. In domestic affairs the Great Depression overshadowed all else. To Canadians faced with the problem of surviving during these years of economic and social dislocation, world problems aroused little genuine concern. True, the events in Europe, Africa and Asia were the subjects of articles, radio broadcasts and pessimistic speeches which warned of expanding aggression and foretold war. But most Canadians continued to believe they were secure from the affairs of other continents. Canadians were intentionally a peace-loving people having little influence in world affairs, and the prospect of involvement in war was inconceivable.

Industrial Depression

The Depression was worldwide but Canada was one of the countries hardest hit. Nationally, the west suffered most, especially Saskatchewan. The search for the causes of the Depression has spawned many theories but some facts are clear. The optimistic 1920s had been years of overexpansion and overpro-

duction. Large amounts of credit had been extended for speculative projects which were financially unsound. When the
stock market collapsed, the swollen values of stocks and bonds
dropped sharply. Many business firms became bankrupt while
others, including the major industries, reduced production and
in some years paid no dividends.

Canada could produce far more than it could consume, and
to the secondary industries, based largely in the central provinces, exporting was significant, but to the primary industries
of the west exporting was vital. When other countries were
depressed, they restricted purchases and raised protective tariffs: this economic nationalism further curtailed Canadian
exports.

In spite of the declining prices, some important developments were taking place in the Canadian economy. As early as
1916 new methods of electrolysis had improved the refining of
copper and zinc received at the Trail smelters from Kimberley
mines, and by 1930 British Columbia was one of the world's
leading sources of lead and zinc and also produced silver, copper and gold. In 1914 copper, zinc and silver had been discovered at Flin Flon on the Saskatchewan-Manitoba border, but
not until 1927 was a method of processing the ore found and
the necessary financing arranged; production began in 1930.
Subsequent years of silver, copper and zinc mining marked the
beginning of base metal production in the western Canadian
Shield. During the early 1930s mineral prices were low but by
1936 the buildup of world armaments created a demand and
higher prices for copper, lead and zinc. Gold held its price
during the Depression years, and a new field at Lake Athabasca
showed possibilities. In Alberta, coal remained the most
important mineral, though Turner Valley oil began production
in 1936. Other industries did not recover as quickly as mining;
lumbering, pulp and paper production, fishing and fruit growing all suffered. Between 1929 and 1933 Canada's income from
exports dropped a ruinous 67 per cent.

Wheat growing suffered the most of all industries. The
1928–29 season had left a surplus of wheat on a glutted world
market. The pools, which had paid $1.50 a bushel on the
expectation of a 1929 price of at least $1.60, were unable to
obtain anything like that price and were saved only by loans

from the federal and provincial governments. By the end of 1930 the pools owed $23 million, when the price per bushel was 50 cents; two years later it had dropped to 32 cents, the lowest price since the beginning of western wheat exports.

In 1935 the federal government established the Canadian Wheat Board to control the sale of all wheat, oats and barley. After 1974 the board was restructured to become the sole purchaser and seller of feed grains for export, while feed grains and other crops were marketed interprovincially by private agencies. In the late 1930s, through government aid and the new board, the pools survived and began a period of recovery. Much of their energy and investments were concentrated on encouraging a variety of co-operatives such as stores, petroleum depots, credit unions and insurance companies. The stronger co-operatives organized educational programs, established magazines and newspapers, disseminated information through radio and encouraged co-operative social activities. Saskatchewan and Manitoba led in the co-operative movement, which had some success in Alberta and British Columbia.

Although the price of wheat was low, farmers might have managed had the prairies not been struck by five years of drought. In Saskatchewan it was actually nine years, beginning in 1928 and climaxing in 1937–38. Along with drought came grasshoppers, Russian thistle, early frosts, hailstorms, wind, and soil erosion. As the soil dried, the searing wind carried it away in dust-laden clouds. Where crops had been planted the soil might be blown away from the roots, or it might cover the plants so deeply that they could not grow. A farmer at harvest time might have wheat fields six inches (15 cm) high with stalks a foot (30 cm) apart. All of the southern prairies suffered. In 1930 wheat production totalled 420 million bushels, but in 1935 it was less than 270 million, the lowest since 1924. After 1933 world markets began to recover, but this did little to help the farmer who had nothing to sell. Despite little or no income, they still had fixed commitments: farm taxes, depreciation, and interest on debts for land or machines. Many farmers gave up and left. An estimated quarter of a million people migrated from the prairies in the decade 1931–41, some to the moister lands farther north, some to the cities where they added to the number of unemployed, and many to the United States.

A vicious circle was established. Industries could not sell their goods and laid off workers, whose reduced buying power resulted in further industrial cutbacks and layoffs. During the 1920s the provincial governments had increased their budgets with taxes on gasoline, motor vehicle and liquor sales, but they had spent recklessly on roads, railway grants and resource development. Municipalities had also increased taxes via increased property assessments when construction was flourishing. Now people could not pay taxes and revenues fell. The provincial and municipal debts remained to be paid, essential services had to be carried on, and there was an ever-growing demand for relief.

The Individual

Every citizen in Canada was affected by the Depression. Some were fortunate to keep their jobs, though their income might decrease and tenure of employment was uncertain. When a lumber mill threatened to close on the west coast, the workers agreed to continue without wages for a share of the profits: at the end of the month each received $25. The standard beginning salary for teachers in British Columbia was $960 per year, but rural teachers might receive part of their pay in kind (such as pigs) while some city teachers received no December cheques because municipal funds ran out before the end of the year.

The drastic fall in wages was felt especially in the west. While the average decrease in Canada from 1928 to 1933 was 48 per cent, Saskatchewan had the highest decline at 72 per cent, followed by Alberta, Manitoba and British Columbia with 61, 49 and 47 per cent respectively.

Everyone was familiar with the men who went from house to house offering to do any kind of work for a meal. Long queues were seen at the soup kitchens. Many volunteered their help to charitable institutions to alleviate distress. Parents found it increasingly difficult to keep their children in school and many promising students never reached high school graduation because they had to help their strapped families. Even university graduates were happy to obtain unskilled work.

Wives and mothers had the difficult task of providing nutritious meals and keeping clothes repaired so the children could go to school "decent," and many women undertook part-time, poorly paid work to earn a few extra dollars.

If the family with some income found life difficult, for those unemployed or living in the drought areas the problems were often insurmountable. Malnutrition caused ill health, yet the ill could not afford doctors and hospitals. Dental care was an impossibility. Clothes were made from any material and sugar sacks made practical underwear. Often, especially in winter, children could not attend school because they had no warm clothes; in fact, the school might be closed because there was no money for janitors or fuel. For those able to attend there was always the problem of buying books and supplies.

And yet, with all the shortages, most people were living in comparative comfort, for while wages were low, so were prices. There was a reluctance to buy durable goods or luxuries, and cars were kept running longer. There were still dances and parties. This was the greatest age of the moving picture, with extravaganzas of all kinds being shown in theatres whose fairy-tale appearance contrasted sharply with the misery outside. At home the radio offered lectures, news, comedies and stories. Magazines were cheap and appealed to all tastes. To some people, the Depression meant unfortunate restraints which altered their lives little; the hardships of many of their fellow citizens were kept at a distance along with those disturbing military aggressions in Europe and Asia.

R. B. Bennett

Like most people, politicians were unprepared for the sudden economic collapse at the end of 1929. Prime Minister King predicted that the setback was only temporary, then insisted that the federal government did not have the constitutional power to assist victims of the Depression; such powers were under provincial jurisdiction. Constitutionally he was right, but the provinces were handicapped by greatly reduced revenues and mounting welfare costs. When he finally agreed to provide the prairie provinces with relief grants, the gesture was too late to save him.

Before the election of 1930 he made another concession to a long-standing demand of the west when he turned over control of natural resources to Manitoba, Alberta and Saskatchewan. By that time most of the arable free land was gone and the transcontinental railways were completed. The original purpose of federal control of crown land for the systematic development of the country was gone, and the financial returns were a minor part of the federal budget, though they would be a significant addition to provincial income. In 1930 the potential government revenue from forests, mines and petroleum was unrecognized. Fifty years later they would make the western provinces wealthy, and the division of income from natural resources would fuel new discord between governments, both federal against provincial and provincial against provincial.

The new leader of the Conservatives was Richard B. Bennett, a Calgary millionaire who was highly regarded in financial circles. He promised to promote industry behind tariff walls and to "blast" Canada's way into the markets of the world. A dynamic and colourful orator, Bennett conveyed the confidence and energy of a successful businessman, and Canadians responded by returning 137 Conservatives to parliament. The Liberals were reduced to 38 and the remaining 20 seats were won by an assortment of independents.

Bennett was the first prime minister from the west but he was not of the west, for his strength was in the industrial centres. In the prairies his support rose from one seat to 23, but although he received 11 of 17 seats in Manitoba and 7 of 14 in British Columbia, he won only 8 out of 21 in Saskatchewan (up from zero) and 4 of 16 in his home province of Alberta. True to his election promise, his first action was to raise tariffs on the theory that this would protect manufacturers and maintain Canadian employment. The response of other nations was retaliatory high tariffs. Although the tariff did protect the domestic market, this was not large enough to absorb the volume of manufactured goods that could be produced.

As the Depression continued, federal-provincial cost-sharing agreements were reached, and the Bennett government spent over $134 million in relief from 1930 to 1933. Millions were spent on public works such as the Trans-Canada Highway as well as public works of municipal and provincial governments, the federal government usually paying half the cost in the west; but these contributions did not stop the decline.

During Bennett's term the Commonwealth of Nations was established, in 1931. The Imperial Economic Conference was held in Ottawa in 1932—an attempt to create a Commonwealth trading bloc, but in the end bilateral treaties were negotiated between attending countries. Canada gained preferential tariff rates for the sale of a number of primary products in return for tariff concessions to British exporting manufacturers. But the gains were minimal given the extent of the decline in European and American markets during these years.

Two positive domestic achievements of the Bennett government were the creation of the Bank of Canada in 1934 and the Canadian Broadcasting Commission in 1932. The latter, which established a publicly owned network in French and English, was later reorganized as the Canadian Broadcasting Corporation (CBC) and included television. The CBC has developed into one of the most positive forces towards Canadian unity, making possible simultaneous experiences throughout the country in even the most isolated communities. A hockey game in Montreal is watched, live, in Vancouver; and Canadians coast to coast may tune in to the minister of finance presenting his budget proposals to parliament. The Canadian Radio-television and Telecommunications Commission (CRTC) was established in 1968 to regulate all public and private broadcasting, including radio, television, cable, and commmunity antenna systems. This federal body was faced by increasing provincial demands for local control over some phases of these influential media.

The Unemployed

It has been estimated that approximately 25 per cent of Canada's wage earners were unemployed in 1935. They and destitute farmers on relief totalled 1.5 million. There was no established policy on social welfare, no unemployment insurance, no public health insurance ("medicare"), no guaranteed income supplement.

To alleviate the distress, the Bennett government in 1931 passed the Unemployment and Farm Relief Acts, but increasing amounts paid to the provinces were never enough. The unemployed, seeking work or at least relief from idleness, moved across the country on freight trains, usually stopping for short periods in the cities. Vancouver and other locations along the British Columbia coast were popular destinations, especially during the mild winters. In an effort to scatter the restless unemployed and to get them out of the cities, relief camps were set up across the country, some accommodating 2,000 men. Here they received board plus 20 cents a day and a little extra for cigarettes in return for building and maintaining roads and bridges, publicized as government make-work projects. To the men isolated in the camps, the dreary depressing days passed without purpose or future.

In 1935 the men from the camps, joined by unemployed from Vancouver, began a trek to Ottawa to demand work and wages. Riding the freights they converged at Regina where the government ordered them to stop. While the men waited, a delegation advanced to Ottawa where they received little sympathy and no promises from Bennett. Upon their return to Regina a riot broke out between marchers and police, in which one man was killed, many were injured and property damage ran into thousands of dollars. A few days later the men were dispersed in trains provided by the Saskatchewan government. A royal commission later blamed the riot on communist influences, perhaps missing the point that 1,300 disgruntled men could not be expected to wait in idleness for two weeks without trouble.

The Depression years, which saw thousands of unemployed willing to work for a pittance, were disastrous for the trade union movement. Conditions were fertile for the growth of communism but its appeal was weakened by the Regina riot which many people believed was communist inspired. Both the Trades and Labour Congress (TLC) and the Co-operative Commonwealth Federation (CCF) were led by moderate anticommunists, and communists were unable to win influential positions in either organization. It was at this time in the United States that the American Federation of Labor (AFL), which represented skilled workers, was being challenged by the Committee of Industrial Organization (CIO) which included unskilled as well as skilled workers. Their rivalry spread to Canada through the international unions and the labour movement was weakened by the contest between the crafts-oriented TLC and the broader-based Canadian Congress of Labour (CCL).

Bennett's New Deal

The Depression reached its lowest point in 1933 and for the next few years there was slow recovery, but it was not obvious. A Royal Commission on Price Spreads, under H. H. Stevens of Vancouver, revealed that in the retail trade many large businesses were overpricing their products. After embarrassing the government with his findings, Stevens resigned from the cabinet to start his own Reconstruction Party. Bennett, recognizing that drastic action was needed, impressed by Franklin D. Roosevelt's New Deal in the United States and facing an election, announced his own "New Deal" which promised to establish unemployment insurance with equal contributions from employers and employees, to define minimum wages, set hours of work, regulate marketing, oppose monopolies and unfair business practices, and to plan rehabilitation for the prairie provinces.

Many people blamed the Conservatives for the Depression and were dubious of this sudden about-face. The party itself was split by its leader's change of policies. The Liberals campaigned under the slogan "King or Chaos" and avoided making any but vague promises. To complicate matters, three new political parties were promising reforms: the CCF, Social Credit and Reconstruction. In the election of 1935, the Conservatives retained only 39 seats against the Liberals' 171. Saskatchewan and Manitoba voted overwhelmingly Liberal while British Columbia split its votes. The CCF took only 7 seats (3 in British Columbia and 2 each in Saskatchewan and Manitoba), the Social Credit 15 (all in Alberta), and Stevens was the sole Reconstruction Party MP.

Many of Bennett's reforms were later referred to the Privy Council which upheld only three: criminal code amendments against unfair business practices, an act to control monopolies, and a farmers' creditors act to alleviate the debt burden of farmers.

Co-operative Commonwealth Federation

Before the Depression, farm and labour groups had been working towards political co-operation. Under the leadership of such men as J. S. Woodsworth, M. J. Coldwell and T. C. Douglas, preliminary moves were made in Calgary in 1932 to form a Co-operative Commonwealth Federation of farmers, labour and socialists. Woodsworth has been recognized as one of the great parliamentarians of Canada. As a Methodist minister he worked for many years among the poor immigrants of Winnipeg, then resigned from the church and worked on the Vancouver waterfront where he became involved with labour organizations. He was one of the leaders arrested in the Winnipeg Strike. Woodsworth was a devoted pacifist, strongly anticommunist and a socialist. Often reviled for his socialist ideas, he never faltered in pursuing his aims. He died in 1942 and did not see many of his idealistic policies enacted into law by the Liberal governments. He is still remembered by members of all parties for his steadfastness against powerful opposition and for his devotion to the goal of a better society for all men and women.

M. J. Coldwell worked as a teacher and principal in Alberta and Saskatchewan for twenty-four years. He was consumed with the "well-being of the have-nots." He was president of the Canadian Teachers' Federation and later president of the Saskatchewan Independent Labour Party, a Regina alderman, chairman of the Calgary conference of farmer and labour groups in 1932 and eventually national secretary of the CCF. He continued to travel throughout Saskatchewan into the rural communities spreading CCF doctrine. First elected to the House of Commons in 1935, he served for twenty-three years, succeeding Woodsworth as leader of the party in 1942. He retired from active politics after his defeat in the Conservative sweep of 1958, but his reputation as a statesmen continued undiminished. In the words of Prime Minister Trudeau, "He was a politician, a parliamentarian, a humanitarian, and a man of courtesy and grace."

The founders of CCF were farmers, labour leaders and intellectuals. It differed from most protest parties in that it not only was provincial but also aimed from its founding to become national. The national convention in Regina in 1933 drew up the party's credo, "The Regina Manifesto," which called for the replacement of capitalism, the elimination of class exploitation, and for widespread government economic planning including the nationalization of such key industries as railways, banks and public utilities. As short-term objectives the new party advocated rural electrification, slum clearance and public works. There were proposals for government medical insurance as well as state-run hospitals and dental insurance. In general the CCF hoped to introduce into Canada an evolutionary socialism similar to that advanced by the British Labour Party.

The CCF's support was at first firmly agrarian. Although the unions sympathized with the movement, for many years they contributed very little active support. The aims of the landowning farmers and the middle classes of Saskatchewan were different from those of the wage-earning workers in industrial centres. The leaders of organized labour were not involved in the early organization of the party; in fact, they were not convinced that the unions should even be politically oriented. Given its limited appeal in urban Ontario, the movement remained strongest in the west. Avowedly socialist, the party disturbed many people to whom socialism was synonymous with communism. It gained adherents slowly as is shown by the disappointing results of the 1935 federal election; early provincial results were little better. The CCF had few funds and felt the opposition of business and the press. Its strength lay in the dedication of its members and their active participation in numerous local associations. They were fortunate in having in parliament a small group of hard-working, capable members who never failed to press for reform and whose influence belied their small numbers.

Social Credit in Alberta

William Aberhart was born in Ontario and in 1915 became a Calgary school principal. Here he became interested in a fundamentalist wing of the Baptist Church and became a lay preacher. A persuasive speaker in an era of evangelism, Aberhart built a large following and eventually established the

Calgary Prophetic Bible Institute. In 1925 he began preaching on radio and acquired a new audience in British Columbia, Saskatchewan and the neighbouring states.

In 1932 Aberhart became a supporter of "social credit"the unorthodox monetary theories of Maj. C. H. Douglas, a Scots engineer. Douglas maintained that a fundamental weakness of the capitalist system was that consumer spending power was never sufficient to equal potential production, the result of the existing financial system. To offset this disparity between consumer spending and production, Douglas proposed that the government issue "social dividends" in the form of cash payments to all citizens. Before long Aberhart was expounding his version of Social Credit over the radio. Albertans with little money to spend and impoverished by debt could see that the stores were overstocked, and the promise of a monthly dividend of twenty-five dollars made sense.

When the United Farmers of Alberta government refused to endorse Aberhart's policies, candidates for Social Credit entered the provincial election of 1935. The Social Credit Party swept the polls taking 56 seats against only 5 Liberals and 2 Conservatives; the UFA was completely wiped out and never recovered. Five days after the election, the Calgarian Bennett was defeated in the federal election.

Aberhart was an aggressive man who suffered no opposition and believed that government should be controlled by "experts": once in power he and his cabinet dictated policies. None of his caucus had been elected before, and the first two years were devoted to mastering the techniques of governing, so there was little opportunity to introduce radical change. As the UFA had learned many years earlier, new theories must be modified to the established system of government. Although the Depression was waning when the Social Credit Party took office, the farmers in the south suffered between 1934 and 1937 from grasshopper plagues, frost, and the drought and soil erosion of hot summers. It is estimated that 5,000 farmers in southern Alberta left their farms during these years. Given such problems, the new legislators had little opportunity to experiment with reforms.

Pressured by his followers, Aberhart did pass a number of items of provincial legislation aimed at controlling banking, credit and finance, but these were ruled outside provincial jurisdiction by the Alberta Supreme Court and eight were disallowed by the federal government. Aberhart was now able to claim that his attempts to institute reform were frustrated by the government in Ottawa and by the financial powers. No dividend was ever paid. For a short time a form of scrip was issued which acquired value as each week the holder bought and affixed a stamp until they added up to the face value. The experiment was short-lived, but the phrase "funny money" would come to haunt the Social Credit Party.

The provincial government was completely dominated by Aberhart, who contented himself with a conventional administration of the province. Encouraged by their provincial success, many adherents of Social Credit dreamed of expanding to the national level, but although Alberta elected 17 federal members in 1935, the party never lived up to its expectation of challenging the old federal parties.

Bracken and Anderson

All the western provinces were severely strained financially as debt charges and government costs mounted, with the added drain of relief spending. In Manitoba, John Bracken's government held on. He continued to lead his coalition, gaining Liberal support in 1932, against some opposition from the Labour Party and the CCF, but he was never in serious danger. The drought and unemployment had caused serious derangement of the province's finances, and in 1932 Bracken suggested a union of the three prairie provinces to reduce administration costs—a proposal that the others did not seriously consider. In the 1936 election Bracken was able to attract the new Social Credit members to his coalition.

In Saskatchewan, J. T. M. Anderson's coalition Conservatives suffered from their connection with the federal Conservatives. Because of the depressed conditions in the province, in 1931 the United Farmers of Canada (Saskatchewan Section) determined to enter politics and formed the Farmers' Political Association under the leadership of George Williams. In the cities, M. J. Coldwell was organizing the Independent Labour Party. In 1932 the two groups united to form the Farmer-

Labour Party which shortly became the CCF (Saskatchewan Section). In the election of 1934 J. G. Gardiner's Liberals were returned after four years out of office, while the Farmer-Labour Party, which had obtained 24 per cent of the votes but only five seats, was the official opposition. This was the first time since 1912 that the Saskatchewan legislature had only two distinct parties, but in the ensuing years dissenting voters were torn between the new rival parties Social Credit and CCF (SS). Gardiner resigned as premier to join Mackenzie King's cabinet and W. J. Patterson became premier. Undoubtedly assisted by the split in the opposition parties, the Liberals were again successful in 1938, but the CCF had ten seats and Social Credit two.

Tolmie and Pattullo

When the Conservative Dr. Tolmie won the 1928 election in British Columbia, the province's industries were reaching one of their most prosperous periods. Vancouver was the only western city to continue expanding both in population and financially after World War I, and eventually it passed Winnipeg to become Canada's third largest city. Today 50 per cent of British Columbians live in the province's southwest corner. The remainder are scattered throughout the province, mostly in valleys separated by high mountain ranges. Thus B.C. tends to become regionalized, not only between interior and coast but also among the separate interior communities. Agricultural land is scarce, and found in pockets which tend to be put to specialized intensive farming, such as the fruitlands of the Okanagan Valley, the wheatlands of the Peace River valley, or the dairy farms of the lower Fraser Valley. Scattered throughout the province are isolated lumbering and mining camps as well as fish canneries.

Instead of independent farmers working in a vast continuous area, B.C. had a large force of hired workers, some of them employed in the towns and cities but many living in small scattered camps. Dependent on daily wages for survival, they were for many years exploited by their employers. The conditions were ripe for the introduction of trade unions, which were recognized only after many years of bitter struggle. The dangerous, low-paying work and unhealthy camp conditions in the early days led to bitter confrontations between employees and employers and created a gap of mistrust which has never been completely bridged. Against the power of the employers, often supported by the government and press, the workers formed strong unions which have largely retained this attitude of militant confrontation. Today strikes are common, not only by labourers against industrialists, but also by civil servants and professional classes against governments.

In prosperity the Tolmie government had little to worry about, but the rapid decline after the stock market crash had immediate repercussions in British Columbia's primary industries as orders dried up and exports declined. Production was curtailed and men were laid off. In the cities, especially Vancouver, construction fell off and business dropped. The unemployed from the lumbering, mining and fishing centres poured into Vancouver and by December 1929 they were demonstrating.

The pleasant and easygoing Tolmie did not know how to handle this sudden crisis. His cabinet had been attempting to restrain government spending and he would not spend money until he received assistance from Ottawa, which was slow in coming. Meanwhile, more unemployed arrived in Vancouver escaping the harsher climate of the other provinces, adding to the already serious problem. When the Bennett government finally made a grant of $900,000 for relief, the money was passed on to the municipalities for distribution. The province undertook a vast public works program, setting up relief camps in an effort to reduce the burden of unemployed in the cities. British Columbia had about one-third of the relief camps in Canada.

Meanwhile, the provincial Liberal Party under Thomas Dufferin Pattullo was being reorganized. Tolmie, with a discontented party and unable to solve the problems of the Depression, suggested that a coalition government be formed. But Pattullo, sensing victory, refused the offer. As the election of 1933 approached, the new CCF party under the leadership of such people as Ernest E. Winch and Dorothy Steeves gained adherents. The Liberals won 34 seats, the Conservatives only 3 (Tolmie himself was defeated), and the CCF became the official opposition with 7 seats.

Pattullo was an MLA, had worked for the federal government in the Yukon, had been mayor of Prince Rupert and had strong ties with the interior. He has remained a figure of controversy, some chroniclers depicting him as an honest, generous man while others describe him as aloof and stubborn. Pattullo's policies were in contrast with his predecessor's. He believed that the government should not be reducing expenses but should be spending money and encouraging industry in order to alleviate unemployment. His government increased the relief scale and passed the Work and Wages Act which limited hours of work and fixed a minimum wage scale. Financial assistance was given to primary industries. He eliminated relief payments to nonresidents of the province. A broad public works program was begun, including the Fraser River bridge at New Westminster that bears his name. These steps were but a palliative, for in 1935 the unemployed began their "March to Ottawa" from Vancouver.

Pattullo's policy of "Work and Wages" brought the province close to bankruptcy. Because of the influx of unemployed from other provinces, he revived the western demand for "Better Terms" and an increase in grants from Ottawa. He insisted that these be received with no strings attached and that the province retain complete control of its finances, but both Bennett and Mackenzie King refused to make such grants unless they had some control over expenditures. Pattullo also failed in his attempts to unload the Pacific Great Eastern Railway on the federal railway system. Thus, in spite of their both being nominally Liberals, there was increasing animosity between Pattullo and an unsympathetic King. In 1937 the provincial electorate approved Pattullo's policies when his party won 38 seats to the Conservatives' 8. The socialist groups were handicapped by internal dissension: the CCF remained at 7.

Although conditions had improved by 1936, there were still many unemployed and Vancouver continued to be the recipient of immigrants fleeing the prairie drought. When in 1938 it was announced that no relief would be given to unemployed from outside British Columbia, a mob subsequently occupied the post office, the art gallery and the Hotel Georgia. After two weeks, the RCMP cleared the buildings, and before the demonstration ended a riot spread through the business section.

The Rowell-Sirois Commission

In 1935 the Liberal Party returned to power in Ottawa after the low point of the Depression had passed; the country was gradually recovering, though there was a short slowdown in 1938–39. One of the new government's first acts was to revise Bennett's unemployment scheme, receiving the consent of all provinces to bring unemployment insurance under the federal government; the British parliament amended the BNA Act to make this possible in 1940.

Early in 1936, following a visit by Mackenzie King to President Roosevelt, a moderate reciprocal trade agreement was made with the United States from which the west benefited. Both countries lowered their tariffs on a large number of specified items. The listed imports into Canada included automobiles, agricultural machinery, books, films, and some natural products such as cotton and vegetables. The benefits to Canada included the free export of many agricultural products, fish, minerals such as nickel and asbestos, lumber and wood pulp.

The drought that had ruined so many wheat farmers eased in some regions in 1935 and production revived. In that year the federal government established the Canadian Wheat Board, which was continually troubled by grain surpluses that had to be stored and therefore required large federal subsidies.

The Depression emphasized the complexity of Canadian federation, the variety of regional interests and the limited constitutional rights of the federal government in its attempts to interfere with provincial rights. In 1937 King established a Royal Commission on Dominion-Provincial Relations (the Rowell-Sirois commission) to investigate Canadian fiscal and constitutional problems.

The commission pointed out that the original Fathers of Confederation had planned a strong central government by specifying the powers of the provinces while retaining the residual powers to itself. In the ensuing years a series of decrees by the British Privy Council had, in fact, given residual powers to the provinces for regulating wage levels, hours of work, trade unions and public health. Moreover, areas under provincial jurisdiction, such as education, social services and highways, had expanded far beyond the limits anticipated in 1867. The provinces had become responsible for very costly services on limited revenue resources, since the major powers of taxation rested with the federal government. The commission also noted that regional disparity was increasing.

The *Rowell-Sirois Report* made several significant recommendations to eliminate inequalities among the provinces, among them a system of "adjustment grants" to provide each province with adequate funds. Unemployment relief, which had been administered haphazardly during the Depression years, should become a federal responsibility. The provinces were to allow the federal government full powers for the collection of direct taxes personal income tax, corporation tax and succession duties.

The report was brought before a dominion-provincial conference in 1941 when delegates from Ontario, Alberta and British Columbia refused to discuss it, fearing that it would lead to further centralization. Instead, in the midst of war, agreements were made between the federal and provincial levels of government allowing the former more financial and economic powers for the pursuance of the war effort. The report was laid aside, but its recommendations were not forgotten. It had given influential expression to the belief that the state had a responsibility to act positively for the social and economic welfare of the people. This belief, following the Depression and strengthened by the war effort, was to have a profound effect in postwar Canadian politics and to encourage welfare legislation. The problems of division of powers, division of taxes and the responsibilites of each level of government would be reconsidered after the war.

While Canada was recovering from the Depression, events abroad were inexorably drawing the country into its second great war. The war demands on industry and manpower would end the Depression decisively.

Background to War

During the 1930s Canadians were beset by internal social dislocations and were only minimally concerned with the critical events in Asia and Europe. They held certain assumptions in international affairs. National autonomy, achieved so recently, had to be preserved at all costs, and any outside interference, whether by a national or international body, was to be avoided. As a trading nation, Canada's best interests would be served by avoiding international commitments that would antagonize customers and restrict freedom of trade. As a North American nation isolated from the historic rivalries in Asia and Europe, Canada could only be adversely affected by involvement in the wrangling of those regions.

Canada had insisted on membership in the League of Nations as a sign of its growing autonomic status, but even before the covenant was signed Canada had tried unsuccessfully to weaken article 10, which established a system of collective security under which League members undertook to enforce mutual peace throughout the nations of the world. Thus from the beginning Canada was lukewarm in supporting League action against aggression.

In defence of Mackenzie King's policy of neutrality, it has to be recognized that past involvement in foreign affairs had been a divisive force in Canadian affairs. For instance, when Italy invaded Abyssinia in 1935, the League voted for sanctions against Italy, yet when the Canadian representative suggested that essential oil be added to the list of banned exports, King repudiated his plan. And to Canadian businessmen the growth of foreign military strength meant increased orders for armaments, which required minerals and other products that Canada could supply. Italy, for example, ordered the light, nonsplintering sitka spruce from the Queen Charlotte Islands to be used in airplane wings.

From 1935 to 1939 Canada increased its defence expenditures slightly but maintained its permanent force at less than 4,000 men. A small number of Canadians did recognize the threat of militarism and dictatorship. Pickets in Vancouver protested the loading of ships for Japan carrying iron, copper and scrap metals. Some people became actively involved abroad. Approximately 1,250 volunteers fought in Spain to support the democratically elected government against the dictatorship of Francisco Franco.

Beginning of War

When Germany invaded Poland, Britain declared war, and a week later, on 10 September 1939, the Canadian parliament, with only three dissenting votes, supported an independent declaration of war.

Within a short time measures had been taken to organize the country for war. The War Measures Act of 1914 was proclaimed to be in force again, granting the cabinet extraordinary powers through orders-in-council. Steps were taken to suppress suspected subversive organizations and intern some aliens, to increase the armed forces, to establish censorship, and to lay the foundations for a wartime economy. Volunteers from all parts of the country joined the navy, air force and army. The northern bush pilots were important assets to the RCAF (whose 220,000 members made it the fourth largest air force) as well as the RAF. One of Canada's main contributions to the war was the organization and maintenance of the Commonwealth Air Training Plan, a scheme that brought over 130,000 airmen from all parts of the Commonwealth to train in Canada.

For two years it was a European war and Canadian forces were shipped from eastern ports and airfields to Britain. The first action seen by Canadian troops in Europe was at Dieppe on 19 August 1942. The 5,000 Canadians formed the bulk of the 6,100-member striking force in this ill-fated sally. The 3,000 men killed, wounded or taken prisoner included 346 of the 503 Queen's Own Highlanders from Winnipeg, 339 of the 523-man South Saskatchewan Regiment, and 174 of the Calgary Tank Regiment.

Following the reciprocal agreements of 1936, co-operation between Canada and the United States grew. Prime Minister King kept in personal contact with President Roosevelt and believed that he had considerable influence as a mediator in cementing good relations between Roosevelt and Winston Churchill. When Britain declared war, the American neutrality laws handicapped Roosevelt in his desire to assist Britain, but for a week he was able to supply goods to "neutral" Canada. At various prairie border points, planes and materials were landed and hauled into Canada by Canadians.

In August 1940, the Ogdensburg Agreement established the Permanent Joint Board of Defence which co-ordinated North American defences. By the Hyde Park Agreement of 1941, Canada and the U.S. undertook to complement each other's war production.

The Pacific War and Japanese Evacuation

While the European war was being fought, Japan, a member of the Axis, continued its war in China, and Britain and the United States were bringing pressure on Japan to limit its military expansion. On the Canadian west coast there was increasing opposition to the resident Japanese. King agreed to stop shipment of wheat and timber to Japan but he did not want to take too drastic measures for fear of Japanese retaliation against Canadian missionaries and traders. He was worried that British and American policies might involve Canada in a war with Japan. Because such a war did not seem imminent, however, Canada willingly sent two battalions to Hong Kong in 1941 to relieve the British troops of garrison duty.

On 7 December 1941 the Japanese bombed Pearl Harbor and the United States entered the war. Canada, along with Britain, immediately joined the United States in declaring war on Japan. Japanese forces spread rapidly through southeast Asia and the Pacific. In Hong Kong, Canadian troops became involved in their first battle of the Second World War. The partially trained, poorly equipped force, which included members of the Winnipeg Grenadiers, held out for seventeen days before surrendering on Christmas Day. Of the 290 Winnipeg Grenadiers, 139 were dead. Of the 1,975 Canadians involved, 557 died in battle or the prison camps.

The military position of western Canada was drastically changed by the Pacific war. No longer were the hostilities far across the continent and the Atlantic, for now western Canada, and particularly the Pacific coast, was threatened. During the first two years of war, Canada's Atlantic defences had been strengthened but only minimal attention had been given to those of the west coast. Now these became vital, and to remedy their vulnerability, they were strengthened and new posts were established along the entire coast.

Invasion did come to the Pacific coast. In June 1942 Japanese forces occupied the two westernmost Aleutian Islands, Attu and Kiska, and bombed Dutch Harbor, an American base on Unalaska Island: Japanese troops were on North American soil, threatening Alaska and occupying sites for possible air attacks into western Canada. Japanese submarines ranged from the coast of California northward. A British freighter was sunk in Juan de Fuca Strait. A submarine shelled Estevan Point light-house on Vancouver Island but did no serious damage—the first and only attack on Canadian soil by foreign troops since the Fenian raids of 1867.

In the autumn of 1944 the Japanese launched 9,000 balloons carrying high explosives or incendiary bombs. Carried by the prevailing winds, they floated over western Canada and the northern states. The objective was to cause forest fires and uncertainty in western North America as well as to raise Japa-nese morale. Of the few balloons that reached Canada, most dropped in British Columbia, but some were discovered as far east as Manitoba. The Japanese experiment did little damage and was abandoned.

As mentioned, when the war began in 1939 Canada made moves to suppress suspected subversive organizations and a number of aliens were imprisoned. Although there was some prejudice against people of German, Austrian or Italian origin, no extreme demonstrations occurred like those during the First World War. Many such people on the prairies were third- or fourth-generation Canadians and in some communities they made up the bulk of the population. This toleration, however, did not extend to the Japanese on the west coast.

Canada, the United States and Mexico all evacuated the Jap-anese from coastal areas and transferred them inland. In Can-ada thirty-eight Japanese who were suspected of being subver-sives were arrested immediately after Pearl Harbour. Japanese-language schools and newspapers were closed. Prime Minister King was dubious at first about taking overt action, for he feared retaliation against the Canadians captured at Hong Kong; but fears of Japanese raids and possible disorders from the anti-Oriental elements on the west coast forced him to agree to evacuation in February 1942.

In Canada, all coastal Japanese were assembled in centres

and distributed to inland camps as far east as Ontario. Japanese assets, such as fishing boats, motor vehicles and businesses, were seized and auctioned off for a fraction of their worth. Families were broken up. No distinction was made between recent arrivals and those who were born in the country—Nisei—or were naturalized. In all, 23,000 were moved, three-quarters of them Canadian-born. The speed of evacuation caught both the Japanese and authorities unprepared, and the makeshift camps hastily assembled meant months of suffering before federal aid alleviated conditions.

A few Nisei had joined the Canadian forces before Pearl Harbor and had fought in Europe, but west coast opinion was opposed to their enlistment. Premier Pattullo feared that if they were recruited they would demand the franchise. But after the first panic had subsided, the co-operation of some Nisei was sought: in 1945 a quota was set on 150 Nisei volunteers who did valuable work not only in battle but also as interpreters and translators during wartime and the occupation of Japan.

After the war almost 4,000 Japanese returned to Japan. Most remained in Canada but established themselves far from the west coast. (The 1971 census showed 15,600 Japanese Canadians in Ontario but only 13,785 in British Columbia. Alberta had only 4,460, Manitoba 1,335 and Saskatchewan 315.) Led by the Nisei, they took steps to recover their losses and to regain citizenship rights. The compensation they received was far below actual losses.

In 1947, when the Canadian Chinese Immigration Act of 1923 was repealed, full citizenship rights were extended to Chinese resident in Canada for five years. In 1949, Chinese and Japanese Canadians were enfranchised.

Controls and Reform

During the First World War, inflation had caused prices to rise rapidly followed by demands for increased wages and worker strikes. Mackenzie King was determined to avoid a repetition of those conditions. In 1939 the Wartime Prices and Trade Board was created and later its powers were strengthened; eventually it imposed a total freeze on wages and prices. No other Allied nation was able to match Canada in the success of these anti-inflation measures. Rationing was established for many items such as butter, sugar, tires, gasoline and alcohol, and food coupons limited the amount of specified goods that could be purchased. Every clothing item carried a label stating the price as set by the government. Because automobile production had been displaced by war industries, secondhand cars were in demand and ceiling prices were set for every model. (After the war, when automobile production revived, would-be new car buyers would wait a year for delivery.) Propaganda in support of the war was organized and censorship imposed.

The National Service Act in 1942 classified essential jobs and forbade people holding them to move to higher-paying work. Jobs in agriculture and education were among those categorized as essential. The shortage of manpower combined with the demand for materials of all kinds meant full employment. Labour unions almost doubled their membership during the war, from 359,000 in 1939 to 711,000 in 1945. As the unions gained strength, they demanded more recognition and opposed attempts to control their activities. When the federal government established a number of labour boards, labour accused them of favouring the employers, and the employees' newly won right to organize and to collective bargaining was ignored. As a result, during the years 1941 to 1943, militant strikes were common in almost all industries, even such strategic war industries as coal mining, steel production, aircraft building and munitions. In 1943 there were more Canadian strikes than in any previous year. The war effort was being seriously handicapped, and the federal government was forced to establish the Wartime Labour Relations Board in 1943 which discouraged labour strife by accepting the right of labour to organize and by encouraging collective bargaining and arbitration.

The War Industries Control Board was headed by Clarence Decatur Howe, who in 1940 had been appointed minister of munitions and supply. In 1913 Howe had been appointed by the Board of Grain Supervisors to build elevators. From this start, he formed his own company as a consulting engineer, working always with the farmers' co-operatives and specializing in the construction of grain elevators. He became familiar with the west and its grain problems as his elevators spread across Canada and north to Churchill. He never forgot his "own association with the west." In 1935 he was elected member of parliament for Port Arthur, which he had developed as a grain terminal. Howe first served in the cabinet as minister of railways and marine. He was responsible for the National Harbours Board and introduced the bill establishing the Canadian Broadcasting Corporation. Later he became minister of transport and then, in wartime, moved to minister of munitions and supply.

Howe brought his proven abilities as an organizer to one of the most demanding and important war departments, with a budget in the billions of dollars. Under his leadership Canada produced ships, tanks, rifles, ammunition, artillery and aircraft. New factories were built across the nation. The number of shipyards increased from fourteen to ninety, many on the west coast. To ensure production, Howe insisted on federal control of essential materials such as lumber, oil and steel, and set up numerous crown corporations. One of them, Polymer Limited, created a new chemical industry with its manufacture of synthetic rubber to replace the imported natural rubber cut off by the war. Towards the end of the war, Howe was made minister of reconstruction, responsible for postwar reorganization and the encouragement of new industries to take advantage of the wartime-trained manpower. Later, as minister of trade and commerce, he was influential in adjusting grain exports to postwar requirements. During the Korean War, he was appointed minister of defence production. Howe served under three prime ministers and, next to them, was the most powerful figure in government. He was a driving man who acted with authority and was impatient of delay. In wartime rapid decisions were necessary, but in peacetime his authoritative, dominating approach was not acceptable and eventually led to bitter opposition which accused him of being rigid and unbending. Ten years after the war, his great wartime contributions were overshadowed by his dictatorial actions in forcing closure of the House debate on the Trans-Canada Pipeline.

Although Mackenzie King won the election of 1940 with an overwhelming 178 Liberal seats, he recognized that CCF successes in provincial elections indicated a growing force of pro-

test. In order to weaken that party's appeal as well as to gain
the support of the labour unions, the government introduced a
number of reforms: farm improvement loans, a fisheries support program, the Industrial Development Board, the National
Insurance Act, the Veteran's Insurance Act and unemployment
insurance. By 1946 the Dominion government was paying 75
per cent of the old age pension introduced in 1927. One of the
most innovative actions of the King government was its family
allowance legislation, passed in 1944 and scheduled to take
effect in July 1945, after the election. The vote on second reading of this bill is a rare example of unanimous agreement
among the Liberal, Conservative, CCF and Social Credit members. On third reading *Hansard* did not even record the vote
but merely recorded the bill as passed.

Defence of the North Pacific

An overland route from the United States to Alaska through
Canada had been discussed intermittently since the mid-1930s.
In 1938 Premier Pattullo had visited President Roosevelt and
reported to Prime Minister King that Roosevelt was prepared to
lend up to $15 million for a highway. King was dubious about
permitting American financial penetration of Canada and
feared also that the U.S. might use the road for the movement
of troops through a neutral Canada in a war with Japan. That
year a Canadian-U.S. commission was appointed to explore the
financial and political problems of such a road, but there was
little enthusiasm at the federal levels and its research dragged.

The war with Japan demanded close co-operation between
Canadian and American defences. Air bases in British Columbia, mainland Alaska and the Aleutians were used by both
commands and the protection of shipping became a joint
responsibility. The port of Prince Rupert boomed as a base for
American troops bound for Alaska and the north Pacific. But
the ocean route, which was supplying materials to Russia as
well as protecting the coast, was vulnerable to Japanese submarine attacks so inland routes became a necessity, especially
after the Japanese occupation of Attu and Kiska.

Three major projects were undertaken. Air routes were
extended from the central United States through Edmonton

along a Northwest Staging Route to Alaska. Edmonton became a centre of activity, teeming with Americans. From there the Edmonton, Dunvegan and British Columbia Railway carried goods to Dawson Creek, from which point a new artery, the Alaska (or Alcan) Highway was built by the U.S. Army and Canadian civilians. The highway was begun in August 1942 and the 1,600 miles (2570 km) to Fairbanks were passable within a year. Because speed of construction was essential, the road at first detoured around such obstacles as swamps and gullies and it was not until the following year that bridge construction was begun and the road upgraded. At the end of the war in 1946, maintenance of the 1,200-mile (1930-km) Canadian portion was transferred to Canada, which in 1962 turned the British Columbia section over to the provincial Department of Highways. Since that time the road has been upgraded and partially paved.

The third project was the building of an oil pipeline over mountainous terrain from Norman Wells to the refineries at Whitehorse. At an estimated cost of $130 million, the Canol pipeline was the largest defence undertaking authorized by the Canadian government and part of the joint defence agreements with the U.S. Necessary to ensure oil supplies during wartime, this costly scheme was abandoned after the war. In that period of crisis, no time was spent on preliminary impact studies of the environment or effort made to protect native rights.

On 11 May 1943 a bloody American assault on Attu killed almost all the Japanese garrison of 2,300 and regained the island. Kiska had a larger garrison and elaborate plans were made for its invasion. Canada asked to be included in the project and thus 5,300 Canadians were in the assault force of 34,000. When the troops arrived at Kiska on 13 August, they found that the Japanese had deserted the island. For the first time a Canadian force had served under American command, and for the first time had left directly from Canadian shores prepared for offensive action.

The Allied occupation of Attu and Kiska lessened the threat of air attack on western Canada, but the flow of war materials along the Northwest Staging Route and Alcan continued since Alaska was useful to the Allies for another reason: from there war materials were shipped on Russian vessels to Siberian railway terminals without fear of Japanese attack since these two nations were not yet at war.

The Permanent Joint Board of Defence proved its value during the war, especially in the north Pacific, and continued into the postwar years. The rise of the Cold War, along with improvements in aircraft and the advent of missiles capable of crossing the high Arctic, led in 1958 to the establishment of the North American Aerospace Defence Command (NORAD), permitting joint defence posts in Canada's north. The agreement is periodically renewed in spite of opponents who believe that the presence of American forces will inevitably draw Canada into an American war.

The Politics of Wartime

Mackenzie King vividly remembered the disruption caused by conscription in the First World War and was resolved that it should not be repeated. He recognized that there was strong opposition not only in Quebec but also from the labour unions, the CCF, various pacifist religious groups, and even in his cabinet. To strengthen his position he suddenly called the election of 1940. Although his overwhelming majority indicated the support of the people, dissatisfied groups remained, especially in the west.

In an attempted compromise on the conscription issue, Mackenzie King introduced in 1940 the National Resources Mobilization Act, which gave the government wide controls including the right to conscript men for training and service in Canada but which explicitly forbade conscription for overseas duty. This act was followed by national registration, which required all people over sixteen to carry registration cards. Then in 1942 King called for a plebiscite asking the electorate to release the government from its pledge to refrain from full conscription. The result was overwhelming approval, except in Quebec where it obtained less than one-third support, thus verifying King's belief that conscription would split the country.

Following the Normandy invasion in 1944, Canada began to fall behind in maintaining manpower levels, so after trying vainly to postpone the crisis the prime minister was forced to concede: an order-in-council approved the dispatch of 16,000 home-service conscripts to Europe. Very few of them were actually sent and this, combined with King's obvious reluctance, lessened his opposition in the country. The 1945 election returned the Liberals with a reduced majority of 125 seats, and although the Conservatives had increased theirs from 39 to 67, the new challenge was the CCF's 28 seats and the 10 Social Credit seats from Alberta.

The Cost of War

Since 1867 the federal government had shown a tendency to assume ever-greater powers and this centralization was accentuated during the 1939–45 war when national problems took precedence over local ones. Centralized economic control was essential for directing the heavy taxation requirements for war. This was achieved by new federal-provincial tax rental agreements by which the provinces vacated the fields of corporation and income taxes to the federal government in return for direct subsidies, thus enhancing the powers of the federal government in relation to those of the provinces. This federal predominance was to remain a major factor in postwar politics and has been increasingly challenged. Other means of raising money were found in excess-profit taxes, compulsory savings and war savings stamps. Most borrowing was through Victory Loan bonds purchased by Canadian citizens to be repaid after the war. Before the First World War, Canada's national debt was $134 million. By 1918 this had increased to $314 million and by the end of the Second World War was over $11 billion.

The costs of war cannot be measured only in dollars or materials—the amount of waste or destruction. National and international economic and social patterns were destroyed and would take many years to adjust to normal conditions. The loss in lives ran into millions. Of the 780,000 Canadians who served in the war, 37,476 were killed in action. Thousands of others were injured, many of them crippled or hospitalized for life. Few families in Canada were unaffected by the casualty toll, and the loss and disruption of war would never be forgotten.

Industrial Development

With the heavy demands of war, Canada's primary and secondary industries expanded at an unprecedented rate, though during the last year production began to slacken. By 1944 agricultural production had increased 30 per cent. Forest production replaced Britain's lost Scandinavian sources. Mining expanded to meet the war consumption of copper, lead, nickel and zinc. Above all, the war brought increased demands for such secondary goods as pulp and paper, iron and steel products, electrical equipment, airplanes, trucks and high-octane gasoline. New techniques and products were introduced, such as electronic equipment and synthetic rubber, and remained integral to the economy after the war. It has been estimated that 70 per cent of Canada's wartime production went to its allies.

Experiments were being carried out in Britain and the United States towards the development of atomic bombs and by 1939 scientists had determined that nuclear fission and atomic power could be achieved using uranium. The Eldorado Mine on the eastern shore of Great Bear Lake had been working a deposit of pitchblende, which contains uranium, between 1933 and 1940; when the Americans needed large amounts of uranium, the government of Canada bought a majority interest in Eldorado and revived production. With an assured supply of Canadian uranium, the United States was able to expand its research and prepare the bomb that was to change the power structure of the world.

The Conflict Ends

At the end of the war Canada was a different nation from that of 1939. The unemployment and Depression of the '30s had given way to new industries, a wide export market and full employment. Canada's contribution to the war effort in both men and materials had brought it to the forefront of world powers. Canada was a signing member of the United Nations in 1945, where it asserted its position as a leading middle power and accepted its responsibilities as a member of the international community in search of permanent peace. The war had confirmed Canada's ties with Britain and had increased its economic and military connections with the United States.

Domestically, Canada in 1945 was on the brink of an era of unprecedented expansion. A wealth of raw materials combined with a strong industrial and commercial economy allowed the country to look forward to the fruits of peace. The coming years would see the emergence of the west as a major force in Canada's economic, social and political development.

Chapter Nine

POSTWAR YEARS:
THE WEALTHY WEST

For twenty years after the war western Canada followed earlier-established patterns of population and industrial expansion. In the 1960s, certain national and international developments suggested radical changes for the west. New mineral and energy sources broadened Canada's economic base. The revival of Japan and other Pacific nations as well as the international recognition of the Chinese communist government opened new trade opportunities and made Canada a Pacific as well as an Atlantic power. The proliferation of air travel and communications ended Canada's isolation from world affairs. Postwar applied science, as opposed to "pure" science, affected entire cultures, transforming everything from major industry to home entertainment. Technological advances enhanced the fears that a new war would devastate mankind; Canadians, situated between Russia and the United States, watched with trepidation the vacillation between cold war and détente. Increased regionalism within Canada itself threatened the unity of the country: tensions grew between provinces, between provincial and federal governments and between the regional interests of west and east.

Agriculture

Although the rapid growth of secondary industries continued after the war, prairie wheat remained the foundation of not

only the prairie economy but also the transportation industry
to both coasts. In the postwar period agricultural production
fluctuated from year to year, responding to the habitual uncer-
tainties of frost, floods, drought and plagues. The shortage of
water has now been alleviated by dam construction. In 1958 a
provincial-federal agreement was reached by which the largest
earth dam in Canada was constructed on the South
Saskatchewan River and a smaller one on the Qu'Appelle. The
final cost of the project, completed in 1967, was $196 million,
of which the federal government paid 75 per cent. The dams
created a lake 140 miles (225 km) long which could supply
water for the irrigation of up to 400,000 acres (160 000 ha), as
well as provide domestic supplies, recreational facilities and
power generation. With the agricultural improvements resulting from scientific research and advanced technology, and
with the stabilizing control of the Canadian Wheat Board,
farmers were able to mitigate the setbacks of poor crop years
and achieve more stability. The Wheat Board became the sole
marketing agency for prairie wheat, oats and barley, though
after 1974 domestic marketing of feed grains was permitted on
the open market.

The strong postwar demand for wheat in western Europe
declined as continental agricultural production returned to
normal. Canada faced strong competition from other wheat
producers—Australia, Argentina and the United States—and
world production began to outstrip demand. Despite international agreements, the price declined. The major prewar markets of Europe which had taken over 60 per cent of Canada's
wheat took less than 20 per cent in 1977–78, while the United
States market dropped from 20 per cent to less than 2 per cent
in the same period. In 1969 a two-price system was established
for wheat sold in Canada which set a guaranteed floor price. In
1970 the government took drastic measures to reduce the surplus by the Lower Inventory for Tomorrow (LIFT) program:
farmers were paid six dollars per acre (0.4 ha) for wheat acreage converted to summer fallow and ten dollars per acre to
convert to perennial forage acreage.

The Canadian wheat trade was saved by the increased
exports to the People's Republic of China, the Soviet Union,
Japan and other Asiatic countries. Canada's recognition of the

People's Republic of China in 1970 was followed by a large growth of trade. Whereas China trade was $105 million in 1965, it reached a record $438 million in 1974, after which it declined slightly. Between 1965 and 1972 only once were wheat exports less than 90 per cent of Canada's total exports to China; in 1977 wheat still totalled 84 per cent. A large percentage of Canada's limited trade with Russia is in also wheat. As a result of a long-term sales contract in 1969, the Soviet Union was Canada's largest market for wheat in 1972–73; its purchase of 147.9 million bushels was 30 per cent of Canada's total wheat exports and 85 per cent of total exports to Russia. When the United States restricted its sale of wheat to Russia because of the invasion of Afghanistan, Canada set a limit on sales of 4.2 million tons (3.8 million t) for the 1979–80 year. In the following year Canada eased its restraints and sold almost 6.6 million tons (6 million t). (Later in 1981 the American ban was lifted.) Canada's early relaxation of the embargo paid dividends, for in 1981 Canada made a five-year agreement to supply Russia with a minimum of 27.5 million tons (25 million t), for an estimated $5 billion. Until then wheat sales to Russia were unreliable because they depended largely on the variable Russian harvests. Japan has become Canada's third largest wheat market.

The change in Canada's wheat export patterns has had repercussions in western Canada, such as growing discontent with the inefficiency of grain handling. Shortages of railcars have meant slow delivery to ports. When the grain does arrive, the west coast ports do not have the facilities to handle it with expediency. Every day grain ships lie idle in Vancouver's outer harbour: for the crop year 1977–78 Canada paid an estimated demurrage on them of $17 million to $20 million. To relieve these bottlenecks, the federal government continues to promise better transportation and storage facilities. Major construction is planned or underway for Churchill, Vancouver and Prince Rupert; completion of the proposed projects will take several years, but the expanding Asia markets, for which there is so much competition, make them essential. Revisions to the National Harbours Board proposed in 1981 would give ports more local participation in planning, but the federal government would retain control. Meanwhile, farmers continue to struggle with natural crop hazards as well as uncertain storage facilities, deliveries and sales, for which they blame the disinterest and unreliability of the federal government.

Minerals

World War II had given impetus to Canadian mineral production. For instance, Canada supplied 80 per cent of the Allied nickel requirements. In 1940 when the mine at Yellowknife opened, Canada ranked second to South Africa in gold production, but the wartime government felt that the miners were more essential in other fields and gold mining decreased. Mineral production continued to accelerate after the war and included newly important minerals for modern science and industry—platinum, cobalt, titanium, molybdenum, tantalum, tungsten and potash. Air routes and new mining technology opened new sites.

In 1959 uranium was discovered at Lake Athabasca. The nickel-copper mine at Thompson, Manitoba, was made profitable by a railway. Similarly, a railway was constructed to the new lead-zinc mine at Pine Point on Great Bear Lake, which was brought into production in 1965. Important for Saskatchewan was the discovery in the southeast of the largest high-grade potash deposits in the world. In 1962 the first successful and largest potash mine was opened near Esterhazy, and by the end of the decade nine other mines were producing. The government controlled production and sales through the Potash Corporation of Saskatchewan. Copper, molybdenum and asbestos were discovered in British Columbia. Asbestos was found in the Yukon and tungsten in the Northwest Territories. From the end of the war until 1976, the value of Canadian mineral production increased thirty times.

Petroleum and Natural Gas

Crude petroleum in varying quantities is found in many parts of Canada; early explorers to western Canada had recorded oil seeps, but the presence of commercial amounts was not recognized until 1912–14, when shallow wells were discovered at Turner Valley resulting in a short speculative period which ended with World War I. The first major crude oil well was brought into production in Turner Valley in 1936, but war again interrupted expansion. During the war Norman Wells fields supplied the Canol pipeline, but this was abandoned after the war. By 1944 production in Turner Valley was declining and there had been little progress in the search for large reserves.

In February 1947 the Leduc oil field was discovered seventeen miles (27 km) south of Edmonton. Until then Canada had imported 90 per cent of its oil, mostly from the United States and Venezuela. After the discovery at Leduc, the federal government planned to make Canada less dependent on imported oil, which was nonetheless cheaper than Alberta's. Two major pipelines were built across Canada. A network of feeder lines carried oil to the main trunk lines at Edmonton. From there the Interprovincial Pipe Line extends through southern Ontario to refineries at Montreal; en route it receives Saskatchewan and Manitoba crude oil. The Trans Mountain Oil Pipeline carries oil from Edmonton to refineries in Burnaby, near Vancouver. Subsidiary lines from both major trunk lines carry export oil to U.S. refineries. See Map 12. Thus Alberta oil was to serve Ontario, western Quebec and the west while imported oil supplied eastern Quebec and the Maritimes.

Before 1960 the United States was the biggest producer of oil, which was controlled by a few companies. The American and some European companies opened oil fields in other parts of the world, including Canada; the richest of them would be in the Arab states. By 1970, while the demand for oil was rising rapidly, U.S. oil production had begun to decline and the Middle East fields became vital to western economies. In 1960 the Organization of Petroleum Exporting Countries (OPEC) had been formed by thirteen countries including some Arab states, Venezuela and Nigeria. (Canada, except for a small amount of exports to the U.S., is an importer of oil.) In 1973 the OPEC member nations demanded and got almost double the previous price for oil from the oil companies; at the end of the year the world price was $5.04 a barrel U.S. funds, slightly higher than the Canadian price of $3.80 Canadian. The world price escalated rapidly until in 1981 OPEC set it at $36 U.S. ($40.80 Canadian).

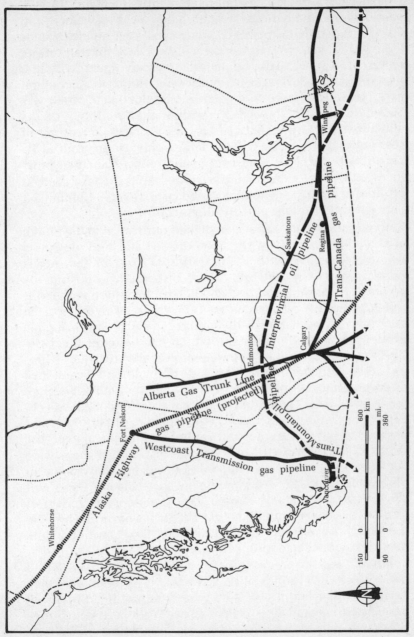

MAP 11: OIL AND GAS PIPELINES

The rise in oil prices combined with the decline in U.S. production and the discoveries at Leduc awakened interest in Canadian petroleum possibilities. Almost two hundred fields were tested, many of them successfully. These spurred further research; in some years the major companies spent $1 billion on exploration, development and production of oil and natural gas. The total value of Canadian oil production in 1980 was $9.1 billion, of which Alberta contributed $7.9 billion. Alberta contains over 70 per cent of Canada's recoverable reserves of conventional crude oil but consumes only 18 per cent of its production. Sixty-four per cent goes to other Canadian provinces and the remainder to the United States. Saskatchewan produces about 12 per cent of Canada's oil, British Columbia 3 per cent and Manitoba a small amount.

Exploratory wells have been drilled northward to the mouth of the Mackenzie River, the Beaufort Sea and into the Arctic Islands. Alberta's northern oil sands are one of the largest known reserves in the world. The four major deposits underlie an area 27,000 square miles (70 000 km^2) in eastern and northern Alberta. The recovery of oil from these reserves has been and remains a challenge to modern science. The principle product is synthetic crude oil, which can be refined as gasoline, jet fuel and other petroleum products. By 1980, Great Canadian Oil Sands and Syncrude Canada had begun two open-pit mines. In the Syncrude agreement of 1975, development funds were committed by the governments of Alberta (10 per cent), Ontario (5 per cent) and Canada (15 per cent), and because of the vast amounts of capital and technical expertise required to develop oil sands properties, most of these were controlled by major oil companies through twenty-one-year renewable leases from the provincial government. Depressed oil markets in 1982–83 caused capital to dry up and most sands projects were put on hold. Cumulative government revenues from leases to the end of 1978 were $35.5 million, while royalties amounted to $110.2 million.

Natural gas was found in western Canada in the 1870s and began to be used locally about 1900. It was never of more than local importance until 1954–59 when the first interprovincial pipelines were built. The Trans-Canada Pipeline system begins near the Alberta-Saskatchewan border, where it collects Alberta and Saskatchewan gas, and extends through Montreal along the St. Lawrence Valley with connections to American pipelines. The Westcoast Transmission Company collects gas by lateral pipelines from northeastern British Columbia, western Alberta and the Northwest Territories to its pipeline running from Fort Nelson to the American border at Sumas, south of Vancouver, and has branch lines serving many communities throughout the province. (See Map 12.)

Natural gas is often found together with oil, and Manitoba is the only western province without it. About 75 per cent of Canada's producing gas wells are in Alberta. From 1967 to 1978 western Canada's natural gas production doubled, from 43 867 million m^3 to 87 223 million m^3 a year. Of the latter figure, Alberta had 75 329, British Columbia 8724, Saskatchewan 1643 and the territories 527.

Expansion of the oil and natural gas industries has brought new wealth to the three westernmost provinces. Related industries have sprung up, along with the production of such by-products as sulphur, propane and butane. Thousands of new jobs have been created, resulting in the growth of cities and nonagricultural activities. In 1980, when the average unemployment rate for Canada was 7.8 per cent, British Columbia had 6.8 per cent, Manitoba 5.5 per cent, Saskatchewan 4.4 per cent, and Alberta 3.7 per cent, the lowest in Canada. The pipelines may surpass the transcontinental railways in size of construction. Export sales of oil and gas to the United States have not only become of major significance in the balance of trade but also demanded closer co-operation and, sometimes, caused tensions between the two countries.

Both federal and provincial politics have been affected by Alberta's oil and gas. Whereas the higher prices of early Canadian oil in relation to other sources had handicapped Canadian exploration and sales, the rapid rise of world prices made Canadian oil comparatively cheap and encouraged exploration for new reserves. Furthermore, higher prices could be charged for the Canadian product which would mean greater profits, to be divided among the oil companies, the federal government and the provincial governments. As world prices continued to soar so did the possibility of immense revenues.

The division of profits from natural resources brought about a confrontation between the provinces—especially Alberta—and the federal government. Numerous federal-provincial conferences failed to reach a compromise. The provinces asserted their claims to control their resources from which they could raise revenues by leases and royalties; the federal government controlled interprovincial and foreign trade and could levy taxes on exports. The first serious clash occurred early in 1974 when Alberta raised its royalty rates but the federal government declared them nondeductible for federal tax purposes, which meant that oil companies would be paying taxes as well as royalties.

The oil and gas industries have long been a problem to the federal government, which has tried to establish some basic policies. In response to the growing opposition to large profits leaving the country through American oil companies, attempts have been made to ensure more Canadian control. In the 1950s, by federal-provincial agreement, the construction of the Trans-Canada natural gas pipeline was planned by a consortium of American and Canadian investors. After long negotiations, C. D. Howe arranged for an all-Canadian route from Alberta to Sarnia rather than one through the United States. Options for construction were signed and a deadline was set, but the Conservatives and CCF were against the American investors and obstructed the bill. In order to meet the deadline, Howe introduced a closure motion and the legislation was passed in June 1956 only hours before the deadline. His despotic action was a major factor in the defeat of the Liberals and the success of John Diefenbaker's Conservatives.

In 1975 the Canadian government established the crown corporation of Petro-Canada whose head office is in Calgary. Petro-Canada was to assist the federal government in formulating national policies to increase the Canadian presence in the petroleum industry. Its mandate permits it to explore for oil and gas or any other form of energy; to reproduce, refine and market them; and to deal with oil-supplier nations. It took control of the government's 45 per cent share in Panarctic Limited, an exploratory consortium operating in the Arctic. It acquired the federal government's 15 per cent share in Syncrude, an interest in the Hibernia field off Newfoundland, as well as interests in various other oil, gas and pipeline companies. And it acquired several hundred retail gas stations stretching from coast to coast. Petro-Canada's goal is to achieve self-sufficiency of supply for Canada.

The short-lived Conservative government of 1980 considered returning Petro-Canada to the private sector, a policy that contributed to its defeat since many Canadians objected to returning a profitable enterprise to American-controlled companies. The succeeding Liberal government reinstated the policy of gaining Canadian control of the industry and strengthened Petro-Canada, which was encouraged to invest more heavily in the north, enter the retail market and take over foreign-controlled companies.

The importance of Alberta oil, natural gas and other minerals to the Canadian economy can be seen in the 1976 statistics for Canadian mineral production. Crude petroleum accounted for 26.8 per cent of the total value, followed by natural gas at 16 per cent, iron ore (from eastern Canada) at 8.1 per cent, nickel 8.0 per cent, copper 7.3 per cent and zinc 5.6 per cent. Alberta produces 45 per cent of all Canadian minerals. British Columbia ranks fourth with 9 per cent, followed by Saskatchewan at 6 per cent and Manitoba at 4 per cent. In 1976 exports of petroleum and natural gas totalled over $4 billion.

Possessing most of Canada's energy supplies, Alberta has become the wealthiest province in Canada. Many corporations and financial institutions established their head offices or major branches in the booming cities of Calgary and Edmonton. The centre of Canada's economy, which historically had been in Ontario, is moving to the west. Since its oil is a nonrenewable resource, Alberta has sought to ensure its future with the Heritage Savings Trust Fund, funded by its gas and oil royalties. This fund is earmarked to improve the quality of life in the province, provide capital for other investments and diversify and expand Alberta's economy. It has grown through investments and loans—often to other provinces at comparatively low rates. Before the oil fields are depleted, Alberta plans to have established a sound base for secondary industries to maintain prosperity. To diversify its energy base, the province controls 51 per cent of the Alberta Energy Corporation which has interests in natural gas, pipelines, coal, petrochemicals and forests.

In 1978 the value of Canada's oil imports was $3.4 billion while its exports, all to the United States, amounted to $1.5 billion. Because Canada has its own oil supplies, the domestic price has been kept low. In 1981 when world prices were approximately $40 Canadian a barrel, Canadian oil was selling for only $17.78. To equalize the costs across the country, the federal government subsidizes Maritime refineries for selling their imported oil below cost (in 1980 the subsidy amounted to $3.2 billion) and intends to continue the subsidy with its revenues from western oil profits.

As Alberta's Heritage Fund grew, other provinces, especially Ontario, reacted, claiming that this money should be shared by all Canadians. The problem of division of profits was aggravated by the BNA Act by which Alberta has control of its natural resources but not their export. Furthermore, Ottawa has the right to override provincial powers "in the national interest," which, for example, allows it to establish the price of oil.

In 1980 the federal Liberal government determined to decrease its budget deficit, running into billions of dollars, with greater profits from the oil resources. Unable to reach agreement with Alberta's Conservative premier, Peter Lougheed, the federal government unilaterally imposed a tax on oil and gas which raised their price to all Canadians as well as foreign buyers. The increase of 18 cents a gallon (almost 4 cents a litre) on gasoline was felt by all consumers. And the producing provinces reacted bitterly. British Columbia claimed that the tax on natural gas resulted in a decrease in export sales, which would mean either a deficit budget for the province or restrictions on development funds and essential government services. The western provinces claimed that the tax was driving many companies to abandon their exploratory activities and to move to the United States where profits were higher. Premier Lougheed took the offensive by threatening to cut back oil production by up to 180,000 barrels a day, in three stages beginning in March 1981. This decrease in supplies would more than offset the federal government's increased income because the shortage would have to be made up with oil imports on which the government granted a subsidy. Provinces having oil supplies or potential oil supplies, including

British Columbia, Saskatchewan and Newfoundland, as well as the territories, strongly supported Alberta's stand. Ontario, which depended on Alberta oil, was threatened most by a reduction in supplies. The Alberta stance aggravated the tension between the west and the federal government and between the west and Ontario.

In 1981 the federal government and Alberta reached a compromise agreement, followed by comparable federal agreements with the other provinces having oil or the prospect of oil. All levels of government accepted that Canadian oil prices will eventually rise to near—but not reach—world prices. Formulas were devised by which profits from higher prices will be divided among the oil-producing provinces, the federal government and private enterprise. The agreements were expected to encourage further exploration and development.

Coal

As early as the 1850s coal mines were operating on Vancouver Island to supply steam vessels. Railways and the steel industry were a great stimulus to the industry, as was the conversion from wood for home heating. The first prairie coal mines were worked in 1877 near Lethbridge, but the best coal was later discovered in the Crowsnest Pass area. Soon after 1900 coal began to displace wood. Canadian production increased from 630,000 tons (570 000 t) in 1867 to 15 million tons (13.5 million t) in 1913, then declined during the war years because of transportation problems and the shortage of manpower, though by 1924 there were still about 400 mines in Alberta alone.

For the next fifty years, coal production declined absolutely as a result of the conversion of steamships and railways to oil, the conversion to oil and gas for home heating, and the increased use of electric power. Recovery began in the 1970s with the resurgence of Japan. After its outstanding postwar recovery, Japan was drastically in need of raw materials: its major Canadian demands were for copper and forest products, but it also invested in the development of the coal areas of Alberta and British Columbia and, for example, the molybdenum mines at Endako, B.C. It was the Japanese market that

opened the great coal fields of southeastern British Columbia
and southern Alberta. In 1981 British Columbia reached an
agreement to supply Japan with 8.5 million tons (7.7 million t)
of coal per year for fifteen years from mines to be opened in the
northeastern part of the province, an immense project requiring a combined public and private investment exceeding $2.5
billion. It includes the building of eighty miles (130 km) of new
rail spur from the British Columbia Railway and the upgrading
of the BCR and CNR to Prince Rupert. Both provincial and
federal governments are involved, but Premier W.R. Bennett of
British Columbia was determined to maintain control of this
resource and therefore most of the responsibility for development is provincial, meaning a period of heavy provincial
indebtedness. Whether in the long run the ambitious plan
becomes a provincial liability or asset will not be known for a
decade.

Canada faces competition for the Japanese and other Pacific
coal markets from China, Australia, the Soviet Union and the
United States. To satisfy Japanese demands, a special loading
port was established at Roberts Bank near Vancouver, where
kilometre-long trains unload the coal, yet by 1980 the port was
unable to handle the traffic and plans were underway for
extensive expansion. Of the total Canadian coal exports in
1976, almost all went to Japan, and of this British Columbia
and Alberta produced 95 per cent.

The Japanese trade has accentuated the shortage of west
coast port facilities. With the Panama Canal and the expansion
of postwar Pacific trade, Vancouver became Canada's leading
port, handling the largest number of vessels and the largest
amount of cargo. The opening of the northeast B.C. coal mines
requires the upgrading of railways and the construction of new
port facilities. The project is also resulting in the opening of
other mines and industries in northern British Columbia, the
construction of a new town (Tumbler Ridge) in the wilderness,
and necessarily rapid improvements in Prince Rupert's port
facilities. These are being co-ordinated with much-needed new
procedures for handling prairie grain and potash.

By 1980 the world had been faced with the energy crisis.
Western Canada is fortunate in having a surplus of energy, but,
unless new large fields are discovered, Alberta's oil is pro-

jected to run out within a decade. Expectations of vast new
fields in the Arctic regions and off the Newfoundland coast,
and improved extraction techniques for the Athabasca oil
sands promise to supplement the shortages, but these fields are
as yet unproven. There is enough natural gas for at least twenty
years, while the known coal reserves are almost unlimited. The
huge capital investment needed for the expansion of western
mineral and petroleum resources has caused the Vancouver
Stock Exchange to become a major trading centre.

The western provinces are rich in electrical energy. Alberta
obtains 95 per cent of its electrical energy and Saskatchewan
70 per cent from thermal power. On the other hand, British
Columbia, Manitoba and the territories obtain almost all their
electricity from hydroelectric power, a renewable resource.
Studies of the feasibility of tapping more northern rivers have
been underway for many years. Western Canada will be supplied for the foreseeable future by its great reserves of coal and
water power, but other energy sources must be discovered to
replace the threatened shortage of petroleum.

Trade

Approximately 70 per cent of Canada's trade is with the
United States. Since World War II Canada's dependence on
Britain and the European Common Market has declined so that
today they take only 12 per cent of its exports. The greatest area
of expansion has been the Pacific Rim, where Canada is a major
trading nation. Japan has now supplanted Britain as Canada's
second largest trading partner, taking over 7 per cent of its
exports, or, excluding the United States, 20 per cent of exports,
totalling $4.4 billion in 1980. Ninety-five per cent of Canada's
exports to Japan are raw materials, and of the fifty-four principle commodities, forty-eight come from the western provinces
and the Yukon. The leading exports to Japan are coal, rapeseed,
copper, wheat, wood pulp, lumber and fish roe. On the other
hand, 67 per cent of the imports from Japan go to Quebec and
Ontario. As western Canada strives to increase its export trade
in raw materials, central Canada seeks to restrict the imports of
competitive manufactured goods; yet as western exports
increase they must be balanced by imports. Whereas the west-

ern provinces favour a policy of free trade, Ontario supports strong protective tariffs, a conflict that has long affected Canadian politics and deepened the rift between western and central Canada.

Present-day wheat exports depend on the markets of the Soviet Union, China and Japan. Efforts are being made by governments and private enterprise to expand the variety of commodities sold to these countries, as well as to increase trade with other Pacific countries, such as Taiwan and Korea. At the same time, large amounts of capital from Japan and Hong Kong are being invested in Canada, helping to open new resources and to establish new industries. The expansion of Pacific trade offers almost unlimited opportunities to Canadian businessmen in the fields of resource development, transportation facilities, investment opportunities and industry.

Canada–United States Relations

History shows that Canada cannot ignore the pressures and influences of the United States. The threat of annexation has been a perpetual thorn, and though it has been minimal in recent years, it has not been eradicated, as the Constitution crisis of 1981 revealed when a minor movement for annexation was organized on the prairies. More insidious are American influences on cultural life, subtly affecting patterns of living, communications, recreation and the arts. Canadians follow American politics closely, for American leaders and policies may affect directly industrial growth and individual well-being.

During the last century Canadian and American economies have become increasingly interwoven, bringing advantages and disadvantages for Canada. It has meant prosperity and a high standard of living, and comparatively low defence expenditures because of the country's faith in American protection. On the other hand, since World War II Canada has become dependent on American trade. Canada's need for funds for research and resource exploration has encouraged vast amounts of external investment capital. Foreign ownership is more prevalent in Canada than in any other country in the Western world. In the nation's formative years most of this capital came from Britain, but since the 1920s American investment has dominated. In 1975, of the total $69 billion invested in Canada by nonresidents, the United States held $53 billion or over 75 per cent. The profits from these investments seriously affect the Canadian balance of payments. In 1973 it was stated in the House of Commons that 99.9 per cent of the petroleum industry and 83 per cent of the combined oil and gas industry were controlled by foreign investors. Many Canadian corporations are subsidiaries of multinational corporations centred in the United States.

Through the investments of the Canada Development Corporation (CDC) established in 1971, the Canadian government hopes to develop and maintain strong Canadian controlled and managed corporations in the private sector of the economy. The Foreign Investment Review Agency (FIRA), established in 1974 to assess non-Canadian business ownership, was revised in 1979 to make foreign acquisitions more difficult. As mentioned earlier, Petro-Canada is buying foreign-controlled companies and encouraging Canadian control in the petroleum and natural gas industries. The National Energy Program (NEP), started in 1980, aims to achieve 50 per cent Canadian ownership—government and private—of the domestic petroleum industry by 1990. This trend towards government control, restrictions on foreign ownership and special tax allowances for Canadian companies met with opposition in the United States, which threatened retaliatory measures against the NEP. The first two policies also met with some opposition in Alberta which requires large amounts of capital for northern development. Faced with internal and external opposition, the federal government temporarily modified the NEP though the long-term objectives remained.

Labour unions continue to increase annually in Canada; in 1977 there were 579 unions with a total membership of 3.3 million, or 37.6 per cent of the nonfarm labour force. The largest group is the Canadian Labour Congress, which doubled its membership from one million in 1956 to 2.3 million in 1981; by that time most industrial and public sectors were unionized and its rate of growth levelled off. The CLC has been handicapped by the increase in automation and suffers from internal problems. The public service unions, such as the Canadian

Union of Public Employees (CUPE), grew faster compared to the older trade unions and have different problems. Attempts to encourage Canadian unions have led to disputes with members of international unions. Altogether, over one-half of Canadian union members, including some of those in the CLC, are affiliated with international (American) unions. In recent years the CLC has promoted stronger political ties with the New Democratic Party.

The dependence of both business and labour on the United States has been a source of dissatisfaction, if not alarm, to many Canadians. Organizations such as the Committee for an Independent Canada oppose American control and "takeovers," and have won some legislative restrictions which have had little actual effect. Western Canada has a history of susceptibility to American infiltration. The prairies are a vast open space where an arbitrary boundary has been unable to prevent ideas and traffic from entering freely. The mountain ranges and coastal waters of British Columbia create natural north-south passages to the United States rather than to the rest of Canada. The war years demonstrated the importance of air and land routes from the central states through Canada's northwest to Alaska, and the postwar years saw the co-operation of the two nations in developing northern defence posts. Today the increasing air travel to the Orient follows the "Great Circle" route from the United States across Canada. Since the west depends on exports of primary materials and imports of manufactured goods, it has always favoured more liberal trade agreements with the United States, as opposed to the high-tariff, protective policies of central Canada.

A recession in the United States is watched with trepidation in the western provinces, especially in British Columbia. If American construction declines, the effect on the forest industry whose main markets are in the United States may be widespread unemployment and sympathetic business losses. Similarly, other major primary and secondary industries such as mining and pulp and paper are dependent on economic conditions in the United States.

Several noteworthy co-operative projects by the two countries have affected the west, especially British Columbia. In 1909, following the bitter Alaska boundary dispute, the Perma-

nent International Joint Commission was established to settle
boundary disputes and regulate the use of waters common to
both nations. The commission has continued to be successful
in settling minor disputes. The Fur Seal Convention of 1911,
renewed in 1953, saved fur seals and sea otters from extinction.
In 1923 the International Salmon Fisheries Commission inaugurated a joint effort, including the construction of fish ladders
on the Fraser River, to conserve and enhance salmon stocks.
An agreement reached on halibut fisheries in the same year
was the first truly Canadian treaty in that there was no British
signatory. In 1961 the Columbia River Treaty (modified in
1964) established a major hydroelectric power and flood control system. Since the discovery of northern natural gas and oil,
agreements for their transportation to the United States have
required major negotiations extending over several years.

The close connections between Canada and the United
States have led to many disagreements of varying intensity.
Minor problems include the attempts by Canada to restrict
southern businesses from draining away their advertising dollars to American radio and television stations transmitting
across the border. British Columbia has had a long-simmering
dispute with Seattle which wants to raise its Skagit Valley
hydroelectric dam to obtain more power, flooding a considerable part of the valley in B.C. In Manitoba there is opposition to
the proposed Garrison diversion project which will provide
irrigation for North Dakota but will affect the flow of the Red
River, create irrigation problems in Manitoba and harm its
inland fisheries. Such local problems, though arousing a certain amount of acrimony, are eventually settled though only
after long negotiations. Other problems, such as the transportation of oil and gas and the division of fisheries, are more complicated and demand years of discussions at top political levels.

Technological improvements have permitted fishing nations
to extend their hunt into all parts of the oceans and Canada has
become alarmed by the foreign depletion of stocks off its
coasts. In 1964 it established a nine-mile (14.4-km) Canadian
fishing zone beyond its three-mile (4.8-km) limit, and in 1971
extended this zone on the west coast to a limit running from
the northern end of Vancouver Island to the Queen Charlotte

Islands. On 1 January 1977 it unilaterally extended its fishing zone on both coasts to 200 miles (320 km). Later in the year, faced by similar actions by other Pacific nations, the United States also adopted the 200-mile zone, leading to disputes along the Pacific coast. The two countries disagree on the course of the new fishing boundaries off Juan de Fuca Strait and from Dixon Entrance, so that in each area there is a mutually claimed triangle with apex at the coast. Both countries have seized fishing vessels for poaching. Canadian halibut fishermen have protested against overfishing by Americans. Such nagging incidents are reminiscent of the Alaska boundary dispute and will undoubtedly take years of patient negotiation before mutually satisfactory agreements are reached. One reason for the slow progress in fishing agreements lies in the American system of government, as was illustrated by the eastern fisheries dispute. Although the two countries signed a treaty, it had to be ratified by the United States Senate, where lobbying interests caused delay. When a change in government occurred in 1981, the American attitude hardened, so that negotiations on eastern fisheries must be reopened.

The discovery of oil in Alaska has meant a decade of debate over its transportation to the United States. A project to build a natural gas line along the Alaska Highway has been approved, but the transport of oil has presented a more complicated problem. The original plan was to ship it by large tankers to a southern port, but the record of tanker disasters throughout the world led to strong opposition, especially since they were to enter the narrow waters of Juan de Fuca Strait and Puget Sound. Alternative overland routes have been proposed, but all have faced opposition because of the costs and the dangers to the environment. Not the least problem is the vociferous demands of native peoples for recognition of their rights, consideration of their lifestyles and recompense for the use of their land. Ultimately, because of American energy requirements, routes for the distribution of northern oil and gas will be established. Before that is accomplished, there will be difficult negotiations by native groups and provincial, state and both federal governments.

The political, economic and social patterns of the United States are thus of vital significance to western Canada. American monetary policies can restrict the investment of capital so necessary for the development of primary and secondary industries. This is especially true of risk capital needed for the discovery of new petroleum and mineral resources. American tariff policies may reduce exports to the United States as well as increase American competition in world markets. New leaders may change government policies, and personal clashes between the leaders of the two countries have had repercussions in foreign, monetary and tariff policies and on business opportunities. The activities and successes of American unions often affect their Canadian counterparts. American restrictions, such as gasoline rationing, customs regulations and taxation on conventions held outside the United States, affect Canada's tourist industry. The proximity of pollution-spreading projects may alarm citizens of both countries, and Canadians may demonstrate against nearby American nuclear or military bases. Infiltration of American communication media affects Canadian attitudes and lifestyles. Internal dissension between provincial and federal governments creates uncertainty for Americans planning investments in Canada. Because of the open north-south communication routes, western Canada is open to American pressures; only through strong federal-provincial cooperation can this magnetic pull to the south be nullified by west-east bonds. Acrimony between western provincial and federal governments weakens these west-east ties and in so doing delays the fulfillment of independence, self-sufficiency and unity desired by nearly all Canadians.

Chapter Ten

POSTWAR YEARS:
THE WESTERNERS

The New West

Duating the early years of growth the west had been controlled from central Canada— was dependent on it financially, commercially and politically. During the war and postwar years this dependence lessened, and as western Canadians became more prosperous and self-sufficient their attitudes towards Canada changed.

The wider economic base which resulted from the discovery of new resources broadened the market possibilities and cushioned the effect of fluctuating prices. With new resources came wealth and greater economic autonomy. Capital flowed into the region. Multinationals and conglomerates began major research and development projects in natural gas, oil, oil sands, hydroelectricity and coal.

The changing patterns of international power influenced Canada's economy. Specifically, the emergence of the Pacific Rim as a potential market and source of capital investment had direct repercussions in the west. China and Russia became Canada's major markets for grain. Imports from Japan of both capital and goods influenced the economy of the entire nation, but the west, with its proximity to Asia, was most affected. As wheat, fish, minerals and forest products were shipped to Asia (and liquefied gas exports were planned for the future), there was an increasing demand for better transportation services and the upgrading of western ports, including Churchill.

Much of western growth was made possible by new technol-

ogy. Air routes crisscrossed Canada to Europe and Asia.
Sophisticated instruments for mineral exploration and better
airplanes revolutionized the old hit-or-miss methods of prospecting. New techniques made feasible the extraction of harder
to reach minerals and petroleum. Hydro power could be
brought from far distant rivers. Scientific studies led to
improved agricultural output. Telecommunications reduced
the precarious isolation of remote communities.

The mineral wealth, changing trading patterns and technological advances have allowed styles of living which are far
removed from those of thirty years ago. The west's resources
and growing educated population have made it the wealthiest
region of Canada, and westerners are self-confident and aggressive in their demands for political recognition. Perhaps most
significant is their optimistic spirit, the belief that the future of
Canada lies in their hands.

Changing Agricultural Patterns

When the first settlers arrived in the west they obtained 160
acres (64 ha) of farmland either by purchase or by homesteading. With horses or oxen they broke the land, and as years
passed they tried to buy additional quarter sections. Most of
their labour was by hand, and as late as the 1930s special trains
carried unskilled labourers to the harvest. Lack of capital and
power machinery limited the amount of land a farmer and his
family could handle. For example, power threshing machines
were so expensive that usually one machine, either hired or
bought co-operatively, was used to work several farms.

The 1950s saw revolutionary changes. Electrification spread
to rural areas. The introduction of powerful mechanized farm
machines made larger farm units workable; in fact, large
acreages were necessary to pay for those expensive machines,
which lost money every day they were idle. Within a few years
little casual labour was used, but the skilled machine operators
expected higher wages and other farm costs increased. Often
the small farmer could not compete as organizations with capital turned agriculture into a modern business enterprise: financial balances became the responsibilities of farm managers and
trained accountants. Experimental farms studied the use of fer-

tilizers and insecticides as well as the potential use of soils.

Rural lifestyles were revolutionized. While many independent farmers sold out, many others adjusted to the changing methods and no longer had to strain physically from dawn to dusk. Regular hours for skilled farm workers were established. Modern transportation allowed farmers to operate from a population centre providing supermarkets, shopping centres, entertainment and other amenities. Once an individual struggling from day to day, the farmer became a businessman; but in some ways the problems did not change, for farming was still affected by the weather and other natural hazards and by new government policies. It was increasingly affected by the competition of world trade, the growing world demand for food, the crop yields of other nations, and by shifting international alignments and trade agreements.

The original prairie towns and villages had been settled along railway lines which carried passengers, brought supplies and took away the harvest. The advent of automobiles, buses and trucks eliminated most passenger traffic and many of the supply services. Faced with mounting losses, the railways closed numerous short, unprofitable lines, which meant that grain had to be carried to more distant gathering depots, adding to the farmers' costs. Many independent farmers viewed this extra burden as a betrayal by the railways, for the original settlers had believed the railways would always serve them. The farmers' belief in federal government disinterest was also strengthened.

When they arrived at their homesteads, prairie settlers would first select the location for a home (which would become a more solid structure with time), probably on a high spot in the quarter section. From here the surrounding land stretched into the distance, broken only by the odd clump of trees, the schoolhouse, the elevator by the railway and the community centre. At night they saw clear starlit sky and sometimes the northern lights. In winter they smelled crisp cold air, in spring the scent of flowers, in summer and autumn the warm smell of wheat. Above all they felt the unfettered freedom and independence of the open spaces, and were comforted by the small dots in the distance signifying the homes of their nearest neighbours, breaking the isolation and inspiring a co-operative spirit of mutual interest and assistance. These men and women and their descendants were the backbone of the prairie provinces. Although they might leave the living of the farm, they would never forget or forsake the freedom of the open land.

Changing Population Patterns

The great immigration period inaugurated by Clifford Sifton ended with the First World War. After the war, immigration continued sporadically, amounting to little during the Depression but increasing again after World War II. The overall pattern was steady immigration combined with a steady natural population growth. Between 1920 and 1980 the population of Canada grew from 8 million to 25 million.

In recent times most immigrants have been drawn to the industrial regions of central Canada but many have settled in the west. Since 1951 British Columbia's population has shown the greatest percentage increase of any province, rising steadily from 1,165,000 to 2,500,000 in 1980. Alberta's growth slowed between 1931 and 1951 but since that time doubled to 1,838,000 in 1976 and by 1980 had passed two million. (Calgary is the fastest-growing city in Canada.) Although it has grown in population, Manitoba, the first western province settled, declined in percentage growth from 9.5 per cent in 1951–56 to 3.4 per cent in 1971–76. By 1976 it had passed one million, but it has grown comparatively little since that date. Its proportionally slow growth resulted in a decrease in Manitoba's representation in the House of Commons. Saskatchewan suffered losses in the 1930s but began a slow recovery that lasted until 1966. Its representation in the House of Commons decreased the maximum three seats. Then in 1974 its broadening economic base brought prosperity and attracted workers. Since 1976 Saskatchewan has been growing at the rate of more than ten thousand people a year, reaching 970,000 in 1980. The territories grew steadily, increasing fivefold from 1921 to 1980 when the Yukon had a population of 21,600 and the Northwest Territories, 43,000.

At the beginning of the twentieth century, roughly 60 per cent of Canadians were living in rural areas and 40 per cent of the labour force was engaged in agricultural pursuits. During the First World War the pattern changed: by 1921 the urban population surpassed rural. This process of urbanization has continued with only minor interruptions, so that today 70 per cent of the population lives in urban areas.

In the three prairie provinces in 1921, 65 per cent of the population was still rural, but with increased mechanization and improvements in agricultural technology, the off-farm flow picked up. In 1941 the prairies were still 60 per cent rural, when the Second World War accelerated the movement to the cities. The 1951 census showed 56 per cent rural; by 1978 over 65 per cent was urban. This overall figure, however, does not reflect even distribution, for Saskatchewan was only 55 per cent urban while Manitoba had jumped to 70 per cent and Alberta to 75 per cent. In British Columbia the change was even more impressive: in 1921 it was still 55 per cent rural; in 1931 it was 57 per cent urban; in 1961, already 75 per cent urban.

Two notes must be added regarding this trend towards urbanization. Despite fewer farm owners and the reduction in farm labour, the actual land under cultivation and the quantity of agricultural products have increased. In 1941 Saskatchewan had 125,000 farms; in 1966, 79,000, and in 1976, 69,500. In the same period the average size of a Saskatchewan farm was, respectively, 432 acres (175 ha), 807 acres (327 ha) and 939 acres (380 ha). Secondly, although villages and towns have increased in number and size, the greatest population flow has been to large cities. In British Columbia over one-half the population lives in Vancouver and its environs, in Alberta over one-half in Edmonton and Calgary, in Manitoba over one-half in Winnipeg, and in Saskatchewan one-third lives in Regina and Saskatoon.

The greatest influx of European immigrants to Canada occurred in the first years of the twentieth century, and the flow has continued. The first settlers took out homesteads and sought wage work in order to pay for them and to survive through the early years. The shovel, the wheelbarrow, the pick; fish canning and sawmilling, represent the unskilled occupations they held, working long hours in deplorable conditions for minimal wages. Gradually they became established, cleared the land, expanded their crops, moved from sod huts to wooden houses and sent their children to school. Two, sometimes three generations passed before an alien people became assimilated.

Some groups, such as the Doukhobors, Mennonites and Hutterites, did not wish to be assimilated. For instance, the Hutterites claimed that since they were an agricultural society, they were not subject to certain taxes. In 1934 the Supreme Court of Canada disallowed this claim, judging that they were, in fact, involved in industry indirectly. The 10,000 Hutterites believe that all things are held in common and no person really acquires any personal assets, and were therefore opposed when the government introduced universal social security numbers in 1973 (while implementing the Canada Pension Plan). Although they have been obliged to accept federal regulations, the 75 per cent of Hutterites living in 104 colonies in Alberta reached an accommodation with the province, and there the feeling of unfair government involvement is lessening. British Columbia has not yet resolved the problem of the Doukhobors' internal conflicts, which have resulted in the breaking of laws, though property damage and demonstrations have declined in recent years.

Most immigrants sought to become assimilated and were ambitious for their children's education. Their descendants have adopted scientific methods of agriculture and have entered business, the professions and government. Such families joined the mainstream of Canadian life and melded with the population. At the same time they never forgot their homelands or lost their innate desire to visit them and refresh ancestral roots. As Canadians, they have enriched the country's cultural life by maintaining ethnic skills and arts, encouraged by the federal policy of multiculturalism.

Each new wave of immigrants followed a similar pattern, experiencing a period of prejudice and hardship while they held unskilled labouring jobs, from which they rose by hard work and frugality until they, too, competed with other Canadians. In recent years, as technology replaces unskilled labour and unemployment increases, opposition to the importation of alien workers has grown. Although immigration laws discriminating on the basis of race, religion or sex have been relaxed, they now favour people trained in the particular skills needed in the country and speaking one of the two official languages. Exceptions are made for refugees.

Before 1967 Europeans accounted for at least 75 per cent of the immigrants entering Canada, but within a decade they dropped to about 35 per cent. Asian immigrants from Southeast Asia, India, Hong Kong and Pakistan now account for about 25 per cent. Many of these newer minorities still hold low-paying jobs and live in urban enclaves. In recent years, there have been incidents of discrimination or even violence against the "visible minorities," symptomatic of the underlying intolerance of a sector of Canadians.

In 1901, 57 per cent of the population was of British descent and 30.7 per cent, French descent. In 1971 they had come closer, dropping to 44.6 per cent and 28.7 per cent respectively. The percentage of people speaking English only in 1971 was 76.1 per cent; French only, 18.0 per cent; both languages, 13.4 per cent; neither language, 1.5 per cent.

Since most French-speaking Canadians live in Quebec, these figures are not representative of western Canada, where 55 per cent of the population is of British descent and only about 2 per cent is French—many concentrated in francophone communities such as St. Boniface where 17,000 people are of French descent. There are over forty ethnic groups in the west, and Germans and Ukrainians far outnumber the French on the prairies. In British Columbia there are more Chinese. The people of western Canada regard French-speaking Quebec as a legitimate part of the Canadian federation, and provincial governments have addressed the needs of bilingualism in their education systems. But in the majority view, Quebec's internal problems are significant to the west only so far as they affect Canadian unity or threaten the Atlantic outlets for western exports, and there is limited sympathy for special status in the greater multiethnic and multicultural society.

Canadians are developing a national culture based on multiculturalism. Whereas eastern Canada was opened by the French and British, western Canada was settled and developed by a greater variety of peoples, so that through assimilation, cooperation and tolerance, western Canadians will be the base upon which a truly national identity is established.

The Cities

The population of western Canada almost doubled in the postwar years as a result of natural increase and immigration. Unlike the early settlers, most of the newcomers were not agricultural, and the existing population was becoming more urbanized: cities grew and urban problems become more pressing.

The scarcity of urban land resulted in rising real estate prices. As in the east, most early city cores became the centres of finance and industry, forcing the spread of homes far from the centre, creating urban sprawl. Suburban retail and service centres followed, while in the city core the banks and other financial institutions erected skyscrapers to conserve valuable land space. People who wished to live near the centre were forced into high-density areas of apartment complexes. Older buildings of historic significance were ruthlessly demolished, and older sections of the city away from the financial district were allowed to deteriorate into slum areas.

As the urban population spread out, dividing and blacktopping valuable farmland, services such as water, sewage and roads became necessary. In order to co-ordinate these services, the cities extended their boundaries, or regional planning boards were established. The division of costs became a source of disagreement between neighbouring communities. Because people who lived in the suburbs worked in the city, the burden of providing roads and transportation fell on the city; museums, art galleries, civic buildings, recreational centres and other necessities of urban life were located in the city and paid for by its taxpayers, but they were used by the entire region. Meanwhile, demands for housing in the suburbs resulted in land speculation: large-scale housing projects were rapidly put together, often of poor construction and design, which foretold a short life or a future slum area. One of the major responsibilities of regional boards was to preserve parkland and recreational areas against the pressures of housing.

The satellite municipalities had their own expansion problems but to lesser degree. Nevertheless, municipal services, education and land requirements made increasing demands on the public finances of every community.

As the gateway to western settlement, the hub of railways, the centre of the grain trade and the distribution centre for goods to the farmlands, Winnipeg was the metropolis of the west. It became less dominant after 1914 when the Panama Canal opened Pacific outlets for grain, and the virtual collapse of the western economy during the Depression caused its further decline. In the postwar years, mechanization of agriculture and the declining farm population lessened Winnipeg's importance as a distribution centre. The automobile and airplane reduced the importance of railways for passenger transport, but they continued to be major bulk carriers. On the other hand, the new industries of the west demanded machinery and construction materials, which Winnipeg supplied. Old and new manufacturing concerns acquired a diversified industrial base. Winnipeg also continued as a leading western financial centre, being the headquarters for a number of large insurance companies. As the provincial capital, Winnipeg had a growing federal and provincial civil service.

Winnipeg has continued to grow (to 599,500 people in the metropolitan area by 1980), though not as fast as other western cities. Although its economic patterns have changed, the result is a prosperous, stable and growing city.

Beginning as a railway centre on Pile of Bones Creek in 1882, Regina achieved brief notoriety during the Rebellion of 1885. It was first important as the North West Mounted Police headquarters and the capital of the North-West Territories. In 1903 it was incorporated as a city and two years later became the capital of the new province of Saskatchewan. Located in the heart of one of the richest wheat-growing regions in the world, Regina was soon the major distribution centre. As Saskatchewan's economy has become more diversified, the capital has continued to grow both in population (154,000 by 1980) and facilities. By the 1980s it was experiencing a downtown building boom, and in 1980–81 housing starts increased 150 per cent. Its imaginative and enthusiastic citizens have changed the city from a bare prairie town to an attractive capital.

Unlike Winnipeg, Regina is not the hub of railways and must share the distribution of materials with Saskatoon, the centre for potash, uranium and oil exploration. It has doubled its population in thirty years and now approaches Regina in size. The cities of Saskatchewan may never be great metropolitan centres but they remain livable places and their futures are assured as distributing centres for industry and resources.

Edmonton traces its history as far back as 1795 when the first fur posts were established. For nearly a century it was the largest community west of Winnipeg. In 1905 it was selected as the capital of Alberta. The city has always been important as a transportation centre, from the time when the fur brigades headed west to the Pacific and north to the Mackenzie River, and again as the beginning of the staging route to the northwest during World War II. After the discovery of oil at nearby Leduc in 1947 and the opening of northern oil and gas fields, the city became an even more active distribution centre. It is on the international air routes and serves the vast north. The growing city (numbering 569,000 people by 1980) has expanded in all directions and in recent years has adopted a metropolitan attitude.

Edmonton has an impressive location high on the banks of the North Saskatchewan River. Its serenity and beauty, the legislative buildings, Fort Edmonton, and a system of parks along the river all belie the intense commercial activity. Edmonton gives the impression of a city that foresees an inevitable great future but has not lost touch with its historical and cultural beginnings.

The North West Mounted Police established Fort Calgary in 1875 at the junction of the Bow and Elbow rivers, joining a few scattered missionaries, traders and settlers. The settlement grew slowly until the railway arrived eight years later. The city of Calgary was incorporated in 1884 with a population of under 500, but with the railway, cattle ranching and the opening of nearby mines, it grew to become the largest city in the territories. During the great immigration era at the turn of the century, Calgary's population soared from 4,392 in 1901 to over 40,000 in 1911. From that point growth was steady until after World War II when developments in oil and natural gas changed the pattern again and the city boomed. The metropolitan population in 1980 was 550,800.

Canada's fastest-growing city has been called the most "Americanized." Many financial and commercial establishments have moved their headquarters there, and powerful American corporations have set up offices. The rapid growth has created an urban sprawl and homes are springing up many kilometres from the centre. To visitors the city is a nightmare of torn-up streets and new skyscrapers competing with each other for space. There is an atmosphere of excitement and urgency in Calgary's working life. Some of the richest people in Canada, some comparatively newly rich, live there. Indications are that in a few years Calgary will displace Toronto as the financial centre of Canada. Meanwhile, construction goes on. Calgary exhibits the spirit of new power, new wealth and initiative characterizing western Canada.

Vancouver was transformed from a lumber milltown by the arrival of the CPR, and its future as a great port was brought closer by the opening of the Panama Canal. Four railways serve the city, major highways link it to the rest of Canada and the United States, and international air routes expedite travel in all directions. Today Vancouver has access to the expanding Pacific markets in the Americas, Australia and Asia. Its hinterland, providing raw materials for export and markets for manufactured imports, extends to Saskatchewan in the east and the Yukon in the north.

The expansion of industry and trade combined with the mild south coast climate continue to attract newcomers to Vancouver. The city is shaped like a huge mitt between the Fraser River and Burrard Inlet, its small thumb containing the core of commercial and industrial activity, and the rapidly increasing population (1.25 million by 1980) has created a shortage of living space. Although many homes have been constructed on the mountainous north shore, most of the urban sprawl has been into the Fraser Valley, threatening to destroy one of the few agricultural areas of the province—bitterly decried by many but with limited effect.

Vancouver is suffering from growing pains and requires urban planning. Major changes are under way: by 1990 the city expects to have new rapid transit systems, new sports and cultural facilities, a new convention centre, new bridges over the internal waterways and a modernized harbour to expedite the handling of deep-sea cargo.

The capital of British Columbia, Victoria, is very conscious of its historic origins and attempts to maintain its British tranquillity. The provincial government is a major employer and tourism has become a major industry, encouraging the preservation of parks and heritage buildings (and even cherished old customs such as afternoon tea).

Until recent times Victoria maintained its slow pace, but a rapidly increasing population (230,600 in 1980) attracted by the temperate climate of Vancouver Island has changed the city's atmosphere. Although attempts are being made to preserve its hereditary flavour, the city has succumbed to pressures for more suburban housing and shopping complexes. Victoria is still a tourist's delight but the "little bit of old England" is being swamped by modern city life.

The Arts

In early times every small community met its own recreational and social needs. Schoolhouses often doubled as community halls, where home arts and crafts were displayed and entertainment consisted of school concerts, singing and amateur theatricals, holiday sporting events, and all-night dances with a fiddler, someone drumming on chair rungs, and perhaps a piano player. The visit of a political candidate was an excuse for an assembly or a picnic with outdoor games. Before 1900 many towns had theatres which brought visiting artists and lecturers.

The proliferation of the arts in the last fifty years has coincided with the growth of cities. Citizens with more education, wealth and leisure time demanded higher standards from writers, artists and performers, and created training opportunities for local talent. Every major western city and some of the smaller ones had its own symphony orchestra. A wide variety of theatrical groups and dance companies were founded. Sponsors attracted the finest of the world's artists. Many Canadians, both individuals and groups, became world famous in the literary, performing, applied and fine arts. To serve a growing need, impressive new theatres, art galleries, museums and libraries were built in every city.

The majority of westerners trace their origins to Europe and its rich cultural heritage. Appreciation of the arts and love of history were transposed to western Canada, as were the comparable traditions of the many Asiatic groups. Western native groups, though their traditional cultures were not "swamped" or displaced by the European presence as early or so extensively as were the eastern tribes, were equally in danger of not being able to maintain their arts and customs for new generations; but the cultural resurgence of the last thirty years suggests that the danger is past. The historic backgrounds of almost every ethnic community are preserved in local museums or memorials and annual festivals.

The increasing demand for high-calibre artistic and athletic events does not automatically generate the necessary funding: no major artistic group in the west is financially independent and each survives only by subsidy—from individuals, corporations and all levels of government. In 1977 federal cultural expenses were $800 million, of which 70 per cent was spent on broadcasting, 7.6 per cent on historic parks, 5.4 per cent on museums and 4.8 per cent on the performing arts. Attempts to establish guaranteed revenue sources resulted in provincial cultural funds, government-run lotteries and the Canada Council. In 1977 the Manitoba Arts Council (founded 1965) budgeted $636,000 and the Saskatchewan Arts Board (1949) budgeted $794,000. The British Columbia Cultural Fund (1967) established an endowment fund which eventually totalled $20 million. Alberta passed a Cultural Development Act in 1947 and in 1979 allotted $85 million to its Department of Culture. The Canada Council (1957) receives its income from three sources: an annual parliamentary grant ($59.7 million in 1977), interest from an endowment fund established by parliament, and private donations.

The apparently large grants are not enough to assist all the arts. Government funds may fluctuate uncertainly from year to year, and there is always the problem of choosing the individual or organization most worthy of assistance. The success of the arts depends on the dedication, sacrifice and continuous efforts of many individuals and groups. From them are emerging distinct art forms which express the historic origins, special traits and hopes of western Canadians.

Native Organizations

After forty years of deprivation following the disappearance of the buffalo and the establishment of the reserve system on the prairies, the native peoples began to organize in their struggle for better conditions, including greater self-government. They had legitimate grievances concerning their treaty settlements—or lack of treaties. Poverty and underemployment did not go away. There are 574 Indian bands in Canada, two-thirds of them in the west and north. United action began among the more concentrated bands of British Columbia, most of whom lived on nontreaty Indian lands, occupied and developed by whites without compensation. (In 1916, for example, the province withdrew 33,000 acres, or over 13 000 ha, of reserve without Indian consent.) In 1915 the Allied Tribes of British Columbia was formed with representation from most regions. In the following years similar organizations were formed across Canada, including the Assembly of First Nations (formerly the National Indian Brotherhood, a federation representing status Indian groups), Native Council of Canada (representing Metis and nonstatus Indian groups), Manitoba Indian Brotherhood, Federation of Saskatchewan Indians, Union of British Columbia Indian Chiefs, Indian Association of Alberta, Yukon Native Brotherhood, the Dene Nation and the Metis Association of the Northwest Territories. Similarly, the widely scattered Inuit formed the Inuit Tapirisat of Canada, whose potential influence has been weakened by initial internal disagreements over priorities, but whose union is expected to ultimately resolve them. Although "status" native peoples are all under federal jurisdiction, general agreement among them has also been made difficult by the fact that those people north of 60°, the Yukon Indians, the Dene and the Inuit, either do not have treaties or, where treaties exist, do not have reserves and land claims settlement is outstanding—unlike most of those in the provinces.

Five groups have evolved, each with its own individual problems: the treaty or "status" Indians on reservations; those who have left the reserve and nonstatus Indians; Indians of the north, such as the Dene, without land settlements; the Metis, and the Inuit.

The Inuit

Until the Second World War practically the only contact the Inuit had with white people was through the trading posts, the

NWMP, scattered missions, isolated government stations and the irregular visits of whalers and trading vessels. Via such contacts many goods and services were introduced that made life easier, but contact also had deleterious effects. The people of the Mackenzie delta, for instance, who once numbered 2,500, were reduced to 250 by 1908 after the collapse of whaling. The Inuit continued to be a scattered nomadic people depending on marine mammals, fish and migratory animals. Since 1951 their number has doubled, two-thirds of them living in the Northwest Territories.

The postwar world revolutionized Inuit life, as northern defences were established, mines were opened, roads were expanded, oil sites were explored, and the airplane, radio and television became commonplace. Although 75 per cent of Inuit still engage in trapping on a full-time or part-time basis, they are increasingly adopting a wage economy based on modern skills. There are no reserves but the people have tended to gather together in permanent village settlements. The federal government has been responsible for medical services, welfare benefits, schools, and outside education in southern cities. The government also has encouraged band co-operatives, by providing advisers and funds, in industries such as fishing and logging as well as in the production of Inuit art.

Many Inuit are now skilled in industry, commerce, teaching and other professions; some have entered politics. But they remain suspicious of the growing search for natural resources, the expansion of transportation routes and the proposed pipeline construction. They demand employment on these projects but fear the social disruption, the later unemployment and obsolete skills, and particularly the disruption to the environment. Inuit (as well as Dene) are determined to maintain their identity, their language and their culture, and insist that the "opening of the north" must not ignore their aboriginal claims and their right, as a distinct cultural unit in Confederation, to share in the planning and responsibility for the north.

Demands of the Native Peoples

The native organizations continued to petition the federal government, and even the queen, for better conditions, but until 1940 they had little success. After the Depression and war, native peoples benefited somewhat from the greater emphasis throughout the nation on universal education and public health and welfare.

By the BNA Act, native peoples, and their lands, are the special responsibility of the federal Department of Indian Affairs and Northern Development. Technically, although there are almost one million people of native ancestry in Canada, only about 300,000 status Indians are affected by the federal Indian Act. The government spends over a billion dollars a year ($1.64 billion in 1982) administering a wide range of services.

In recent years overlapping federal and provincial jurisdictions regarding native affairs have created more problems. The concerns of nonstatus Indians do not come directly under the federal government and become the responsibilities of the provinces. The Metis, neither white nor native and not under the Indian Act, form a strong, distinctive unit. In the House of Commons in 1974 Len Marchand stated the problems of the Metis: "The people have come under provincial jurisdiction, and by and large they have been left out of society."

Education of status Indian and Inuit children is an obligation of Indian Affairs. The minister is authorized to maintain schools directly or, since 1948, through provincial departments of education which it reimburses. The integration of native children into provincial schools is encouraged, and today over 50 per cent of the approximately 80,000 Indian students in Canada attend provincial schools. On northern crown lands and reserves the federal government co-operates with territorial departments of education, and in recent years policy has been to transfer control to native bands. In 1976–77 Indian enrollment at the elementary level in Canada totalled 71,717, and secondary, 10,589. Students in universities and other postsecondary institutions numbered 3,577; another 6,170 were taking vocational courses.

In the more populated areas Indian students were integrated into the public school system, while Indian and Inuit students from the most remote areas were boarded at regional residential schools, the federal government paying transportation and maintenance costs, or were financed to southern institutions.

In acknowledgement of the impracticality and undesirability of the old policy of enforced assimilation, provincially administered, community day schools gained support, courses were revised to make them more applicable to native life, and vocational programs were expanded. Some universities introduced special courses for native students as well as faculties of native studies. But by 1971–72, native education was far from satisfying the needs. While 86.3 per cent of the population was enrolled in elementary schools, only 13.7 per cent was in secondary schools. The dropout rate was four times the national average and over 90 per cent of Indian children failed to complete high school.

Status Indians and Inuit were not federally enfranchised until 1960, and were subsequently elected to school boards, municipal councils and the provincial and federal legislatures. They continued to press for a greater voice in their own affairs, through the courts and lobby groups, determined to share in the benefits and responsibilities of industrial society while sustaining a changing, yet distinctive native culture.

Although federal-provincial agreements were reached on education, other native policies added to intergovernmental tensions. One of the most frustrating to the native peoples concerns the critical issue of land ownership. In the constitutional division of powers natural resources, including land, are under provincial jurisdiction, but the Indian population, their treaties and reserves, are federal concerns; when bands seek settlement of land claims their requests have been tossed back and forth between the two levels of government since the various parties cannot reach agreement. Public health and welfare is a provincial responsibility and services to nonstatus Indians, including those who were formerly status Indians under the Indian Act, are a reluctantly assumed provincial cost.

Significant developments brought Indian affairs to public consciousness in the 1970s and affected attitudes of whites and natives. In 1971 the U.S. government passed the Alaska Native Claims Settlement Act granting natives almost $1 million and 45 million acres (18 million ha) of land. This served as a criterion for Canadian natives. Although in 1973 the Supreme Court of Canada rejected by a vote of four to three the claims of the Nishga Indians, who had never signed a treaty, to land in

British Columbia, the federal government subsequently announced its new policy of comprehensive claims settlement in nontreaty areas of Canada, by which it is committed to come to terms with Indian land claims and other aboriginal rights. In 1975 the Canadian and Quebec governments reached an agreement with the Inuit and Cree to permit development in northern Quebec of hydro power from the rivers flowing into James Bay. In 1982 a land claims settlement was achieved by the federal government, British Columbia and Penticton Indians by which the province will return 12,243 acres (almost 5000 ha) of unoccupied crown land and pay $1 million to retain other land. The federal government will pay $13.2 million compensation for the remaining acreage now largely held by third parties. This agreement is seen as precedent-setting for the other twenty-one claims still outstanding on the land withdrawn from B.C. reserves without Indian consent in 1912. And claims are finally being settled in the Yukon and western Arctic, as a result of the huge resource-development schemes there.

Five native races speaking seven different languages live in the vast lands of the western Arctic and Mackenzie Valley. The Dene demand to be treated as a distinct "nation." They and the Inuit are seeking to form their own provinces from the Northwest Territories, roughly east and west of a line from the Mackenzie delta to Churchill, which would give each of them control of their own interests and resources as well as political equality within Canada. The explorations for oil and gas in the north and the proposed pipelines have resulted in specific demands by the native peoples, and their right to consultation was strengthened by the 1977 federally commissioned Mackenzie Valley Pipeline Inquiry, which recommended a ten-year delay in construction pending settlement of native claims regarding land, resources, education, health and social services, and new political institutions.

Developments in the north have brought a new crisis to the native people. They are aware of the ruinous effects that aggressive white industrial policies have had on native peoples in the south during the last century and now they are facing the same double threat of dispossession and depopulation. They want to share in the material advantages of modern society— power boats, snowmobiles, electricity, modern heating.

Through television and in northern urban centres they are inundated with the values of the wider society. How can their material aspirations be achieved without resorting to a wage economy and accepting the industrialization of the north? Will they have a hand in northern development or simply be pushed aside as in the past? How can they secure the benefits without losing their hunting grounds, their cultural traditions and their inherent individuality? And are they strong enough to resist the pressures of a continent threatened by critical energy shortages?

The federal proposal to patriate the constitution in 1981 was a catalyst which united the native peoples and the Metis, who all felt that their present special status would become weakened or circumscribed under the proposition. Hearings, widespread demonstrations and even a native delegation to London showed they were determined to use this occasion for the advancement of their interests. As a result, the Constitution Act of 1982 included the following sections:

25. The guarantee in this charter of certain rights and freedoms shall not be construed so as to abrogate or derogate from any aboriginal treaty or other rights or freedoms that pertain to the aboriginal peoples of Canada including
    (a) Any rights or freedoms that have been recognized by the Royal Proclamation of October 7, 1763 and
    (b) Any rights or freedoms that may be acquired by the aboriginal peoples of Canada by way of land claims settlement.

35. (1) The existing aboriginal and treaty rights of the aboriginal peoples of Canada are hereby recognized and affirmed.
    (2) In this Act "aboriginal peoples of Canada" include the Indian, Inuit and Metis peoples of Canada.

The Western Identity

Although historically part of the British Empire and joined together by the BNA Act, Canada has always been a union of regions and this regionalism remains. The west was annexed by Canada and for decades was an outpost of central Canada, but did not have the same traditions. True, westerners study early Canadian history and recognize the significance to democracy of the Quebec Act, the Constitutional Act, the Rebellions of 1837, Lord Durham's Report and the BNA Act uniting eastern Canada, all shaping the political and economic conditions in the country today. But none of them involved the west directly.

Western Canadians have their own historical preoccupations—the fur traders, the gold rushes, Louis Riel, the problems of native peoples, the coexistence of many ethnic groups, the development of natural resources. Westerners recognize that central Canada opened the west for its own profit—railways and financial institutions moved in to expand the market and investment opportunities of the east. This was accomplished by a federal government, controlled by eastern interests, which assisted these groups with protective tariffs, discriminatory railway rates and other legislation at the expense of the west.

After the west was populated, when the provincial governments were more experienced and the region proved to have more riches than wheat, westerners demanded recognition of their contributions to the nation. The government in Ottawa is still demonstrably controlled by the combined Ontario/Quebec vote and the west wants this veto power broken, in order to achieve a greater voice in both national and international affairs. It sees increased western control of resources and greater provincial powers as helping to redress the outflow of wealth in the past.

Westerners are, first of all, Canadians, but they see Canada as a federation of regions, each with its own problems. Whereas certain responsibilities necessarily belong to the federal government, local problems, westerners believe, are best understood by provincial governments, which are now capable of managing their own affairs. They should have full control of those provincial responsibilities outlined in the BNA Act, on the premise that strong, self-governing units will in fact make a stronger and more united country.

Chapter Eleven

POSTWAR YEARS: POLITICS

Mackenzie King

P RIME Minister Mackenzie King was re-elected in 1945 with a clear but reduced majority. King, however, was aging and in 1948 he retired; two years later he died. In recent years, many biographers have tried to interpret this enigmatic, lonely man. Seldom did he demonstrate positive leadership until he was pressured by public opinion. Yet through political acumen he held his party together and guided the country through some of its most difficult years. All successful Canadian prime ministers must have the ability to compromise, and in this approach to government Mackenzie King was supreme.

Louis St. Laurent

The Liberal Party has selected alternatively English and French leaders. Mackenzie King's successor, Louis St. Laurent, was a prominent Quebec corporation lawyer who had been the prime minister's chief Quebec lieutenant. St. Laurent gained the respect and admiration of both French and English for his administrative abilities and his warm personal appeal. His term marked a period of expansion and optimism in both domestic and foreign affairs, but politically showed little change from the policies of the King government.

The St. Laurent government continued the policy of extending and defining Canada's sovereignty. The word "British" was
dropped and "Dominion" downplayed in Commonwealth ter-
minology. In 1949 the Canadian process of appeal to the Judicial Committee of the British Privy Council was abolished and
the Supreme Court of Canada became the final court of appeal.
In the same year the BNA Act was modified to permit the
federal government to amend those sections in which it had
exclusive interest. Also in 1949 Newfoundland became the
tenth province, and Vincent Massey became the first Canadian-
born governor general.

Louis St. Laurent died in 1973 at the age of ninety-two. His
dispassionate approach to politics and his refusal to become
embroiled in interparty bickering were summed up by John
Diefenbaker: "He was motivated by a deep sense of public duty
and believed there could be no greater honour than to serve
one's country. . . . But he never understood the clash of debate
in the House of Commons."

The Diefenbaker Era

St. Laurent had no problem winning the elections of 1949
and 1953, but the Liberal Party after twenty consecutive years
in office had become complacent and arrogant. Symptomatic of
this attitude was the "pipeline debate." Two powerful competing lobby groups wanted to pipe Alberta gas directly to the
United States or, alternatively, to construct a pipeline to eastern Canada that would pass south of the Great Lakes, but C. D.
Howe, minister of trade and commerce, was determined to
bring the gas to eastern Canada by an all-Canadian route. In the
summer of 1956 Howe forced closure on the debate in the
House of Commons. The Conservatives, led by their aggressive
new leader John Diefenbaker, capitalized on Howe's action,
claiming that refusal to debate was a betrayal of parliamentary
rights. Diefenbaker's rousing oratory and strong personality
carried his party to a minority victory in 1957, marking the end
of thirty years of Liberal government. St. Laurent resigned as
leader in 1957 and was succeeded by Lester B. Pearson.

When Diefenbaker took office, he had the advantage of a
disorganized opposition. During the early months of his

administration he outlined programs which promised rapid development of the country under Canadian control. He offered his vision for "One Canada" and the opening of the "New North." In 1958, feeling that he had gained the confidence of the electorate and that uncommitted voters would support a winner, he called another general election, hoping to gain a majority in the House. The Conservatives won an amazing 208 seats, the largest mandate ever given to a prime minister. Even Quebec accorded him 62 per cent of its votes— the first Conservative majority since John A. Macdonald's. The Liberals were reduced to 49 seats, the CCF to 8 and the Social Credit Party had none.

The Conservative legislation was impressive and reflected Diefenbaker's western background. The South Saskatchewan River power and irrigation project was begun, the Board of Broadcast Governors was established, old age pensions were increased, new federal-provincial tax agreements were adopted, plans were made to open roads and railroads to the resources of the north, wheat markets were expanded to China and Russia. Probably Diefenbaker's most significant achievement was the enactment of the Canadian Bill of Rights.

Although he was a powerful orator and critic, he did not have the leadership abilities necessary to hold his party and cabinet together. Conservative leaders have always been English-speaking and since the time of Macdonald have failed to find strong Quebec lieutenants: Diefenbaker never understood Quebec and was unable to establish a strong collaborator. In his attempts to assist farmers, fishermen and other low-income groups, as well as to develop the north, his government spent almost as much money as all previous governments combined. Even so, he was unable to prevent an economic depression and an increase in unemployment.

The electorate's early hopes and enthusiasm had disappeared. Meanwhile, the opposition parties had reorganized; Lester Pearson was now experienced. In 1962 the Conservatives won only a minority of 106 seats, while the Liberals rose to 99 and the former CCF, now the New Democratic Party (NDP), rose to 19. Even the Social Credit Party revived, winning 30 seats, almost all in Quebec. Diefenbaker clung grimly to power and avoided making major decisions regarding defence or the economy. Meanwhile, his party and cabinet were racked by internal quarrels; three ministers resigned over defence policies and others followed. In February 1963 the united opposition defeated the government, and in the ensuing election the Liberals won a minority decision with 129 seats. The Conservatives were reduced to 95 and the NDP and Social Credit to 17 and 24 seats respectively.

John G. Diefenbaker

Diefenbaker was born in 1895 of German-Scottish ancestry. In 1903 the family moved to the west where he witnessed the struggles of the early settlers and the agonies of the Depression years. As an attorney, he won a reputation for supporting the underprivileged. Ever a fighter, he lost five federal election campaigns before becoming a member of the Conservative opposition in 1940. His attempts to win the party leadership were unsuccessful until 1956. To many in his party he embodied popular radicalism, and he never lost contact with the people, especially the farmers, nor forgot his early struggles on behalf of the least privileged. Diefenbaker rejected the Conservative Party's reputation as the party of the business establishment, believing it could appeal to all levels of society. He was a monarchist, and while in opposition never failed to question any legislation, however minor, that threatened Canada's loyalty to the royal family or the British connection. Diefenbaker did not become prime minister until he was sixty-one years old. After his defeat in 1963, the disorganized Conservative Party demanded a leadership vote, and in 1967 he was replaced by Robert Stanfield.

Twenty years before, the Conservative Party had been weakened by the business-oriented Ontario faction's opposition to the National Progressive policies of John Bracken, which had resulted in his replacement by George Drew. To westerners, Diefenbaker's defeat in the convention was another example of the power of Toronto's Bay Street—its opposition to western influence and its determination to retain control of the Canadian economy. The west never lost its love for Diefenbaker. He won a record thirteen elections in succession and continued to sit in the House of Commons until his death in 1979. He never ceased to be a dominant figure in debate as he relentlessly needled the Liberal government. Especially honoured in his home province of Saskatchewan, Diefenbaker will always be remembered by both supporters and opponents for his dedication to the "average Canadian" and his vision of "One Canada." After his death, his influence held in the west, which continued to reject the Liberals.

Lester Bowles Pearson

Lester Pearson was only two years younger than Diefenbaker but differed from him sharply in background and personality. Beginning in 1948, he won eight federal elections. As minister of external affairs, he brought more prestige to Canada for his responsible leadership of the middle powers than had any previous Canadian. He was present at the formation of NATO, president of the UN General Assembly, and instrumental in the formation of the United Nations Emergency Force (1957) which alleviated the Suez crisis and for which he received the Nobel Peace Prize.

Pearson was a friendly man who combined the qualities of humility and humour. As one who worked for world peace, he was proud to be a Canadian. Réal Couette eulogized him: "He worked for the national unity of Canada. He never said anything in the west against the east or in the east against the west. He always tried to convince the Canadian people, whether they spoke French, Ukrainian, Italian, English, or any other language, that their first duty was to be a genuine Canadian."

He had been little involved in domestic affairs; indeed, he had shown small interest in them. Said one Liberal backbencher: "He came as a professional in diplomacy but as an amateur in politics." His first few years as leader of the opposition were difficult and humiliating, requiring him to face the cutting oratory of the experienced Diefenbaker, but Pearson stubbornly continued to master the techniques of parliamentary debate.

Pearson was always handicapped as the leader of a minority government after both elections of 1963 and 1965. In spite of early indecisions, the government nevertheless had a number of solid achievements: reforms in parliamentary procedure; a new nonpolitical procedure for the redistribution of Commons seats; minimum income levels for old-age pensioners and the promise to reduce eligibility from age seventy to sixty-five by 1970; liberalization of divorce laws; the extension of vocational and technical education; the abolition of capital punishment; collective bargaining for the civil service; a transferable Canada Pension Plan; medicare; and the provincial option to withdraw from federal-provincial shared cost programs. In 1968 he instigated federal-provincial conferences for revision of the constitution and appointed a Royal Commission on Bilingualism and Biculturalism. Apart from the unification of the armed forces, probably his most controversial action was the adoption of a new Canadian flag.

In 1968 Pearson resigned as leader of the party and died in 1973. As his Nobel Prize citation states, he was a man who had "strong faith in the final victory of the good forces of life."

New Leaders

In the election of 1968, both major parties offered the voters new leaders. The Nova Scotian Robert Stanfield had a reputation for honesty and sincerity, and the Conservatives hoped that his middle conservative stance would heal the wounds of the bitter convention that had dismissed Diefenbaker. The scars remained, however, so that it was largely Diefenbaker's own continuing loyalty to the party that held it together and kept it strong in the west.

Upon Pearson's resignation, the Liberals selected Pierre Elliott Trudeau as leader. A university graduate and widely travelled, Trudeau was first elected in 1965 from Quebec and became minister of justice. In the 1968 federal-provincial conference, he ably presented his strong belief in federalism. This conference was a turning point, for television cameras conveyed his stimulating personality to the nation.

In 1968 he was sworn in as prime minister and three days later asked for dissolution. The Liberal slogan of a "Just Society" paled beside the "Trudeaumania" sweeping the nation. The Liberals won 155 seats with 45 per cent of the vote, while the Conservatives dropped to 72 seats. The federal Social Credit now consisted of the Quebec-based Ralliement des

Créditistes holding 14 seats, while the NDP won 22. For the first time since 1962 Canada had a majority government.

The Trudeau Government

Under the strong leadership of Prime Minister Trudeau, the new government acted decisively. Changes to parliamentary procedure gave more responsibilities to committees. Amendments were made to the criminal code, ranging from new laws on abortion and homosexuality to bail procedures for young offenders. The voting age was lowered to eighteen. Consumer protection and improved welfare laws were introduced. One of the most significant early pieces of legislation was the Official Languages Act, which established English and French as coequal languages for the civil service, crown agencies and federal courts in bilingual districts where the minority group amounted to at least ten per cent of the population. In foreign relations, the Trudeau government continued support for the UN, NATO and NORAD, and it was among the first to recognize the People's Republic of China.

In a few years the enthusiasm of the early Trudeau government waned and its policies became more housekeeping than innovation. The prime minister had demanded secrecy and solidarity in his cabinet and as the years passed his attitude was perceived as dictatorial. Commission reports and other information were buried in bureaucracy and not presented for either public or parliamentary debate. At a time when all western nations were plagued by inflation and unemployment, the Trudeau government was unable to check the trend in Canada. The Canadian dollar fell in relationship to the American, which in turn was suffering in relation to other currencies. Budget deficits resulted in an ever-increasing national debt. Trudeau's support declined and after the elections of 1972 and 1974 the Liberals were again a minority government.

Trudeau was suspect in the west for many reasons. Even in the decisive victory of 1968 he had not swept the west, except in British Columbia where he won 15 out of 23 seats. Although there were slight Conservative gains, many former Conservative seats went to the NDP; in Alberta the Conservatives retained 15 out of 19 members. Trudeau's majority in the

House was dependent on his solid support in Quebec, and his
government was accused of giving Quebec most-favoured treatment. Bilingual legislation fuelled the resentment of those
provinces whose other ethnic minorities far outnumbered the
French but received no special consideration. Trudeau was also in conflict with those provinces demanding greater autonomy.

When he was finally forced to call an election in May 1979,
he faced a discontented nation, especially in the west.
Although his support of federalism was largely responsible for
the defeat of Quebec Premier René Lévesque's "sovereignty-
association" plebiscite, the strong separatist movement could
conceivably bring further federal concessions to Quebec and
there was an anti-French backlash. Labour unions were restless
as inflation eroded away their gains. Wheat was not moving
because of the lack of storage and shipping facilities. Taxes
were increasing while the national debt was reaching stagger-
ing figures. The decline in world trade was reducing exports.
Alberta and the federal government were in confrontation over
the price of oil, export policies and the division of profits.

Upon the resignation of Robert Stanfield in 1974, the Progressive Conservatives had selected as leader an Albertan,
Charles Joseph Clark, who had been first elected to the House
of Commons in 1972. Almost unknown nationally, he presented a quiet, serious figure who did not compete in show-
manship with the earlier Trudeau or Diefenbaker. He came to
the leadership when many people had turned against the dominating Trudeau and were looking for someone who could offer
stability in uncertain times. In his quiet, positive way Clark
seemed to be such a man.

High on the Conservatives' campaign list were offers to
make mortgage interest tax deductible, to expand grain-han-
dling facilities 50 per cent in five years, to make Canada self-
sufficient in energy, to introduce a freedom of information act,
to hold a referendum in the Northwest Territories on provincial status. They promised to increase provincial control of
communications, fisheries and culture as well as provincial
jurisdiction over offshore resources. The federal NDP under Ed
Broadbent had the strong support of some union leaders but
also retained some of its earlier CCF policies. For westerners it
promised a national petroleum company, ceilings on mortgage

rates, assistance to consumer associations and co-operatives, retention of the Crowsnest freight rates, and upgrading of Churchill and Prince Rupert into major ports, as well as pledging to work in conjunction with native peoples for solutions to their problems. Under Broadbent the party's policies were left-of-centre, a position formerly claimed by the Liberals.

The election of 1979 was not so much a vote for the Conservatives as a protest vote against Trudeau. Joe Clark, still under forty, became the youngest prime minister in Canadian history, and the leader of a minority government with 136 out of 282 seats. Of the 114 Liberal seats, only 3 were west of Ontario. Of the 75 Quebec seats, 67 were Liberal, 6 were Créditiste, but only 2 were Conservative. The NDP rose to 26 seats, of which 17 were from the west. Against the solid Liberal opposition, Clark was dependent on the support of other parties, and when his policies differed from the NDP he was dependent on the precarious support of the Créditistes.

The Conservative government was determined to reduce the federal deficit and to restore the economy: in parliament's second month it introduced a budget which included a number of tax increases, the most controversial being an excise tax of 18 cents on a gallon (almost 4 cents per litre) of gasoline, on the promise that Alberta would receive more money for its oil at the wellhead. The Conservatives were convinced that the other parties would not risk another election and a clear Conservative majority, but their gamble failed when the Liberals and NDP combined to defeat the budget—and the government—while the Créditistes abstained.

After his defeat Trudeau had resigned as party leader but now, faced with a new election, he was persuaded to return. The Liberal strategy was to concentrate on southern Ontario and to stress that Clark's budget meant an immediate substantial increase in the price of gasoline. The strategy succeeded. In January 1980 the Liberals were returned with a clear majority of 146 to the Conservatives' 103 and the NDP's stronger 32. Of the total Liberal seats, 125 were from Quebec and Ontario; except for 2 in Winnipeg they had no seats west of Ontario. A dividing line had been established between Ontario and the west.

For sixty years the Canadian government has been domi-

nated by the Liberal Party. The Conservatives have held power
for three short periods, under Bennett, Diefenbaker and Clark.
These three successful leaders were from the prairies, yet they
were dependent on national support; apparently none was able
to understand Quebec and all failed to discover a strong
Québécois collaborator who could win the French vote. To
offset the inherent anti-Conservative attitude in Quebec, the
Conservatives depended on the support of industrial and commercial Ontario, so that the swing in that province nullified
Clark's success in the west. Among sullen, discontented westerners, the election fuelled the belief that they were the pawns
of a government controlled by central Canada.

Inflation, labour unrest, high interest rates and a multibil-
lion-dollar national deficit remained unsolved. Because of his
energy policies and attempts to strengthen the federal government, Trudeau appeared to the west to be insensitive to its
aspirations. The prime minister became wholly absorbed by
"patriation of the constitution" from Britain. Federal-provincial conferences, dating from the Rowell-Sirois Commission of
1940, continued to be held in an attempt to reach agreement on
constitutional amendments, but Trudeau's position as a strong
federalist could not accommodate the premiers' demands for
greater autonomy. No province in Canada had a Liberal government; at the same time, the policies and demands of the various provincial leaders were widely divergent. Nevertheless,
the western provinces were united in their opposition to unilateral changes in fiscal arrangements proposed by Ottawa, and
they all agreed that they should participate in negotiating international tariff agreements. Above all, they insisted on control
of natural resources.

Trudeau's determination to override opposition and unilaterally patriate the BNA Act alienated all provinces except
Ontario and New Brunswick. He was challenged in the
Supreme Court of Canada, which in 1981 ruled that while unilateral amendment by the federal government was legal, precedent required provincial agreement. Under pressure of this
decision, the federal and provincial governments did reach a
compromise agreement on an amending formula and bill of
rights. Future amendments will have to be approved by seven
provinces, representing 50 per cent of the population: thus

Ontario and Quebec each lost its veto power, to the satisfaction of the west. Quebec refused to accept this formula and withdrew its support but was overridden by the approval of the other nine provinces. The amended constitution, the Constitution of Canada Act, passed the Canadian parliament on 2 December 1981 and, after acceptance by the British parliament, came into force on 17 April 1982. Many problems remain to be resolved: interpretations of the bill of rights, provincial and federal responsibilities, and the protection of the rights of women and native peoples.

In the eighty-six years since Laurier's success in 1896, the Liberal Party has been in power for sixty-seven. This trend has not carried through in the four western provinces, however, which almost always have found themselves in opposition. Only twice have dramatic federal leaders, Diefenbaker in 1958 and Trudeau in 1968, aroused enthusiasm in the west.

In federal elections Manitoba steadfastly supported Macdonald and the Conservatives until the collapse of Borden's Union government. After a decade of fluctuating allegiance in the 1920s, it turned to the Liberals until the rise of Diefenbaker. British Columbia was steadily Conservative, except for a brief period of support for Laurier, until 1945. For the next thirty years it divided its votes as the NDP became a strong provincial party, and in 1974 returned to the Progressive Conservatives. Alberta, beginning as Liberal, was soon disillusioned and after 1921 supported protest movements—the National Progressives and the Social Credit—until Diefenbaker. Saskatchewan remained Liberal until 1945 when it turned towards the CCF for three elections. Since the Diefenbaker sweep of 1958, the four western provinces, with the exception of British Columbia in the 1970s when it supported the federal NDP, have given majorities to the federal Progressive Conservatives.

The long history of western representation by minority parties has undoubtedly resulted in neglect by the federal government. Repeatedly westerners have tried to establish new political parties that promote their interests, but these have failed when tested against the overwhelming eastern majorities of the older parties. Westerners have felt left out of the governing process and have grown increasingly frustrated by their inability to instigate change.

Saskatchewan

Because Saskatchewan had the largest percentage of rural population of all the provinces and was the most dependent on agriculture, success in Saskatchewan politics demanded the support of the agricultural community. The Liberals kept power by adapting party policies to provincial agricultural needs and maintaining close contacts with the Saskatchewan Grain Growers Association.

The Conservatives never recovered from their short disastrous period in office (1928–34), and the only possible alternative to the Liberals was the CCF, basically a farmers' party. Although it was the official opposition by 1934, the CCF had little early success except in some municipalities. Following the years of drought and Depression, discontent increased in the province during the war years, partly because of opposition to Mackenzie King's policies and to some extent because of desire for change. The CCF modified its socialist policies and avoided such topics as nationalization of industry and collectivization of land. In 1944, under the leadership of Tommy Douglas, it won 53 per cent of the vote and 47 of the 55 seats. It would repeat its success in 1948, 1952, 1956 and 1960, after which Douglas moved to the federal House.

T. C. Douglas, born in Scotland in 1904, was ordained as a Baptist minister in 1930 and was always concerned with people's problems. His first political venture as a Farm-Labour candidate was unsuccessful. Persuaded to run federally, he was elected in 1935 and served until 1944 when he resigned to lead the Saskatchewan CCF. Winning five successive electoral victories, he governed Saskatchewan for twenty years. In 1961 he returned to federal politics as national leader of the newly organized NDP. After ten years he resigned from leadership but continued to sit in the House of Commons until his retirement in 1979.

At only five feet six inches (168 cm) tall, the slight Douglas gave a deceptive impression of shyness and humility, but no one could surpass him in oratory. He commanded all the tricks of public speaking—a thorough knowledge of his topic, a supply of interest-catching anecdotes, and an air of sincerity and strong belief. In debate he was incisive and deadly with repartee.

Upon obtaining power in Saskatchewan, he did not make the error of introducing socialist policies too quickly. For twenty years he eased Saskatchewan towards moderate socialism, defended the west against federal domination, and supported the farmers. He demonstrated that a balance between public and private interests was possible.

Following the success of Diefenbaker, another westerner, the CCF suffered federally and in 1961 was reorganized as the New Democratic Party in an effort to co-ordinate the objectives of farmers and labour. After ten years as federal NDP leader, Douglas resigned in favour of David Lewis. As leader of the first avowed socialist government in Canada or the United States, Tommy Douglas showed that a welfare state with honest and dedicated leadership was practical and compatible with limited free enterprise.

The CCF–Saskatchewan Section did not change its name until six years after the formation of the NDP and even then retained its provincial identity by adopting the name NDP–Saskatchewan Section. The party was fortunate that during its term of office new resources were developed in the province, such as uranium, potash and oil. Although socialist, the party was not revolutionary and never attempted to change the system of responsible government which rested on cabinet control and parliamentary opposition. The CCF proceeded slowly with socialization, assisted by the federal government's initiatives of family allowances (1944), health grant programs (1948), improvements in Old Age Security (1951) and a nationwide Hospital Insurance Act (1957) by which it paid 50 per cent of the costs. This last was probably influenced by Saskatchewan's compulsory prepaid hospitalization plan of ten years earlier, paid for by insurance premiums and an increase in the sales tax from two to three per cent. Alberta and British Columbia followed with similar plans. In 1962, after two years of opposition by the medical profession and an election, the Saskatchewan government established its more controversial medical care scheme, also requiring premiums and an increase in sales tax to five per cent and in corporation tax of one per cent. An earlier attempt had been made in British Columbia in

1936 to introduce a Health Insurance Act which would cover the cost of a physician's treatment for patients earning less than $2,400 a year, but it was opposed by the doctors and postponed indefinitely. In Saskatchewan the government held firm against the near revolt by the medical profession and it had the first medicare plan in North America, a precedent for other provincial and federal governments to follow.

The CCF actually carried out few socialist experiments since the federal government was instituting many welfare policies. In its last years the CCF was responsible for little advanced provincial legislation. W. S. Lloyd, the provincial leader after 1961, was a conscientious man who lacked Douglas's spark. In 1964 and 1967 the NDP lost to the reorganized "Saskatchewan Liberals" under Ross Thatcher.

Thatcher had been a successful federal CCF candidate in three successive elections beginning in 1945, but he was primarily a businessman and "free enterpriser." Disagreeing with CCF policies, he withdrew from the party in 1955 to sit as an independent, and in 1959 accepted leadership of the provincial Liberal Party. At a conference of western Liberals in 1966, Thatcher claimed that the Ottawa Liberals had lost interest in the western groups and he dissociated his provincial party from them. He failed in his first election against Tommy Douglas but was successful against Lloyd.

Thatcher's victories were narrow—only one per cent of the vote separated the two parties in both elections. Lloyd resigned as NDP leader and was succeeded by Alan E. Blakeney, who won a clear majority in 1971, partly on his promise to nationalize at least one-half of the province's potash industry. The Liberals were undermined, too, by a revived Conservative Party which won 7 seats, its first representation with one exception since 1934, though it was far behind the 40 NDP and 32 Liberal seats. In 1975 Blakeney repeated his success, winning 44 seats.

By the 1982 election Saskatchewan was suffering from the Canada-wide recession. The government had established several crown corporations, creating a large bureaucracy of civil servants. Energy costs were increasing as were taxes; farmers were being forced into bankruptcy by high interest rates; unemployment was rising. A too-confident government had lost touch with the people after eleven years in office.

Blakeney was up against a resurrected Progressive Conservative Party led by Grant Devine, an agricultural economist and farmer who strongly opposed the province's socialist policies. In a landmark election the Conservatives won 57 seats while the NDP were reduced to 7. For the first time Saskatchewan was led by a Progressive Conservative government.

When Broadbent's federal NDP agreed to support Trudeau's modified constitutional proposals, Trudeau had hoped that the NDP's strong western base would mean western approval: but Blakeney, siding with Alberta, was firmly opposed. Whereas the federal and provincial branches of the older parties had long been separate entities, the NDP had been unified, so that this new split threatened the party's solidarity in Saskatchewan, the only province in 1981 with an NDP government. The Liberal taint was undoubtedly one factor in Blakeney's defeat.

The Saskatchewan of Grant Devine is vastly different from Tommy Douglas's time. Although the Depression still haunts memories, two generations have passed, and wartime is unknown to many voters. During the Depression thousands left Saskatchewan, so that for many years it was one of the few provinces without population growth. From 992,000 in 1931 the population decreased to a low of 880,000 in 1956, after which it began a steady increase. The loss was responsible for the federal election regulation which limits the decrease in representation per province to three in any one census period. Saskatchewan's representation in Ottawa dropped from 21 in 1945 to 13 in 1968, which it maintained until the election of 1979 when, with an increase in the size of the House of Commons, Saskatchewan's representation was raised to 14.

The labour force, which was 67 per cent agricultural in 1941, is now 67 per cent nonagricultural. Small independent farmers on isolated, self-sufficient operations are being displaced by larger farm businesses requiring large capital outlays and business and technical expertise. The province's uncertain agricultural base has been broadened by the extraction of oil, natural gas, uranium, minerals and potash. Despite all of these developments, the economy is still subject to international market fluctuations. Thirty per cent of the population is now

located in Regina and Saskatoon. Traditionally a farm and university centre, Saskatoon is the fastest-growing city in the province, owing to the South Saskatchewan River dam, new industries, its proximity to the potash and northern uranium mines,
and its federal government offices. From early times
Saskatchewan has been considered a "have-not" province but
by the 1970s its status had changed. Its broad economic base,
growing population and influx of investment capital are indic-
ative of the influence and wealth accruing to western Canada.

Manitoba

Three conflicting interest groups dominate Manitoba politics after 1920: the agricultural interests, largely Liberal and
antiurban; labour; and the British connection. From the early
1920s the National Progressive John Bracken was able to maintain a coalition government with the Liberals and in 1943 even
included the CCF for one year. Coalition resulted in disinterest
and even boredom in provincial affairs, for there was little
disagreement among the leading parties.

In 1943 Bracken left provincial politics to become leader of
the Conservative Party. He hoped to introduce such NPP policies as low tariffs more favourable to the west into the Conservative platform, and insisted that the party be renamed the Progressive Conservatives. A conscientious worker, Bracken did
not have a dynamic personality which would inspire popular
appeal and in 1948 he was replaced as party leader by George
Drew.

Bracken was succeeded as provincial leader by Stuart Garson, who also left to become a federal Liberal cabinet minister
in 1948. His successor to the coalition leadership was Douglas
Campbell, a prosperous farmer. For thirty-five years the coalition government controlled Manitoba. Its moderate and basic
policies, if lackluster, did provide an efficient administration
serving the needs of the province. Manitoba was growing
steadily and there were no spectacular developments. The
major change was the spread of rural electrification. The only
opposition came from the CCF whose support was in the northern agricultural communities and the poorer sections of Winnipeg. During the postwar Cold War years it suffered from its

avowed socialist policies which were perceived as procommunist, and lost the support of many middle-class and ethnic groups. The party began to adopt a more moderate attitude.

Growth in Manitoba had been comparatively slow, both in population and the economy. In 1950 the Conservatives withdrew from the coalition and reorganized in 1954 under a Winnipeg businessman, Duff Roblin. Four years later, shortly after Diefenbaker's sweep, he was successful. After the years of inertia, the Roblin government inaugurated many new projects. Provincial expenditures in health, welfare and education were increased substantially. Schools were consolidated and improved. A major highway construction program was initiated and the water diversion channel that was to save Winnipeg from floods was constructed. The mining community of Thompson was opened and new hydro power projects were undertaken. In 1967 Roblin permitted French Canadians to receive instruction in French during one-half their classroom schedule, "to make up for the grave injustices committed by the Liberals."

This was a period of national inflation, but although wages appeared to increase, farmers and industrial workers made little gains. Immigration to the province was minimal. Although ethnic communities had thoroughly identified themselves as Canadian over three generations, they still felt ignored in spite of government encouragement of political participation and the perpetuation of ethnic traditions.

In 1967, when Roblin resigned and attempted unsuccessfully to enter federal politics, he was succeeded by Walter Weir, who aroused opposition by his proposal (later retracted) to withdraw from the federal medicare program. The Metis and Indians, who had first voted in 1952, were making known the government's indifference to their health, welfare and employment problems. The French minority was upset by the government's indifference to bilingualism. Thus there was fertile field for an NDP program. In 1969 the party had selected as leader Edward Schreyer, the son of a farmer and of German-Catholic background. He had been a teacher and university professor. His strong, attractive personality appealed to many of the discontented. Voted for by the poorer ethnic agricultural communities, the professional middle class, the labouring classes in the cities, the workers in mining districts, and the Indian and Metis communities, the NDP vaulted from third party status and formed a goverment with 28 seats, a majority of one. In 1973 the NDP rose to 31 against 21 Conservatives and just 5 Liberals.

The domination of the British-Protestant upper-class business group which had controlled Manitoba since 1888 had come to an end. The Schreyer government began a series of moderately socialist reforms. It established an ombudsman and a rentalsman to adjudicate landlord-tenant disputes, took steps to preserve small family farms, promoted health clinics, abolished medicare premiums and introduced a limited "pharmacare" program to assist the elderly. An aggressive program was set up to provide public housing. By encouraging native cooperation and creating jobs in government projects, the province improved living conditions for the Indians and Metis. Assistance was given to municipalities in the areas of welfare and education, partly through tax equalization. French cultural groups and French education were encouraged. Family law reforms gave divorced women a fairer share of marriage assets and more financial support, which were precedent setting in Canada. Nationalization was not a major platform of the NDP government but was compatible with its philosophies, and its 1970 automobile insurance plan provoked great controversy.

These many reforms and welfare projects increased the costs of government. After the initial period of reform, the NDP settled into the pattern of established parties in power and came under the control of a politically conscious cabinet. In 1975 the party showed signs of dissension when Schreyer supported federal wage and price controls. The Conservatives under Sterling R. Lyon began an attack on government spending and emphasized its belief in free enterprise. In 1977 Canada as a whole was experiencing serious inflation and unemployment. Wheat prospects were poor after an exceptionally wet autumn. The discontent became tangible when in that year Lyon won a clear majority of 33 seats.

The following year Schreyer was appointed governor general, on which occasion Trudeau remarked, "He is young, dynamic and not from the central Canada establishment." The NDP selected as his successor Howard Pawley, a Selkirk lawyer, who claimed that the party lost "because it kept harking back to its past accomplishments rather than proposing new policies."

Manitoba is the only western province that has not expanded along with the recent discovery of significant new resources. Premier Lyon promised more austerity in government and auctioned off some of the crown corporations. But in a slipping Canadian economy, Manitoba planned to revive its economy with three huge government-funded projects: a $600-million potash mine, an $800-million aluminum smelter, and a prairie-wide power grid using Manitoba hydroelectricity. In the election of 1981 the voters rejected the Conservative plans, which were identified with private business interests, and returned the NDP under Howard Pawley with 34 seats to the Conservatives' 23. The new government faced a business recession, increasing unemployment, a heavy provincial debt and decisions on the mining and power projects.

Alberta

With the death of Aberhart, leadership of the Social Credit Party passed to his long-time disciple E. C. Manning. Much of the appeal of the Social Credit movement rested on the personal popularity of these two sincere, dedicated men. As its long term continued, the party became more conservative, but although it supported "free individual enterprise," it did take some steps towards state control; it expanded welfare and social services and in 1963 began a premium-based medical plan. Supporting free enterprise, it left little for the Liberal and Conservative parties to champion, and their representation remained minimal. Only three times, in 1940, 1955 and 1967, did the Social Credit Party poll less than 50 per cent of the vote, and never was the opposition in the legislature more than nominal.

The CCF had little success in Alberta, which was more urban than Saskatchewan and whose agriculture was more diversified. With prairies, parklands, foothills and mountains, Alberta has a wide variety of resources. Lumbering and mining had made important contributions to the economy long before the oil boom. The economic significance of the agricultural community has been officially recognized through its proportionally greater representation than population warrants. Unions were neither as numerous nor as aggressive as in British Columbia, and the socialists were torn between moderates and extremists; shortly after Manning became premier he was able to turn the postwar fear of communism against the socialists.

By the 1960s prosperity had returned to Alberta largely because of oil revenues. By 1971 there were Albertans who could not remember the Depression and who had never known any other provincial government than Social Credit. The party offered little new in the way of legislation; the decline of Social Credit federally along with the Diefenbaker victories brought a new interest in imaginative government. Manning, though a thoughtful, modest man who had few enemies and wide respect, was not inspiring. When he retired in 1968 his successor, Harry Edwin Strom, tried in vain to revive the earlier enthusiasm for the party. Strom was a soft-spoken southern Alberta rancher who lacked the fluency and personal appeal of the early leaders.

The provincial Conservative Party had been thirty years in the political wilderness and when it selected Peter Lougheed as leader in 1965 it had no seats in the legislature. Two years later, with 11 seats, the Conservatives were the official opposition. In Peter Lougheed they had a young leader who traced his Alberta ancestry back to the fur-trading Hardisty family. He was confident, well educated and had great organizing ability. He appealed to the new urban young vote and had a strong television presence. Promising a healthy agricultural sector and expansion of the petroleum industry, Lougheed led his party to victory in 1971, winning 63 seats while the Social Credit fell to 25. Four years later the Conservatives won an amazing 69 of the total 75 seats, and in 1979 did even better with 74.

The unprecedented income from oil and natural gas and other nonrenewable resources became a critical challenge to Lougheed. In 1971 Alberta surpassed Ontario in the value of its mineral production. Lougheed stood firm on Alberta's right to control its own resources, despite the many outside pressures—the U.S. demand for increased exports, the demands of provinces like Ontario for a share of the profits, the need for imported investment capital, and federal legislation affecting oil and gas exports as well as foreign investment.

When Trudeau returned as prime minister in 1980, to strengthen eastern support for an amended constitution, he determined to impose further federal taxes on oil and gas which would cover the subsidies on eastern oil and reduce the federal deficit. Such action would weaken provincial control of natural resources and reduce the revenues of the oil- and gas-producing provinces. Lougheed became the western voice of protest against the new taxes. Supported by the western premiers, especially British Columbia's Bill Bennett, Lougheed stood firm and threatened to decrease petroleum production, which would force the federal government to increase its imports of subsidized foreign oil and thus gain nothing. The antifederal attitude of western leaders was reflected in new separatist movements as well as more moderate, pro-Canadian groups such as the Canada West Foundation.

Lougheed recognized that Alberta's present wealth is dependent on limited nonrenewable resources, so to protect the long-term social and economic benefits for future Albertans, he set up the Alberta Heritage Savings Trust Fund, which each year receives 30 per cent of the income from nonrenewable resources. By 1980 the assets of the Heritage Fund totalled $6.4 billion. Saskatchewan copied this policy and by 1981 its Heritage Fund passed $1 billion. The Alberta fund has been used for social and economic research, for investments that will strengthen the province's future economy, and for loans to other provinces at favourable rates. Some provinces, especially Ontario, and the federal government believe that these profits should be divided across the nation, but Alberta maintains that they should be accumulated to ensure a strong, economically diversified province in the future.

British Columbia

As the westernmost province British Columbia has always hosted a frontier society, which has been reinforced by modern mining companies and hydroelectric planners seeking new resources. British Columbians have almost a reverence for magnitude and a craving to be the biggest, showing sympathetic approval for the largest railway, the highest dam, the busiest port, the largest ferry fleet, gigantic paper mills, ambitious pipelines and billion- dollar mining ventures.

Provincial politicians have encouraged these grandiose dreams since the time of Richard McBride and his expansive railway policies. W. A. C. Bennett was masterly at covering any weaknesses in government with flamboyant publicity for his railways and dams. His son, Bill Bennett, has projected new hydro dams with more transmission lines, new natural gas pipelines, railway branch lines and vast new mining areas.

The development of natural resources has required a large influx of capital, much of it speculative—for mineral and oil research or railway construction in the wilderness. Other capital is needed to develop the resources on a large competitive scale. From early times politicians have encouraged heavy investment through favourable legislation, land and monetary grants, special resource-harvesting licences, and tax exemptions. This policy unfortunately led to speculation, manipulation and often fraud. Periodic scandals linking business and government have caused a temporary furor and made newspaper headlines, then were usually shrugged off by the majority of people.

The nature of British Columbia industry produced a large employee class. As industry became more complex and controlled by large corporations, the workers were forced into stronger and larger unions for self-protection. Miners, loggers, fishermen, longshoremen and industrial workers formed powerful organizations. Strikes, often bitter and protracted, became a way of life in the province. Various factions of socialists, often supported by the younger population and intellectuals, also opposed the conglomerates, but the unionists and socialists were both torn by disagreement between militant strikers and moderates who patiently petitioned government for protective legislation.

The postwar population growth was accompanied by an increase in government services. Many agencies, boards and crown corporations were established, and a vast civil service was created at both provincial and municipal levels. Civil servants formed their own unions which, in this province especially, adopted the aggressive attitudes common to other B.C. unions. Union aims were to obtain better working conditions not only from private industry but also from the crown corporations and the various levels of government.

The strength of the British Columbia CCF was among the unionists and intellectuals, many of whom were government employees. It was not basically an agricultural organization as in the prairies. Farming in British Columbia is largely intensive, specialized and, except in the interior ranchlands, often a small, family enterprise. Farmers have been generally prosperous and have never suffered the extreme, uneven conditions of the prairies. They have combined to form local cooperatives such as the B.C. Fruit Growers in the Okanagan or the Fraser Valley Milk Producers Association. As businessmen they have had little sympathy with socialist dogma. The established political parties, on the other hand, have wooed their support with special taxes, credit privileges and subsidies. Although the large interior ridings are sparsely populated, they have always been given representation proportionally far in excess of the urban centres.

In 1940 opposition to Liberal Premier Pattullo was increasing. At the Royal Commission on Dominion-Federal Relations, he had been obdurately opposed to granting greater tax powers to the federal government, thus continuing his feud with Mackenzie King. There was discord in his cabinet when some of his ministers recommended a coalition with the Conservatives against the CCF, which Pattullo definitely rejected.

In the election of 1941 the Liberals were reduced from 31 seats to a minority government of 21 seats; the CCF became the official opposition with 33 per cent of the vote and 14 seats, while the Conservatives were reduced to 12 seats. The government's minority position and the growing strength of the CCF led to further cabinet dissension; Pattullo was replaced as premier by John Hart, who formed a union government of Liberals and Conservatives to check the growing socialist threat.

With the support of industrialists, merchants, landowners and investors, the coalition government under John Hart and later Byron Johnson held power until 1952. Eventually the Conservatives felt they were being discriminated against in cabinet offices and in that year the coalition was disbanded.

The two parties were nevertheless united in their opposition to the CCF. To ensure the defeat of the socialists, the government introduced a system of alternate voting, in which voters marked their first, second and subsequent choices on a single ballot; if no candidate obtained 50 per cent of the vote on the first count, the last-runner's second choices would be counted as well, until a clear winner emerged. It was expected that the Liberals and Conservatives would be the top two and thus control the vote, but it was not to be. Victory went to another party entirely—the Social Credit.

The B.C. Social Credit Party had been a minor party in the province. In 1951 the Alberta party had lent advisers and some financial support. More important was the presence of former Conservatives Tilly Ralston and W. A. C. Bennett, two experienced MLAs who brought credibility to the Social Credit. Bennett was a self-made merchant who had built a successful hardware and appliance business in the Okanagan. Twice he had failed to win leadership of the Conservatives.

The coalition government had achieved very little positive legislation, was continually bickering and, was tainted by patronage scandals. Its hospital insurance scheme was not yet a success, and it had failed to solve labour problems, or to keep its promise to aid separate Catholic schools. The alternate voting scheme backfired for former coalitionists when the free-enterprise Social Credit Party led with 19 seats. The Liberals and Conservatives elected 6 and 4 seats respectively. The socialist threat was substantiated by 18 CCF seats, only one behind the leading party. With this election British Columbia became the only province where neither of the two leading parties were the traditional parties. Lacking an official leader, the victors now chose W. A. C. Bennett, who had been in the legislature since 1941.

Within a year another election was called. Once again the alternate voting favoured Social Credit; the results were Social Credit 28, CCF 14, Liberals 4 and Conservatives one seat. Soon after this election the preferential ballot was abolished.

W. A. C. Bennett led British Columbia for twenty years. He personified the ideals of the industrialists, businessmen and middle class who feared the threat of socialism. Prosperous and engaging, Bennett exuded confidence. "My friends," he would repeat over and over, "the problem is simply free enterprise or socialism." He realized that major support came from the rural interior communities and he catered to their needs by establishing regional services and public works projects, but at the same time protected small businesses from government interference.

The government-owned PGE Railway had been an embarrassment to provincial administrations for thirty years. Finally, construction was revived under Premier Byron Johnson. Credit for completing the line to Prince George went to Bennett's government in 1952. Four years later the section between Squamish and North Vancouver was opened. In October 1958 the railway, now called the British Columbia Railway (BCR), reached Fort St. John and Dawson Creek, where it connected with the Northern Alberta Railway. The BCR was pushed north to Fort Nelson, and extensions into other northern sections of the province were envisioned, but a proposed extension to Dease Lake for access to northwestern resources was abandoned because of high costs. In the 1980s a new 200-mile (320-km) projection was planned to serve the new northeast coal fields.

A huge hydroelectric dam—the W. A. C. Bennett Dam—was completed on the Peace River in 1968. After negotiations between the governments of British Columbia, Canada and the United States, the Columbia River Treaty resulted in a series of dams on the Columbia. The Trans-Canada Highway was completed and first-class roads connected the scattered regions of the province. The John Hart Highway from Prince George to Dawson Creek connected the interior to the Alaska Highway. The Westcoast Transmission gas pipeline was constructed from the Peace River to the coast with extensions to Washington state in 1957. Although Bennett was an avowed opponent of socialism, and even while the national Social Credit convention in Ottawa was voting against public ownership, he took over the private B.C. Electric system and established the provincial Hydro and Power Authority. The government took over the private coastal ferry system and made it one of world's largest ferry fleets, and established the Bank of British Columbia as an alternative to eastern-controlled banks.

To further undermine the CCF, Bennett's government introduced homeowner grants, regulations for employee annual paid vacations, and compulsory automobile insurance. At the same time, by revising the fiscal system, he moved many project costs to "contingent liabilities" and within a few years claimed that the province was free of debt. His stable government and balanced budgets promised a sound investment climate which encouraged major industrial expansion.

As the proponent of business, Bennett consistently opposed the strong labour unions. As early as 1954 the Labour Relations Act provided fines and penalties for unions and their officers who contravened new restrictions on strikes. In 1958 secondary boycotts were forbidden and picketing was limited to plants undergoing a strike. Another bill forbid unions to spend payroll deductions for political purposes. In 1967 the principle of compulsory arbitration was established for "essential industries."

The unions realized they needed to be more politically active and turned to the NDP (former CCF), which had core supporters but had been unable to increase its membership in the legislature. By the late 1960s discontent was increasing among social workers, civil servants and teachers as the Bennett government refused their demands for increased funding in a period of accelerated inflation. The combined discontent of labour unions, social agencies, professional government employees and the many people who simply wanted a change resulted in David Barrett's election as premier in 1972, five years after succeeding Thomas Berger as NDP leader.

The new Barrett government moved rapidly to implement its objectives. In 1973 it established the Insurance Corporation of British Columbia (ICBC), which lowered vehicle insurance rates. A land commission regulated land use in agricultural areas, rent controls were established, the B.C. Petroleum Corporation (1973) regulated petroleum and natural gas production, the Mineral Royalties Act increased the mineral tax, and the civil service was reorganized. Through the B.C. Resources Investment Corporation (BCRIC), a holding corporation, the government acquired companies, often to head off bankruptcies and layoffs. A new labour code was drawn up and collective bargaining rights were extended to civil servants. A prescription drug insurance plan and minimum levels for old-age pensions and welfare were inaugurated. Unfortunately, these reforms resulted in a return of provincial indebtedness.

W. A. C. Bennett retired from leadership of the Social Credit Party after his defeat and died in 1979. He had led British Columbia during its most buoyant and successful era of expansion. Undoubtedly the province would have advanced during these years under another leader, but Bennett's leadership was the force that brought organization and status. This was a turbulent and exciting period of immense construction visions, of labour confrontation, of scandals, of unexpected government actions. Bennett might be admired or hated, but he could not be ignored. When he retired no one could question his success as a politician, as a leader and as someone who understood the majority of the people.

Leadership of the Social Credit Party passed to Bennett's son, William (Bill) R. Bennett. The party was reorganized and was able to draw into its ranks several Conservatives and strong Liberals, thus uniting the antisocialist vote and destroying the provincial Conservative and Liberal parties. The Liberals' base as a federal party in the province was also undermined. Business rallied behind Bennett. In the meantime, Barrett's government was handicapped by national problems of unemployment and inflation. Other reform leaders, such as Aberhart, Douglas and Schreyer, recognized that drastic changes need time, whereas Barrett moved quickly, alienating basic industries such as forestry and mining. Some of the more moderate NDP supporters became alarmed by the rapid changes. In the 1974 federal election the British Columbia NDP fell from eleven seats to two, possibly a symptom of the voters' dissatisfaction with the Barrett government. The provincial election of 1975 unified the antisocialist vote and returned Social Credit.

The younger Bennett showed that he had learned his father's strategies and was a strong, capable leader. Advocating a greater provincial voice in Canadian affairs, he characterized his position in Confederation as a "British Columbia Canadian." He moved quickly to reduce the debts incurred by the previous government by drastically raising automobile insurance and ferry rates. Taking a business-oriented stance, the government made concessions to the forest and mining industries. Funds to numerous government agencies were reduced, many, unfortunately, in the fields of welfare and education. Bennett's attempts to limit civil service, health and welfare salaries and to curtail strikes resulted in strong labour opposition.

In 1979 Bennett called an election within a month of the federal election. The resources of the provincial Conservatives and Liberals were also taken up by the federal election. Similarly, the NDP was forced to divide its attention, but it had a stronger grassroots base than the others. Although it gained in number of votes it was unable to unseat the Socreds. The results were 31 Social Credit, 26 NDP and no seats for the other parties. More significant was the popular vote which showed the Social Credit lead drop from 49 to 46 per cent. Now British Columbia had become the only province where neither the Liberals nor Conservatives were even represented. The NDP, meanwhile, handicapped in 1979 by two simultaneous elections, in the following year revealed its underlying strength by gains in the federal election.

The Social Credit government under Bill Bennett faced many problems. As in the rest of Canada, unemployment and inflation continued to rise. Immigrants, estimated at one thousand a week, many from eastern Canada and from Asia, entered the province, increasing unemployment and adding to welfare costs. Inflation rates were among the highest in the country. Nevertheless, the government continued its plans for major construction projects, including power dams, railway and road extensions, a major convention, sports and world exposition complex in Vancouver, and urban passenger transport. In 1979 the government divested itself of BCRIC, offering 95 per cent of ownership to the public: 10.5 million shares were distributed on a basis of five free shares to each eligible resident of the province, and 81.3 million shares were sold to the public, netting $487.6 million for investment in various industries as well as in oil and gas exploration rights.

The Social Credit government has always prided itself on having a balanced budget, and in 1981, with rising costs and declining revenue, it adopted drastic remedies: provincial sales tax was increased from four to six per cent and taxes were increased on liquor and tobacco, personal incomes, corporations, hotel rooms and gasoline; the rates for natural gas, electricity, ferry transportation and automobile insurance were all raised; legislation was passed to limit cost-of-living adjustments to pensions; limits were set on educational and social services.

Blaming Ottawa for provincial ills has long been a practice of provincial politics, and Bennett followed it very far. The long-term issues were provincial and federal policies for fishery conservation, pipeline construction, railway extensions to the northeast coal fields, and offshore resource development. In the constitution patriation crisis the issues were the federal government's unilateral actions and its apparent disregard for provincial rights and problems. When Ottawa passed its National Energy Policy, Bennett claimed that the resulting loss of export markets for natural gas was the reason for British Columbia's financial difficulties as well as for reduced profitability of both exploration and current production. This, he claimed, was the reason for the necessary rise in provincial taxes. His 1982 budget stated: "The government of Canada has a long tradition of fiscal mismanagement. . . . Ottawa does not represent an infusion of *new* money into the Province. Rather it is a return of tax dollars already collected from British Columbians."

As it entered the 1980s the province foresaw an era of great population and economic growth. It had an abundant and secure energy supply in electricity, natural gas and coal. The Social Credit government had two critical problems. Would its positive actions in resource development overcome the discontent caused by inflation, unemployment and higher taxes and offset the threat of the NDP? In its dealings with the rest of Canada, would it be able to retain control over resource development in the province?

The Territories

The former North-West Territories once comprised all of Rupert's Land except for the original Manitoba and British Columbia. In 1898, following the gold rush, the Yukon Territory was separated and soon was given a fully elected council with a federally appointed commissioner. Progress towards self-government has been steady: in 1977 the veto power of the commissioner was cancelled; today the Yukon is much closer to provincial status, having political parties and responsible government. It is still financially controlled by Ottawa, which supplies most of its revenue, and does not have control of land, resources or fiscal matters. Native claims have not been settled. Railway and hydro construction is needed. Although the territory has rich mineral resources and possible future revenue from gas pipelines, the small population of 21,600 living on 207,000 square miles (536 000 km²) will continue to need financial assistance from outside investors and the federal government.

In 1905 Alberta and Saskatchewan were sliced from the territories and in 1912 Manitoba's present northern boundary was set. Later the remaining Northwest Territories were divided into the districts of Mackenzie, Keewatin and Franklin, controlled by the federal government through a commissioner and by a council of representatives from the Anglican and Catholic missions, the Hudson's Bay Company and the RCMP. Representation was modified over the years to include elected members, and in 1975 the council became wholly elected. Between 1899 and 1921 various treaties were signed with some of the native groups.

The territories, constituting one-third of the area of Canada, remained isolated except for the outside contact provided by fur trading posts, missions and supply ships. The Norman Wells oil fields, the Alaska Highway, the air routes to Alaska and defence for the north were all developed in the Second World War, but the region was still detached from the expanding south. In 1974 the federal MP Wally Firth stated:

It is impossible to get to the people through the mails or the newspapers because many of them cannot read. And in addition to French and English, the people of the Northwest Territories speak at least six separate dialects. They are separated not only by distance and climate but by huge cultural differences and equally huge language problems. Travel is made more difficult by the poorly developed facilities in the north. All our supplies have to be brought in either by boat in the summer or by airplane. In most parts the airplane is the only way to get around.

Improved transportation and new mineral, oil and gas

exploration attracted an influx of transient workers from the south. Oil and natural gas potentials are perhaps five times as great as that of Alberta, but the problems of extraction are enormous. The north already produces all of Canada's tungsten, and there are rich mines of zinc, lead, gold and silver. Between 1919 and 1976 annual mineral production rose from $119 million to an estimated $213 million. The proposed pipelines have caused the north to be looked at in a new light and the population has doubled in the last twenty years to 43,000, in eighty communities. There are 16,000 Inuit from four cultural groups, 7,500 Indians (Dene) in sixteen bands representing six different language groups, and 8,000 Metis. The number of tourists increased over ten years from 80,000 to 300,000 a year.

The Northwest Territories Act of 1975 made the Territorial Council a fully elected body of fifteen members, which was later increased to twenty-two. The council became truly representative of the territories when it included Dene, Inuit and Metis. By these changes the territorial government is prepared for provincial status, but before this can occur, accommodation must be made with the native peoples over their claims for land control, aboriginal rights and inclusion in any new form of government. In 1973, out of more than 1,600 Northwest Territories government employees, only 305 were native people.

All native people in the Mackenzie Valley were united in a common cause until 1975 when the Dene declared themselves a nation; in 1976 the Metis Association announced that it did not accept the Dene declaration of claims and made its own. Inuit would like to see the territories divided in two, with the Inuit Tapirisat assuming control over the eastern region. The dissension among the various native groups weakened their bargaining position and delayed political action. All natives have opposed oil and gas exploration and pipeline construction until agreement can be reached with government to settle their land claims, to protect their aboriginal rights, to guarantee employment and to preserve the ecological balance of the land on which their livelihood depends. In spite of their protests, federal studies and agreements continued to be made without their consent.

Because the potential oil and gas revenues are enormous, and northerners suspect that the federal government does not want to surrender that income by granting provincehood, in the 1980s the proposal for a new constitution aroused widespread alarm in the north. The territories could only observe at federal-provincial conferences, and their representation in Ottawa is minimal; but it did serve to unite native groups. The new constitution, which recognizes "existing" aboriginal and treaty rights (at the behest of Premier Lougheed who feared the implications for native control of oil and gas), will perhaps maintain the status quo of the north for many years yet.

Western Leaders

Canadian prime ministers, by avoiding or deferring particular controversial problems of Confederation, have managed to retain office for long periods, and Canadian history may be divided into eras characterized by the reigning prime ministers, from John A. Macdonald to Pierre E. Trudeau. Similarly, provinces tend to support leaders for long terms. Among western premiers who have served for at least a decade are Walter Scott, Tommy Douglas, R. P. Roblin, Richard McBride, W. A. C. Bennett, William Aberhart, E. C. Manning, Alan Blakeney and Peter Lougheed.

In recent years the majority of western representatives in the federal parliament have usually been in opposition to the governing party. The policy of having cabinet representation from each province has thus been difficult, and cabinet members from the west have often been selected for their provincial origins rather than their abilities. There have been some outstanding ministers from the west, like Clifford Sifton, A. L. Sifton, Charles Dunning, J. G. Gardiner and Stuart Garson. Premiers who attempted unsuccessfully to win the prime ministership include Tommy Douglas, Duff Roblin and John Bracken, all from Manitoba or Saskatchewan. British Columbia and Alberta have had few leaders who attained national significance and their lack of a strong, influential voice in Ottawa may have contributed to their discontent. The CCF/NDP, though always a third party, has had some exceptional western parliamentarians, including J. S. Woodsworth, M. J. C. Coldwell, Agnes MacPhail, Grace MacInnis, Stanley Knowles and Hazen Argue.

John A. Macdonald won a by-election in Victoria and both
Mackenzie King and Wilfrid Laurier won in Prince Albert, but
only three westerners have become prime minister—Bennett,
Diefenbaker and Clark. All were Conservatives, and Bennett's
interests were not in the agricultural west. All governed for
short terms that were but intermissions in eighty years of Liberal government. Two western Canadians have been governors
general: A. Roland Michener, from the central Alberta parkland, was appointed in 1967, and Edward Schreyer, former
premier of Manitoba, was appointed in 1978.

Western Alienation

Federal election campaigns build to the climax of polling
day when Canadians watch suspensefully the tabulation of
votes from east to west. In British Columbia no announcements
are made until the polls close at eight o'clock; then the results
from the eastern regions can be revealed. In February 1980 a
wave of dismay spread through the province when it was
announced that the Liberals had already won a majority government of 146 seats. Of these, 125 had come from Ontario and
Quebec. The still uncounted British Columbia votes meant
nothing to the outcome. Later it became clear that, except for
two seats in Winnipeg and St. Boniface, the Liberals had no
representation west of Ontario. The simmering phrase "western alienation" was revived and there were even scattered cries
of "separation."

As Canada has become populated and politically subdivided, different regions have developed their own economic,
cultural and political characteristics. It has become a nation
with variations in wealth, religious beliefs, languages, political
loyalties and industrial interests. Along with unevenly distributed wealth and political power has come rivalry between geo-
graphic regions and between provinces, as well as strong provincial movements for self-determination. The desire of the
west for more autonomy from the federal government has
become more persistent as the region increases its economic
significance in Canadian affairs.

In the western provinces the demand for political autonomy
is combined with aspirations for economic independence from

the Toronto-Montreal axis. The west's estrangement from the
Montreal-Ottawa-Toronto triangle has deep historical roots
that stretch far back to fur trading days when the furs of the
west brought wealth to Montreal merchants. It continued into
the era of settlement when central Canada annexed the west
and forcibly asserted its control over Red River and along the
Saskatchewan. The early settlers were dependent on the east-
ern-based railways, land companies, commercial interests,
industries and financial houses. The farmers' prosperity was
subject to railway planning, discriminating freight rates and
elevator companies controlled by the east for its profit; they
were handicapped by tariff structures established to protect
eastern industries. The wealth of Ontario was largely accumulated through its annexation and colonization of the west.

The well-established Progressive Conservative and Liberal
parties originated in eastern Canada to deal with eastern problems. They have been suspect in the west and are still believed
to be controlled by eastern interests. Attempts to break this
control have resulted in protest parties with national ambitions, which none of them has achieved. In the last twenty
years the dominating Liberal Party has had little support in the
west (except when British Columbia contributed to the Trudeau sweep of 1968). In 1980, while Quebec elected 75 members to the House of Commons and Ontario elected 95, the four
western provinces together had only 77 seats. The west feels
that it is outvoted, has minimal representation in the governing
party, has no veto power, and lacks influential leaders in the
cabinet.

In 1867 the Fathers of Confederation visualized a union of
four provinces with a strong government at Ottawa and lesser
provincial governments controlling "matters of a merely local
or private nature in the province," including law and order,
hospitals, local licensing and education. Since provincial
responsibilities were comparatively limited, provincial income
was limited to "direct taxation." The politicians could not
foresee that there would eventually be at least ten provinces,
many, especially in the west, possessing great economic
resources. As population grew, so did the demands on provincial governments. They required strong leadership and many
large, complex ministries as specialized as those in Ottawa.

Provincial leaders could challenge Ottawa's claim to be the voice of the people.

At the time of the BNA Act the welfare state was not conceived for Canada, and over the years, as it gradually accepted this philosophy of government, the growing costs became provincial responsibilities. When education, roads, welfare, health, and care of the indigent all increased provincial expenditures from limited sources of taxation, the provinces demanded better terms in the form of larger federal subsidies. They insisted on control of the revenue from their natural resources, which resulted in bitter confrontation between the producing provinces, especially Alberta, and the federal government. Other provinces, led by Ontario, claimed that these profits should be shared nationally.

The western provinces also demand a stronger voice in federal policies that affect them, including foreign trade agreements. Why should the farmers be forced to compete in world markets while eastern factories are protected from foreign competition? Why should a farmer be forced to pay high prices for machines or shoes from Canadian factories when, if it were not for tariffs and quotas, cheaper ones would be available? Interest rates are established at the federal level and can affect agriculture, natural resource development and small businesses, whose needs the provincial governments claim to better understand.

Canadian trade faces worldwide competition, and to meet the challenge Canadians must not only be efficient but they must also be reliable suppliers to foreign customers. Here again the west feels neglected. Exports of raw materials and grain are handicapped by the inefficiency of railways, the shortage of trackage and the inadequate port facilities.

In recent years the problem of Quebec "sovereignty" has received much public debate across Canada. In general, western Canadians consider that Quebec has had a disproportionate influence on Canadian politics. Westerners of many ethnic backgrounds appreciate the efforts of the Québécois to retain their own culture, and the western provinces certainly sympathize with Quebec in its aim for greater provincial sovereignty, but in the federal field Quebec is suspected of having more influence than any of the other ten provinces except perhaps Ontario.

Since early history, the west has been comparatively poor, undeveloped and dependent on the east. On the other hand, the central provinces have become wealthy largely through their manipulation of the west. Because of the uneven distribution of wealth throughout the country in 1967, the Federal-Provincial Fiscal Arrangements Act put in place an equalization program: the federal government compensates any province whose per capita revenue is below the national average. In recent years the west has achieved a sound base which has made it largely self-sufficient. The "have" provinces are now Alberta, British Columbia and, recently, Saskatchewan. By the established formula, Ontario, the most populated and industrialized province, now finds itself in the "have not" category, though it is not as yet receiving equalization payments. The wealth that has been found in the west has resulted in the economic power of Canada moving to the west.

The roots of western political discontent lie deep, through many generations of perceived second-class treatment. Now the economic problems of the 1980s, along with Ottawa's authoritarian stand on the constitution and energy, have spawned a number of protest groups, such as West-Fed, Canada West Foundation, Western Canada Concept, and Saskatchewan's Unionist Party, offering a variety of political alternatives ranging from complete independence to union with the United States. Although comparatively small in numbers, they attracted some influential members. They were reminders that all successful Canadian protest parties—the United Farmers, Social Credit and the NDP—began in the west from the same currents of discontent. But the flurry of new protest groups misread the popular attitude towards separation and did not receive the support they expected; the publicity they created soon faded. Only Western Canada Concept, which started in Alberta, remained active and it deferred its original separatist aims in favour of a promise to bring better government to the provinces.

The history of the west reveals that all the major developments were national in scope—the fur trade, the transcontinental railways, two great wars, the Depression, international commitments, pipelines and constitutional change. The many people who have filled the land, both native and immigrant, shared in the growth of a rich democratic nation. Within Con-

federation secondary provincial governments were established
to serve regional interests, and as population and wealth
expanded, the provinces reached maturity and no longer
needed parental guidance from the federal government. With
this historic background westerners are, above all, Canadians,
but they are Canadians who intend to protect and control their
own economic, cultural, social and political destinies.

Appendix

STATISTICAL TABLES

TABLE 1: APPROXIMATE AREAS OF CANADA AND OF
THE WESTERN PROVINCES AND TERRITORIES

	Area (km²)	Percentage of Canada
Canada	9 922 330	100.0
Manitoba	650 087	6.5
Saskatchewan	651 900	6.6
Alberta	661 185	6.6
British Columbia	948 596	9.5
Yukon	482 515	4.9
N.W.T.	3 379 684	34.1

Source: Statistics Canada, *Canada Year Book 1978–79*

TABLE 2: VALUE OF SELECTED MINERAL PRODUCTION, 1980 (IN THOUSANDS OF DOLLARS)

	Manitoba	Sask.	Alberta	B.C.	Yukon	N.W.T.	Canada
Copper	172,255	14,261		723,697	27,527	787	1,856,031
Gold	29,396	7,229		153,491	19,484	68,874	1,021,151
Lead	433			78,107	81,475	57,974	299,134
Molybdenum				296,932			315,423
Nickel	366,468						1,678,607
Silver	21,496	4,215		148,488	101,165	36,368	817,961
Tin				3,663			5,898
Zinc	38,925	4,360		60,036	73,307	179,126	859,880
Asbestos				84,098			641,737
Coal		30,800	302,600	464,800			946,000
Natural Gas		27,371	6,279,598	318,622		41,106	6,692,200
Natural Gas By-products		12,943	1,697,791	30,740			1,741,474
Petroleum	55,263	880,548	7,948,485	192,001		12,320	9,098,104
Potash		986,220					986,220
Sulphur		60	405,720	7,504			414,484

Source: Statistics Canada

TABLE 3: COMPARATIVE VALUES OF MINERAL PRODUCTION

Year	Total* (Canada)	Percentage of Total			
		Man.	Sask.	Alta.	B.C.
1930	279	1.9	0.8	10.9	19.7
1940	529	3.4	2.2	6.6	14.0
1950	1,045	3.1	3.4	13.0	13.3
1960	2,492	2.4	8.5	15.9	7.5
1965	3,743	4.9	8.7	21.4	7.6
1970	5,722	5.8	6.6	24.5	8.6
1976	15,392	3.3	6.0	46.0	9.3
1978	20,261	2.3	7.8	49.7	9.3
1979	26,081	2.5	7.2	49.5	10.3
1980	32,368	2.6	7.1	52.0	8.6

* In millions of dollars

Sources: Statistics Canada, *Canada Year Books* and *Canadian Statistical Review*, April 1981

TABLE 4: CRUDE OIL PRODUCTION (IN THOUSANDS OF CUBIC METRES)

	N.W.T.	B.C.	Alta.	Sask.	Man.	Western Canada	Canada
1947–56	0.43	0.02	93.65	7.44	2.05	103.63	104.21
1957–66	0.86	10.60	246.12	100.89	7.71	368.23	369.94
1967	0.11	3.13	36.68	14.70	0.89	55.51	55.70
1968	0.13	3.53	39.97	14.60	0.99	59.19	59.39
1969	0.13	4.02	44.38	13.89	0.99	63.41	63.60
1970	0.13	4.02	51.74	14.22	0.94	71.07	71.24
1971	0.14	4.01	56.46	14.06	0.89	75.56	75.72
1972	0.14	3.78	67.44	13.76	0.84	85.99	86.11
1973	0.16	3.37	82.98	13.62	0.81	100.94	101.07
1974	0.16	2.99	79.07	11.73	0.75	94.71	94.84
1975	0.16	2.35	64.47	9.38	0.70	80.00	80.11
1976	0.14	2.37	60.86	8.88	0.64	72.89	72.99

Source: Alberta Economic Development, *Industry & Resources 1978–79*

TABLE 5: CANADIAN EXPORT TRADE (PERCENTAGE OF ALL EXPORTS)

	United Kingdom*	United States	Japan
1870	41	51	–
1906	57	35	–
1914	53	38	–
1922	45	40	–
1929	31	36	–
1935	45	48	–
1938	34	39	2
1945	28	30	–
1951	16	59	–
1959	15	60	2
1966	11.2	60	4
1971	7.8	67.5	4.6
1976	4.9	67.6	6.3
1978	3.6	71.5	5.9
1979	4.1	67.8	6.2
1980	4.1	61.8	5.9

* U.K. figures for 1870–1935 include the U.K. and the British Empire.

Sources: Statistics Canada: *Canada One Hundred, 1867–1967*; *Canada Year Books*; and *Canadian Statistical Review*, April 1981

TABLE 6: POPULATION OF WESTERN PROVINCES
AND TERRITORIES (IN THOUSANDS)

	Manitoba	Sask	Alberta	B.C.	Yukon	N.W.T.*
1871	25.2			36.2		48.0
1881	62.3			49.5		56.4
1891	152.5			98.2		98.9
1901	255.2	91.3	73.0	178.7	27.2	20.1
1911	461.4	492.4	374.3	392.5	8.5	6.5
1921	610.1	757.5	588.5	524.6	4.1	8.1
1931	700.1	921.8	736.6	694.3	4.2	9.3
1941	729.7	896.0	796.2	817.8	5.0	12.0
1951	776.5	831.7	939.5	1,165.2	9.1	16.0
1961	921.7	925.2	1,332.0	1,629.1	14.6	23.0
1971	988.2	926.2	1,627.9	2,184.6	18.4	34.8
1976	1,021.5	921.3	1,838.0	2,466.6	21.8	42.6
1980	1,028.3	973.0	2,113.3	2,662.0	21.6	43.5

*Before 1901 figures for Northwest Territories include Alberta, Saskatchewan and Yukon.

Sources: Statistics Canada, *Canada Year Books* and *Canadian Statistical Review*, April 1981

TABLE 7: PROPORTION OF POPULATION DEFINED AS URBAN

	1951	1961	1971	1976
Manitoba	56.6	63.9	70.1	69.9
Saskatchewan	30.4	43.0	52.7	55.5
Alberta	48.0	63.3	73.6	75.0
British Columbia	70.8	72.3	79.7	76.9
Canada	62.9	69.6	76.0	75.5

Source: Statistics Canada, *Perspectives Canada III*

TABLE 8: POPULATION OF WESTERN CANADIAN CITIES

	Victoria	Vancouver	Edmonton	Calgary	Saskatoon	Regina	Winnipeg
1891	16,841	13,709		3,876			25,639
1901	20,919	29,432	4,176	4,392	113	2,249	42,340
1911	31,160	120,847	31,064	43,704	12,004	30,213	136,035
1921	38,727	163,220	58,821	63,305	25,739	34,432	179,087
1931	39,082	246,593	79,197	83,761	43,291	53,209	218,785
1941	44,068	275,353	93,817	88,904	43,027	58,245	221,960
1951	54,584	365,844	226,002	181,780	72,858	89,755	255,093
1961	54,941	384,522	281,027	249,641	95,526*	112,141	265,429
1971	61,761	426,256	438,152*	403,319*	126,449*	139,467*	246,246*
1976	62,551	410,188	461,361*	469,917*	133,750	149,505	560,874*
1976†	218,250	1,166,348	554,228	469,917	133,750	149,593	578,217
1980†	230,600	1,250,000	569,000	550,800	150,000	154,000	599,458

* Boundaries changed since previous census.

† Italic figures are metropolitan area populations. The 1980 figures are estimates.

Source: Statistics Canada, Canada Year Books

TABLE 9: POPULATION BY LANGUAGE OF ORIGIN

	Manitoba	Sask.	Alberta	B.C.	Yukon & N.W.T.
English	727,240	215,685	1,482,000	2,037,000	42,000
French	54,745	26,710	44,440	38,410	1,500
Chinese	3,705	3,390	14,440	46,655	160
Japanese	495	95	1,675	6,450	15
Serbo-Croatian	1,320	395	2,190	5,245	200
Czech	1,900	1,230	4,130	4,380	60
Finnish	480	570	1,060	5,125	30
German	73,375	61,250	79,925	80,970	770
Indo-Pakistani	1,685	645	4,381	19,850	20
Italian	5,875	1,260	13,745	26,715	180
Hungarian	2,200	4,445	6,935	7,900	85
Dutch	7,415	3,030	17,290	21,539	175
Polish	10,215	4,810	9,735	5,665	60
Portuguese	5,455	220	3,445	9,245	25
Russian	925	2,560	1,735	16,055	15
Scandinavian	6,155	8,130	11,870	19,250	80
Ukrainian	60,250	45,920	64,960	22,775	335

Source: Statistics Canada, *1976 Census of Canada: Population: Demographic Characteristics*. Over forty linguistic and national groups are listed.

TABLE 10: CANADIAN NATIVE POPULATION

(Includes Indians and Inuit; inclusion of nonstatus Indians and Metis would increase the percentages by approximately five per cent.)

Year	Population	Percentage of Canadian population
1881	108,547	2.5
1901	127,941	2.4
1911	105,611	1.5
1921	113,724	1.3
1931	128,890	1.2
1941	125,521	1.1
1951	165,607	1.2
1961	220,121	1.2
1971	312,765	1.5
1976	288,938	1.3
1981	318,090	1.3

Sources: Statistics Canada: *1971 Census of Canada*, catalogue 92–723; *Canada Year Book 1978–79*; and *Perspectives Canada III*

TABLE 11: PROVINCIAL PREMIERS

Manitoba

John Norquay		Oct 1878 – Dec 1887
D. H. Harrison		Dec 1887 – Jan 1888
T. Greenway	L	Jan 1888 – Jan 1900
H. J. Macdonald	C	Jan 1900 – Oct 1900
R. P. Roblin	C	Oct 1900 – May 1915
T. C. Norris	L	May 1915 – Aug 1922
John Bracken	coalition	Aug 1922 – Jan 1943
S. S. Garson	coalition	Jan 1943 – Nov 1948
D. L. Campbell	coalition	Nov 1948 – Jun 1958
Dufferin Roblin	C	Jun 1958 – Nov 1967
Walter Weir	L	Nov 1967 – Jul 1969
Edward Schreyer	NDP	Jul 1969 – Nov 1977
Sterling B. Lyon	C	Nov 1977 – Nov 1981
Howard R. Pawley	NDP	Nov 1981 –

Saskatchewan

Walter Scott	L	Sep 1905 – Oct 1916
W. M. Martin	L	Oct 1916 – Apr 1922
C. A. Dunning	L	Apr 1922 – Feb 1926
James G. Gardiner	L	Feb 1926 – Sep 1929
J. T. M. Anderson	L	Sep 1929 – Jul 1934
James G. Gardiner	L	Jul 1934 – Nov 1935
W. J. Patterson	L	Nov 1935 – Jul 1944
Thomas C. Douglas	CCF	Jul 1944 – Nov 1961
W. S. Lloyd	CCF-NDP	Nov 1961 – May 1964
W. Ross Thatcher	L	May 1964 – Jun 1971
A. E. Blakeney	NDP	Jun 1971 – May 1982
Grant Devine	PC	May 1982 –

Alberta

Alex Rutherford	L	Sep 1905 – May 1910
A. L. Sifton	L	May 1910 – Oct 1917
Charles Stewart	UFA	Oct 1917 – Aug 1921
H. Greenfield	UFA	Aug 1921 – Nov 1925
J. E. Brownlee	UFA	Nov 1925 – Jul 1934

TABLE 11: PROVINCIAL PREMIERS (Cont'd.)

Alberta (Cont'd)

R. G. Reid	UFA	Jul 1934 – Sep 1935
William Aberhart	SC	Sep 1935 – May 1943
E. C. Manning	SC	May 1943 – Dec 1968
H. E. Strom	SC	Dec 1968 – Sep 1971
P. Lougheed	C	Sep 1971 –

British Columbia

J. F. McCreight		Aug 1871 – Dec 1872
A. De Cosmos		Dec 1872 – Feb 1874
G. A. Walkem		Feb 1874 – Jan 1876
A. C. Elliott		Feb 1876 – Jun 1878
J. Walkem		Jun 1878 – Jun 1882
R. Beavan		Jun 1882 – Jan 1883
W. Smithe		Jan 1883 – Mar 1887
A. E. B. Davie		Mar 1887 – Aug 1889
J. Robson		Aug 1889 – Jan 1892
T. Davie		Jul 1892 – Mar 1895
J. H. Turner		Mar 1895 – Aug 1898
C. A. Semlin		Aug 1898 – Feb 1900
J. Martin		Feb 1900 – Jun 1900
J. Dunsmuir		Jun 1900 – Nov 1902
E. G. Prior		Nov 1902 – Jun 1903
R. McBride	C	Jun 1903 – Dec 1915
W. J. Bowser	C	Dec 1915 – Nov 1916
H. C. Brewster	L	Nov 1916 – Mar 1918
John Oliver	L	Mar 1918 – Aug 1927
J. D. Maclean	L	Aug 1927 – Aug 1928
Simon F. Tolmie	C	Aug 1928 – Nov 1933
T. D. Pattullo	L	Nov 1933 – Dec 1941
John Hart	coalition	Dec 1941 – Dec 1947
B. Johnson-H. Anscomb	coalition	Dec 1947 – Jan 1952
B. Johnson	coalition	Jan 1952 – Aug 1952
W. A. C. Bennett	SC	Aug 1952 – Aug 1972
David Barrett	NDP	Aug 1972 – Dec 1975
William R. Bennett	SC	Dec 1975 –

TABLE 12: PROVINCIAL BUDGET HIGHLIGHTS

		B.C. 1981–82	Alberta 1979–80	Saskatchewan 1981	Manitoba 1981–82
Expenditures (in millions of dollars)	Total Expenditures	6,610	4,531	1,846	2,381
	Health & Community Services	1,975 (29.9%)	1,706 (37.7%)	719 (38.9%)	918 (38.6%)
	Education	1,172 (17.7%)	661 (14.6%)	401 (21.7%)	502 (21.1%)
	Economic Resources Development & Transport	1,240 (18.8%)	723 (15.9%)	190 (10.2%)	416 (17.5%)
Revenues (in millions of dollars)	Total Revenue	6,636	5,668	1,783	2,161
	Income Taxes	2,190 (33.0%)	1,140 (20.1%)	406 (22.8%)	582 (27.2%)
	Levies & Collections	1,733 (26.1%)	570 (10.1%)	*	479 (22.2%)
	Liquor	338 (5.1%)	151 (2.6%)	80 (4.5%)	87 (4.1%)
	Federal Transfers	1,178 (17.7%)	540 (9.5%)	405 (22.8%)	880 (40.7%)
	Natural Resources	678 (10.2%)	3,146 (55.5%)	599 (32.5%)	†

* included in Heritage Fund
† included in other revenues
Sources: Provincial Budgets

TABLE 13: COMPARATIVE PROVINCIAL TAX RATES, 1981

	B.C.	Alta.	Sask.	Man.
Personal Income (% of federal tax payable)	44.0	38.5	53.0	54.0
Corporation Income (% of taxable income)				
General rate (%)	16.0	11.0	14.0	15.0
Small business rate (%)	8.0	5.0	11.0	11.0
Corporation Capital (%)	0.2	nil	0.3	0.2
Gasoline (% of retail)	20.0	nil	20.0	20.0
Amount per litre	5.32¢	nil	nil	nil
Retail Sales (%)	6.0	nil	5.0	5.0
Meals (%)	nil	nil	nil	5.0
Accommodation (%)	6.0	nil	nil	5.0
Cigarettes (per package)	34¢	8¢	30¢	35¢
Private Passenger Vehicle Fee (range)	$20–$70	$18–$28	$12–$48	$15–$150
e.g.: Chevrolet Citation	$25	$23	$12	$18
Hospital Insurance (annual premium)	nil	*	nil	nil
Medical Services (annual premium)	$102–$225†	*	nil	nil

* Hospital & Medical composite fee: $104 single, $208 family
† $102 single or $225 family

Source: Ministry of Finance, *British Columbia Financial and Economic Review*, March 1981; Ministry of Finance, *1981 Manitoba Budget Address*

TABLE 14: COMPARISON OF PROVINCIAL DEBT PER CAPITA, 1979

	Amount	Rank of province
Manitoba	$3,876	2
Saskatchewan	$2,028	8
Alberta	$1,249	10
British Columbia	$2,662	6
Average for ten provinces	$2,719	

Source: Ministry of Finance, *1981 Manitoba Budget Address*

TABLE 15: CANADIAN ELECTION RESULTS SINCE CONFEDERATION

	Conservatives	Liberals	Unionists	Liberal Conservatives	Progressives
1867	101	80			
1872	103	97			
1874	73	133			
1878	137	69			
1882	139	71			
1887	123	92			
1891	123	92			
1896	89	117			
1900	78	128			
1904	75	139			
1908	85	133			
1911	133	86			
1917		82	153		
1921		116		50	65
1925	116	101			24
1926	91	116			13
1930	137	88			2
1935	39	171			
1940	39	178			
1945	67	125			
1949	41	190			
1953	51	170			
1957	112	105			
1958	208	48			
1962	116	99			
1963	95	129			
1965	97	131			
1968	72	155			
1972	107	109			
1974	97	136			
1979	136	114			
1980	103	147			

Liberal Progressives	United Farmers	CCF	NDP	Social Credit	Créditistes	Communists, Independents and others	Total Seats
							181
							200
							206
							206
							210
							215
							215
						7	213
						8	214
							214
						3	221
						2	221
							235
						4	235
						4	245
9	11					5	245
3	10					5	245
		7		17		11	245
		8		10		10	245
		28		13		12	245
		13		10		8	262
		23		15		6	265
		25		19		4	265
		8				1	265
			19	30		1	265
			17	24			265
			21	5	9	2	265
			22		14	1	264
			31		15	2	264
			17		9	5	264
			26		6		282
			32				282

TABLE 16: FEDERAL REPRESENTATION BY PROVINCES

	Govt.	Number of Seats	Alberta				British Columbia					Manitoba				Saskatchewan			
			*Total**	Lib	Con	NPP	*Total**	Lib	Con	NPP	SC	*Total**	Lib	Con	NPP	*Total**	Lib	Con	NPP
1872	Con	103/200					6	–	6			6	1	5					
1874	Lib	133/206					6	–	6			6	2	2					
1878	Con	137/206					6	–	6			6	1	3					
1882	Con	139/210					6	–	6			5	3	2					
1887	Con	123/215					6	–	6			5	1	4					
1891	Con	123/215					6	–	6			5	1	4					
1896	Lib	117/213					6	4	2			6	2	4					
1900	Lib	128/214					6	3	2			6	2	3					
1904	Lib	139/214					7	7	–			10	7	3					
1908	Lib	133/221	7	4	3		7	2	5			10	2	8		10	9	1	
1911	Con	133/221	7	6	1		7	–	7			10	2	7		10	9	1	
1917	Union	153/235	12	1	11		13	–	13			15	1	14		16	–	16	
1921	Lib	116/235	12	0	0	11	13	3	7	2		15	1	–	12	16	1	–	15
1925	Lib	101/245	16	4	3	9	14	3	10	–		17	1	7	7	21	15	–	6
						UFA													
1926	Lib	116/245	16	3	1	11	14	1	12	–		17	11	–	4	21	16	–	5

					PC	SC			PC	CCF/NDP	SC			PC	CCF/NDP			PC	CCF/NDP
1930	Con	137/245	16	3	4	9	14	5	7	–	–	17	4*	11	–	21	11	8	2
1935	Lib	171/245	17	1	1	15	16	6	5	3	–	17	14*	1	2	21	16	1	2
1940	Lib	178/245	17	7	–	10	16	10	4	1	–	17	15*	1	1	21	12	2	5
1945	Lib	125/245	17	2	2	13	16	5	5	4	–	17	10	2	5	21	2	1	18
1949	Lib	190/262	17	5	2	10	18	11	3	3	–	16	12	1	3	20	14	1	5
1953	Lib	170/265	17	4	2	11	22	8	3	7	4	14	8	3	3	17	5	1	11
1957	PC	112/265	17	1	3	13	22	2	7	7	6	14	1	8	5	17	4	3	10
1958	PC	208/265	17	–	17	–	22	–	18	4	–	14	–	14	–	17	–	16	1
1962	PC	116/265	17	–	15	2	22	4	6	10	2	14	1	11	2	17	1	16	–
1963	Lib	129/265	17	1	14	2	22	7	4	9	2	14	2	10	2	17	–	17	–
1965	Lib	131/265	17	–	15	2	22	7	3	9	3	14	1	10	3	17	–	17	–
1968	Lib	155/264	19	4	15	–	23	16	–	7	–	13	5	5	3	13	2	5	6
1972	Lib	109/264	19	–	19	–	23	4	8	11	–	13	2	8	3	13	1	7	5
1974	Lib	136/264	19	–	19	–	23	8	13	2	–	13	2	9	2	13	3	8	2
1979	PC	136/282	21	–	21	–	28	1	19	8	–	14	2	7	5	14	–	10	4
1980	Lib	147/282	21	–	21	–	28	–	16	12	–	14	2	5	7	14	–	7	7

* Totals include Independent and Labour members.

TABLE 17: FEDERAL THIRD PARTIES IN THE WEST

		Total Seats	Man.	Sask.	Alta.	B.C.
NPP	1921	65	12	15	11	2
	1925	24	7	6	9	–
	1926	13	4	5	–	–
	1930	2	–	2	–	–
CCF	1935	7	2	2	*	3
	1940	8	1	5		1
	1945	28	5	18		4
	1949	13	3	5		3
	1953	23	3	11		7
	1957	25	5	10		7
	1958	8	–	1		4
NDP	1962	19	2	–	*	10
	1963	17	2	–		9
	1965	21	3			9
	1968	22	3	6		8
	1972	31	3	5		11
	1974	17	2	2		2
	1979	26	5	4		8
	1980	32	7	7		12
SC	1935	17	*	*	15	–
	1940	10			10	–
	1945	13			13	–
	1949	10			10	–
	1953	15			11	4
	1957	19			13	6
	1958	–			–	–
	1962	30†			2	2
	1963	24			2	2
	1965	5‡			2	3

* Alberta has never elected CCF or NDP members. Manitoba and Saskatchewan have never elected SC members.
† Includes Le Ralliement des Créditistes.
‡ Créditistes separated.

SELECT BIBLIOGRAPHY

Adachi, Ken. *The Enemy That Never Was: A History of the Japanese Canadians*. Toronto: McClelland & Stewart, 1976.

Akrigg, G. P. V., and Akrigg, Helen. *British Columbia Chronicle*. 2 vols. Vancouver: Discovery Press, 1975, 1977.

Archer, John H. *Saskatchewan: A History*. Saskatoon: Western Producer Prairie Books, 1980.

Barr, John J. *The Dynasty: The Rise and Fall of Social Credit in Alberta*. Toronto: McClelland & Stewart, 1974.

Begg, Alexander. *History of British Columbia from Its Earliest Discovery to the Present Time*. 1894. Reprint. Toronto: McGraw-Hill Ryerson, 1972.

——. *History of the North-West*. Toronto: Hunter, Rose & Co., 1894.

Bellan, Ruben. *Winnipeg, First Century: An Economic History*. Edited by Joan Michaels. Winnipeg: Queenston House Publishing, 1978.

Berger, Thomas R. *Northern Frontier, Northern Homeland: The Report of the Mackenzie Valley Pipeline Enquiry*. 2 vols. Ottawa: Minister of Supply and Services, 1977.

Berton, Pierre. *The Great Railway*. 2 vols. Toronto: McClelland & Stewart, 1970, 1972.

Brown, Jennifer S. H. *Strangers in Blood: Fur Trade Company Families in Indian Country*. Vancouver: University of British Columbia Press, 1980.

Cashman, Tony. *An Illustrated History of Western Canada*. Edmonton: Hurtig Publishers, 1971.

Charlebois, Peter. *Sternwheelers and Sidewheelers*. Toronto: New Canada Publications, 1978.

Cook, James. *The Journals of Captain James Cook on His Voyages of Discovery: Vol. 3, The Voyage of the Resolution and Discovery, 1776–1780*. 2 vols. Edited by J. C. Beaglehole. Cambridge: Hakluyt Society, 1967.

Crowe, Keith J. *A History of the Original Peoples of Northern Canada*. Montreal: Arctic Institute of North America, McGill-Queen's University Press, 1974.

Desbarats, Peter. *Canada Lost, Canada Found*. Toronto: McClelland & Stewart, 1981.

Foran, Max. *Calgary: An Illustrated History*. Toronto: James Lorimer & Co., 1978.

Fowke, Vernon C. *National Policy and the Wheat Economy*. Toronto: University of Toronto Press, 1957.

Frideres, James S. *Canada's Indians: Contemporary Conflicts*. Scarborough, Ont.: Prentice-Hall Canada, 1974.

Galbraith, John S. *The Little Emperor: Governor Simpson of the Hudson's Bay Company.* Toronto: Macmillan of Canada, 1976.

Glazebrook, G. P. de T. *A History of Transportation in Canada.* 2 vols. Toronto: McClelland & Stewart, Carleton Library, 1964.

Gough, Barry M. *The Royal Navy and the Northwest Coast of North America, 1810–1912.* Vancouver: University of British Columbia Press, 1971.

Hearne, Samuel. *A Journey from Prince of Wales's Fort in Hudson's Bay to the Northern Ocean, 1769, 1770, 1771, 1772.* Edited by Richard Glover. Toronto: Macmillan of Canada, 1958.

Hind, Henry Youle. *Narrative of the Canadian Red River Exploring Expedition of 1857 and of the Assinniboine and Saskatchewan Expedition of 1858.* 1860. Reprint. New York: Greenwood Press, 1969.

Holt, Simma. *Terror in the Name of God: The Story of the Sons of Freedom Doukhobors.* Toronto: McClelland & Stewart, 1964.

Howay, F. W., and Scholefield, E. O. S. *British Columbia from the Earliest Times to the Present.* 4 vols. Vancouver: S. J. Clarke Publishing Co., 1914.

Innis, Harold A. *The Fur Trade in Canada.* Rev. ed. Toronto: University of Toronto Press, 1970.

———. *A History of the Canadian Pacific Railway.* Toronto: University of Toronto Press, 1971.

Jackson, James A. *The Centennial History of Manitoba.* Toronto: McClelland & Stewart, 1970.

Johnson, Barbara, and Zacher, Mark W. *Canadian Foreign Policy and the Law of the Sea.* Vancouver: University of British Columbia Press, 1977.

Kalbach, Warren E. *The Impact of Immigration on the Canadian Population.* Ottawa: Census Division, Dominion Bureau of Statistics, 1970.

Kane, Paul. *Wanderings of an Artist among the Indians of North America.* Toronto: Radisson Society of Canada, 1925.

Kendle, John. *John Bracken: A Political Biography.* Toronto: University of Toronto Press, 1979.

Kovacs, Martin L., ed. *Ethnic Canadians: Culture and Education.* Regina: Canadian Plains Research Centre, University of Regina, 1978.

Lipton, Charles. *The Trade Union Movement of Canada, 1827–1959.* 3d ed. Toronto: NC Press, 1973.

Lotz, Jim. *Northern Realities.* Toronto: New Press, 1970.

McCourt, Edward. *Saskatchewan.* Toronto: Macmillan of Canada, 1968.

MacGregor, James G. *Behold the Shining Mountains, Being An Account of the Travels of Anthony Henday, 1754–55.* Edmonton: Applied Art Products, 1954.

———. *A History of Alberta.* Edmonton: Hurtig Publishers, 1972.

———. *Senator Hardisty's Prairies, 1849–1889.* Saskatoon: Western Producer Prairie Books, 1978.

Mackintosh, W. A., and Joerg, W. L. G., eds. *Canadian Frontiers of Settlement.* 9 vols. 1938. Reprint. Millwood, N.Y.: Kraus Reprint Co., 1974. Vol. 3: *History of Prairie Settlement.* Vol. 4: *"Dominion Lands" Policy.* Vol. 7: *Group Settlement.*

Macleod, R. C. *The North West Mounted Police, 1873–1919.* Canadian Historical Association Booklet no. 31. Ottawa, 1978.

McNaughton, Margaret. *Overland to Cariboo.* 1896. Reprint. Vancouver: J. J. Douglas, 1973.

MacPherson, Ian. *The Co-operative Movement on the Prairies, 1900–1955.* Canadian Historical Association Booklet no. 33. Ottawa, 1979.

Milton, Viscount, and Cheadle, W. B. *The North-West Passage by Land.* 1865. Reprint. Toronto: Coles Canadiana, 1970.

Morice, A. G. *The History of the Northern Interior of British Columbia.* 1906. Reprint. Smithers, B.C.: Interior Stationery, 1978.

Morris, Alexander. *The Treaties of Canada with the Indians of Manitoba and the North-West Territories.* Toronto: Belfords, Clarke & Co., 1880.

Morton, Arthur S. *A History of the Canadian West to 1870–71.* 1929. Reprint. Toronto: University of Toronto Press, 1973.

Morton, Desmond. *The Last War Drum: The North West Campaign of 1885.* Toronto: A. M. Hakkert, 1972.

Morton, James. *In the Sea of Sterile Mountains: The Chinese in British Columbia.* Vancouver: J. J. Douglas, 1974.

Morton, W. L. *The Critical Years: The Union of British North America, 1857–1873.* Canadian Centenary Series. Toronto: McClelland & Stewart, 1964.

———. *Manitoba: A History.* 2d ed. Toronto: University of Toronto Press, 1967.

———. *The West and Confederation, 1857–1871.* 4th ed. Canadian Historical Association Booklet no. 9. Ottawa, 1968.

Morton, W. L., ed. *Manitoba: The Birth of a Province.* Altona: Manitoba Record Society, 1965.

Munford, James Kenneth, ed. *Captain Ledyard's Journal of Captain Cook's Last Voyage.* Corvallis: Oregon University Press, 1963.

Ormsby, Margaret A. *British Columbia: A History.* Toronto: Macmillan of Canada, 1958.

Owram, Doug. *Promise of Eden: The Canadian Expansionist Movement and the Idea of the West, 1856–1900.* Toronto: University of Toronto Press, 1980.

Patterson, E. Palmer, II. *The Canadian Indian: A History since 1500.* Don Mills, Ont.: Collier-Macmillan Canada, 1972.

Pethick, Derek. *First Approaches to the Northwest Coast.* Vancouver: Douglas & McIntyre, 1976.

Potrebenko, Helen. *No Streets of Gold: A Social History of Ukrainians in Alberta.* Vancouver: New Star Books, 1977.

Rasky, Frank. *The North Pole or Bust.* Toronto: McGraw-Hill Ryerson, 1977.

Rasporich, A. W., and Klassen, H. C., eds. *Prairie Perspectives 2:*

Selected Papers of the Western Canadian Studies Conferences. Toronto: Holt, Rinehart & Winston, 1973.

Rawlyk, George A.; Hodgins, Bruce W.; and Bowles, Richard P. *Regionalism in Canada.* Scarborough, Ont.: Prentice-Hall Canada, 1979.

Regehr, T. D. *Remembering Saskatchewan: A History of Rural Saskatchewan.* Saskatoon: University of Saskatchewan, 1979.

Rich, E. E. *The Fur Trade and the Northwest to 1857.* Canadian Centenary Series. Toronto: McClelland & Stewart, 1967.

Shackleton, Doris French. *Tommy Douglas.* Toronto: McClelland & Stewart, 1975.

Simpson, George. *The Character Book.* 1832. Reprint. In *Hudson's Bay Miscellany, 1670–1870.* Winnipeg: Hudson's Bay Record Society, 1975.

Smith, Dorothy Blakey. *James Douglas, Father of British Columbia.* Toronto: Oxford University Press, 1971.

Smith, James K. *The Mackenzie River.* Agincourt, Ont.: Gage Publishing, 1977.

Spry, Irene M. *The Palliser Expedition, 1857–60.* Toronto: Macmillan of Canada, 1963.

Stanley, George F. G. *The Birth of Western Canada: A History of the Riel Rebellions.* 1936. Reprint. Toronto: University of Toronto Press, 1960.

————. *Louis Riel.* Toronto: McGraw-Hill Ryerson, 1972.

Stevens, G. R. *Canadian National Railways.* 2 vols. Toronto: Clarke, Irwin & Co., 1960–62.

Thomas, Lewis H. *The North-West Territories, 1870–1905.* Canadian Historical Association Booklet no. 26. Ottawa, 1970.

————. *The Struggle for Responsible Government in the North-West Territories, 1870–1897.* Toronto: University of Toronto Press, 1956.

Thomas, L. G., ed. *The Prairie West to 1905: A Canadian Sourcebook.* Toronto: Oxford University Press, 1975.

Trofimenkoff, S. M., ed. *The Twenties in Western Canada.* Ottawa: National Museum of Man, 1972.

Vancouver, George. *A Voyage of Discovery to the North Pacific Ocean and Round the World . . .* Edited by John Vancouver. 3 vols. London: G. G. & J. Robinson, 1798.

Ward, W. Peter, and McDonald, Robert A. J. *British Columbia: Historical Readings.* Vancouver: Douglas & McIntyre, 1981.

Willson, Beckles. *The Great Company (1667–1871), Being a History of the Honourable Company of Merchants-Adventurers Trading into Hudson's Bay.* Toronto: Copp Clark, 1899.

Wright, Allen A. *Prelude to Bonanza: The History of the Yukon to 1897.* Sidney, B.C.: Gray's Publishing, 1976.

Zaslow, Morris. *The Opening of the Canadian North, 1870–1914.* Canadian Centenary Series. Toronto: McClelland & Stewart, 1971.

INDEX